A MANUAL

OF

PRACTICAL DEVOTION

TO THE GLORIOUS PATRIARCH

ST. JOSEPH.

In loving memory of :
PATRICK J. MCMANAMON
A man truly Catholic
in Faith and practice,
without which it is impossible
to please God.

K.E. GILLETTE

A MANUAL

OF

PRACTICAL DEVOTION

TO THE GLORIOUS PATRIARCH

ST. JOSEPH.

INCLUDING

THE MASSES, NOVENAS, LITANIES, AND OTHER PIOUS
EXERCISES FOR THE FEASTS

OF THE

HOLY SPOUSE OF THE B. V. MARY.

With Motives for those Pious Practices,

DEDUCED FROM

THE EXAMPLES OF OUR BLESSED REDEEMER, THE BLESSED
VIRGIN MARY, THE HOLY ANGELS, THE MOST
EMINENT SAINTS AND DOCTORS
OF THE CHURCH.

TRANSLATED FROM THE ITALIAN OF

FATHER PATRIGNANI, S.J.

Revised by a Member of the Society of Jesus.

TAN Books
An Imprint of Saint Benedict Press, LLC
Charlotte, North Carolina

TAN Books
An Imprint of Saint Benedict Press, LLC
Charlotte, North Carolina
2012

CONTENTS.

SECOND BOOK.

THIRD BOOK.

CONTENTS.

PRAYER TO ST. JOSEPH.

HOLY ST. JOSEPH! hear thy suppliant's prayer,
And take me to thy own paternal care;
For thou whom God selected on this earth
To watch the infant Jesus at His birth,
And guard the Virgin Mother of the Child—
The ever-blessed Mary, undefiled—
O thou to whom such wondrous charge was given,
Must surely now be powerful in heaven!
Be, then, dear Father to my Jesus, be
A father and protector unto me;
Beseech of Jesus that I may obtain
What none through thee have ever sought in vain—
The love of Jesus, with a heart sincere,
Free from the selfishness of hope or fear;
Thus, for God's glory, that I may adore
Jesus, my Saviour, now and evermore.
And thou, O Mary! ever "Blessed," styled,
The Virgin Mother of the Saviour Child,
With Holy Joseph, take me to thy care,
For, thus protected, God *will* hear my prayer!

       Amen.

PREFACE.

ANXIOUS to promote the pious intentions of the author of this work—F. ANTONY-JOSEPH PATRIGNANI, S.J.—we venture to present the public with a translation.

His earnest desire, to use his own expression, was to diffuse more widely the "Devotion to St. Joseph," to re-animate the piety of his devoted children, and, if possible, to induce all hearts to love and venerate him as he deserves.

And does not this great saint, whom God has so eminently distinguished, deserve, in a special manner, the homage of our devotion, respect, and affection? A great many authors and preachers have used their best exertions to exalt by eloquent panegyrics the prerogatives and virtues of St. Joseph, and they have succeeded in rallying around him a multitude of clients, who invoke him as their advocate and spiritual father, and as the dearest object of their love and confidence, after Jesus and Mary. We, in our humble sphere, are now endeavouring to attain the same end, but by a shorter and more easy method, which was adopted in preference by F. Patrignani.

Example, it is unnecessary to say, has far greater influence over the heart and mind, than the most convincing arguments: the latter only gain our approval of what is right, but the former leads us to put it in practice. The examples to be met with in this work are of two kinds, and naturally divide the subject-matter into two parts. The first part exhibits the many interior and exterior practices of devotion in use among St.

Joseph's clients, supplying so many motives for their devotion to him. The second will present to our view numerous instances of the graces and favours which have been granted to St. Joseph's devoted clients. A third part will contain various practices in his honour, and several ways of spreading this devotion.

Patrignani wrote his book in 1709; since his time, the devotion to St. Joseph has undergone many changes in its exterior form. To be content, in a new edition, with presenting the reader with the devotions which were in use then, without giving likewise those which have been adopted since, would be justly to expose ourselves to the reproach of being unpractical. It will easily be understood, then, that some alterations were necessary; but, in permitting these, we have retained, as far as possible, the original text of our author;

and we have generally used notes to explain or enlarge what appeared to us incomplete or incorrect. For several years the Feasts of Saint Joseph have been multiplying; new Pilgrimages and Associations are continually being formed—unequivocal signs of the veneration in which this holy patriarch is held, and, perhaps we may say, of the fruit which this work has produced. We have thought that a short notice of these foundations would not be misplaced; we have, therefore, placed them at the end of the second book. In the third, to the practices already found there, we have added those peculiar to the new Associations, or to the recently founded Pilgrimages. We have, therefore, united in one work, the motives for honouring St. Joseph, and the numerous ways of doing so. But, since the servants of Joseph are also those of Jesus and Mary, we have added

some prayers and hymns to the Sacred
Heart and to the Immaculate Conception,
which will help to satisfy their devotion.

It now remains for us to offer this work,
with our pious author, to the great Saint
who is the object of it, praying him to
supply for its defects, and to accept the
desire we have to increase his honour, to
make him loved by all hearts, and to see
him invoked with confidence by all in
trouble.

PUBLISHER'S NOTES

In his Apostolic Constitution entitled *The Doctrine of Indulgences* published on January 1, 1967, Pope Paul VI promulgated new norms regarding indulgences.

Two points of his Apostolic Constitution should be mentioned here:
1. Contrary to the former regulations, all indulgences, whether *partial* or *plenary*, can now be applied to the faithful departed.
2. With regard to *partial* indulgences, their measurement by days and years has been abolished.

Complete information on the new norms is available in the new *Enchiridion of Indulgences.*

A good summary of the new norms, including lists of the indulgenced prayers and good works, is found in the booklet entitled *New Regulations on Indulgences,* available from TAN Books and Publishers, Inc.

*   *   *

Some of the associations mentioned in this book are no longer active in the United States. However, those wishing to join or receive information on the Pious Union of St. Joseph may write to the address given below, enclosing a stamped, self-addressed envelope.

The Pious Union in Honor of St. Joseph, a crusade of prayer for the dying, was founded by Blessed Father Aloysius (Louis) Guanella (d. 1915) at the Church of St. Joseph's Death in Rome, and made an Archconfraternity by Pope St. Pius X. A similar association begun by Father Hugolinus Storff, a Franciscan in the Mid-West, was canonically erected at St. Peter's Church, Chicago, in 1930 and affiliated with the Archconfraternity. It is not a Purgatorial Society; only the living can enroll.

Pious Union of St. Joseph
St. Peter's Church in-the-Loop
110 W. Madison Street
Chicago, Illinois 60602

WORK OF ST. JOSEPH.

Object of this Work.

THE object of the Work of St. Joseph, is the honour of this great Saint, the increase of devotion to him, and the imitation of his virtues.

To honour St. Joseph is to glorify God in one of His most excellent works—it is to discharge the debt of gratitude we owe to him for the services he rendered to our Divine Saviour and His holy Mother—it is to imitate them and to conform ourselves to the wishes of our dear Lord and the Blessed Virgin, who cannot but be pleased at the homage rendered to a Saint so devoted to them—it is further to correspond to the will of God, who, by the abundance of graces granted to the intercession of St. Joseph, seems, together with the devotion to the Sacred Heart and the Immaculate Conception, to recommend it to our special devotion and confidence. To honour this great Saint is to provide ourselves with a powerful protector during life and at the hour of death.

To spread devotion to the holy patriarch, and the imitation of his virtues, give us a special claim to his affection. By this means we contribute to the spiritual welfare of our brethren, by giving them, in the humble and submissive life of the poor artizan, a preservative against the spirit of the age; and in his powerful intercession and the paternal goodness of his heart, a generous and powerful friend.

Means to employ for this Work.

Our aim is clearly defined as to means: the association trusting principally in the zeal of its members, we will confine ourselves to the following remarks :—

To spread devotion to St. Joseph, the associates should, above all things, endeavour to make the holy patriarch known. In the virtues suggested, they should consider the wants of the persons they address. Regarding the honours to pay him, although in private they be free to follow their own devotion, in the public exercises they should choose in preference what is suitable to the associates in general. The association is composed of persons whose education, habits, and necessities may differ very much; to exact a uniformity in the exercises, would often render them useless, or at least lessen the benefit. Among the different members forming an association, we find the following practices: Some bind themselves each day to certain prayers, to certain acts of charity, or any other virtue, in honour of St. Joseph;

others honour in an especial manner the Seven Sorrows and the Seven Joys of the holy patriarch, by exercises which are appropriate to them. There are associations where each member engages himself to pay him particular honour during one day of the week, month, or year, in the name of all the members; often the associates consecrate particularly Wednesday to the devotion of St. Joseph, and perform different exercises in his honour.

All these practices in honouring St. Joseph have reference to our end. Let those persons who have adopted them add some exercises likely to extend the devotion to the holy patriarch, and the imitation of his virtues ; they can do so perfectly well : and still forming part of their association, can become members of the Work of St. Joseph. The greater part of these practices having been published in the " Devotions to St. Joseph," we refer to that work. As to the last of these practices, the approbation given and the results promised oblige us to pause to make known the Association of Wednesday, formed among the different reunions which have adopted it.

Association of Wednesday.

This practice consists in offering this day to God for the extension of the devotion to St. Joseph, and for the spiritual good of the members of the Work, who make this offering for the same intention. Thus, among the associates of Wednesday, a holy intimacy is formed. Already united for the same end—the glory of St. Joseph—they unite themselves again to obtain the most powerful of means, that of the grace which, in sanctifying themselves, renders their labours beneficial. Charity is the soul of this association; it is the only endowment required from the members. To become a member, the dedication of Wednesday to St. Joseph is necessary; but that suffices. Persons who can do nothing more can beg for the blessings of heaven upon the association, by the merit of their actions and ordinary employments. Those who have it in their power may employ themselves, or others, for the glory of St. Joseph, and add some spiritual exercises for the same object. These exercises are at the choice of the associates and the discretion of the director of each reunion. This important point understood, the following remarks will serve as a guide in the choice to be made.

Exercises in use in the Reunions of Wednesday.

In Angers, Vetré, and Villedieu, and in all the places where the associates have the free disposal of their time, they assemble on Wednesday to assist at the holy Sacrifice of the Mass. The priest, before going up to the altar, recommends the intentions which have been addressed to him to the assistants, and recites after Mass the prayer of the association.

At the end of an exhortation, which takes place every fortnight, the associates concert together on the manner of extending and supporting the Work; each one makes known the result of his efforts, and the aid which he can afford to its progress.

In some parishes, although the consecration of the Wednesday is inviolably maintained, the meeting is deferred to the Sunday evening, to accommodate those who are occupied the other days of the week. Young persons find in these Meetings, attended, as they are, by religious and other devout persons, a preservative against the dangers of the world.

In communities or schools where the consecration of the Wednesday is introduced, if it be not general, those who adopt it may confine themselves to the consecration of the day and some works of piety. If it be adopted by the whole house, superiors may give practices in accordance with the circumstances. Generally, hymns are joined to the exercises noted above. And since the members of the Work of St. Joseph are pre-eminently disciples of Jesus, and children of Mary, they love their meetings to combine with the praises of the holy patriarch those of the Sacred Heart and of the Immaculate Conception. The first hymn, at the commencement of the Mass, is generally to St. Joseph; the second, at the elevation, to our Lord; the third, after the communion, to the Blessed Virgin. The same idea, in the selection of the hymns, is carried out in the monthly meetings of St. Joseph, and when benediction is substituted for the holy Sacrifice of the Mass.

The members of the association are particularly recommended to offer the first Wednesday in the month for deceased members. Those among the members who assist at the holy Mass on that day, offer it for that intention; those who have not that happiness, make at least an offering of the merits of our Saviour in their favour. (*See the Prayers to the Sacred Heart*).

The practice of consecrating the Wednesday is compatible with every rule and every employment. In conforming to the principal requirement, the exterior form may be modified according to circumstances. The associates, besides, do not *contract any engagements;* they have only, after joining the association, to persevere in the offering of the Wednesday. Furthermore, it is to be remarked, that to be a member of the Work of St. Joseph, it is not even absolutely necessary to make the consecration of the Wednesday. Without doubt, it is very advantageous; those who do it derive great help from it during their life, and after death; but as the aim of the Work of St. Joseph is simply to honour our holy patron, and to spread the devotion to him, any person who, without wishing to bind himself to any particular practice, engages to work for the same end, can be admitted as a member. The persons who direct each reunion, inscribe the name, surname, and address of the associates in a register. The list, in detail, of each reunion ought to be forwarded to Angers, to P. N. Louis, Director of the Work, where every information concerning the association may be had.

Prayer of the Associates.

This prayer is said on Wednesday, in private or at the reunion. An indulgence of forty days for the dioceses of Angers, Tours, Rennes, Beauvais, Poitiers, and Nantes.

"O Joseph! who by your fidelity to the inspirations of heaven, merited, in the midst of hard labour, the contempt of the world and the trials of this life, to receive from the Holy Ghost the title of Just, and from God the Father the care of Jesus, His Divine Son, and Mary, the Queen of virgins; we implore of you, now that you are all-powerful with God, to remember us, who still languish in this valley of tears, exposed to the snares of cruel enemies. Obtain for us a contempt for the false goods of this world, victory over our passions, an unbounded zeal in the service of God, a tender confidence in Jesus, your adopted Son, and in Mary, your spouse. O Joseph! be our guide, our patron, our defender at the hour of death. We beg this of you, by the love which you bear to Jesus and Mary. We beseech you to ask the same graces for all those who have associated themselves to us to spread devotion to you. Listen to their prayers, assist their efforts, and obtain, in reward of their zeal, that they may one day be united around your throne at the feet of Jesus and Mary. Amen.

" Sacred Heart of Jesus, have mercy on us.

" Immaculate Heart of Mary, pray for us.

" St. Joseph, pray for us."

At the end of this prayer, a Pater and Ave are added for the different intentions of the associates present at the reunion.

MANUAL OF DEVOTION

TO

The Glorious Patriarch

SAINT JOSEPH.

FIRST PART.

MOTIVES FOR THE DEVOTION TO ST. JOSEPH.

CHAPTER I.

First Motive for Devotion to St. Joseph—the Example of Jesus Christ.

WHEN from His cross Jesus Christ addressed Himself to the ever-blessed Virgin His mother, and, pointing to St. John, said to her, "Woman, behold thy son," undoubtedly He intended to put us all under her protection in the person of that beloved disciple, who then represented the entire body of the elect (*St. Bern. S.*). In like manner, it is most natural to suppose that the Eternal Father, in appointing St. Joseph, as head of the Holy Family, to be the guardian of the lives of Jesus and Mary in their flight into Egypt, wished at the same time to place all mankind under his protection, and to inspire them with respect and veneration for a saint, to whose hands was entrusted the most precious treasure that either Heaven or Earth ever contained, the " Saviour of the world," the " Incarnate Word," the source and centre of the bliss of Paradise. This one motive should in itself be sufficient to inspire us with a particular devotion to St. Joseph; but we have a stronger one still in the example given to us by the Son of the Most High.

The entire life of our Blessed Saviour is a perfect model, or rather we should say a divine model prepared for our imitation. He says Himself: " Behold, I have given you an example, that, as I have done, you also may do " (*John*, xiii.). Let us now see what honour He paid to St. Joseph, that we may imitate Him in that respect. Jesus is the first of all men who honoured St. Joseph; He saw in this holy patriarch the representative of the Eternal Father, who had placed him over Him in this world, so He treated him in every respect as a father; and it would not have been possible for Him to have shown him more filial respect, had he really been His father.

Already, Christian reader, I flatter myself I can read in your heart the pious and eager desire of becoming acquainted with all the particulars of that example of filial piety which Jesus Christ gave us during the life of St. Joseph; but how can you expect to be able to penetrate a mystery concerning which the Holy Ghost has preserved a profound silence? Yes, the Holy Ghost has covered it with an impenetrable veil, since St. Luke, the depository of the secrets of the " Word made flesh," and the privileged historian of the mysteries of His divine childhood, on coming to the recital of the incidents

in the life of the Son of God, from His twelfth until
His thirtieth year, embodies them all in these words:
" He was subject to them."—" Erat subditus illis."
What a mystery! Were eighteen years of the mortal
life of the Son of God spent by Him without exhibit-
ing anything great or wonderful, which might serve
for our instruction? Such an assertion would be
impious. Was the evangelist ignorant of the particulars of the hidden life of our Divine Lord at
Nazareth? Rather, was it not (so to speak) in the
school of the Blessed Virgin that the sacred penman
learned everything that he had to relate? Was it
not from Mary herself that he learned even the most
minute details of the birth of our Redeemer in a
stable, the adoration of the shepherds, the canticle
of the angels, and many other particulars relating to
the mystery of the " Incarnation," so that St. Luke
is called by some writers " the Blessed Virgin's
secretary " ? If, then, so faithful and accurate an
historian as St. Luke has reduced the narrative of
the greater part of our Saviour's life to these few
words, " He was subject to them," we must conclude, that so perfectly did Jesus Christ devote Himself to the practice of obedience, obedience to Mary
and Joseph, that although during that long period
He performed an infinite number of heroic acts of
piety, humility, patience, zeal, and the most exalted
virtues, He seems nevertheless to have had no other
occupation than that of doing the will of others; this
occupation alone, He would have recorded of Himself in the Gospel as being the most noble, the most
glorious, and the most worthy of the Word Incarnate.

But this subjection, this obedience of Jesus Christ,
presupposes that the person whose orders He obeyed,

must have been invested with the right of authority; and hence, in the words of the Sacred Text which we have quoted, do we not find an epitome of the life of the Son of God, and, at the same time, of that of the great St. Joseph? What, therefore, was St. Joseph's occupation during the eighteen years that he lived with Jesus at Nazareth? It was, if we may imitate the brief Gospel phrase, that of "commanding Jesus," a right to which, in the order of a mysterious Providence, he was fully entitled, as being the constituted head and ruler of the "Holy Family." Doubtless, Mary also, as being His mother, had the privilege of commanding Him; but as a father's authority is considered paramount to all others, Jesus rendered to Joseph, in a special manner, the duty of obedience. These are the sentiments of two celebrated theologians, St. Thomas and Pierre d'Ailly. May I be permitted here to address myself thus to the blessed spirits? How often have you not been penetrated with admiration and astonishment, on beholding Jesus deny Himself the liberty of making the slightest movement, speaking a single word, taking rest or nourishment, but in accordance with the precise directions which He received from St. Joseph! But say, ye blessed spirits, what most excited your astonishment? Was it the humiliation of Jesus in obeying St. Joseph, or was it the exalted dignity of St. Joseph's office in commanding Jesus? The just man Noah, when he saw the Ark resting on the mountains of Armenia, required no aid of science in order to appreciate the prodigious weight of the waters of the Deluge: in like manner, Gerson, that devout servant of St. Joseph, discovers in the profound humiliation of Jesus obeying Joseph, the just

measure of our saint's exaltation—the one ascends in
proportion as the other descends; so that, if the subjection of Jesus attests His incomprehensible humility,
it no less proves the incomparable dignity of Joseph;
and all the acts of submission performed by the Son
of God in obeying St. Joseph, are to the latter so
many steps of sublime elevation. When we consider
all this, how can we ever sufficiently comprehend the
sublime dignity of a saint who thus beheld himself
obeyed, respected, and served during so many years
by his Creator and his God? Joshua excited the
admiration of all succeeding generations for having
once miraculously delayed the setting of the Sun,
which at his command actually remained stationary.
But how insignificant was the power of that famous
general when compared with that of St. Joseph, who,
not once, but a thousand times, could either set in
motion or set at rest, as he pleased, God Himself, the
Creator of the Sun and of all Nature! Great in
Egypt, indeed, was the power of that other Joseph,
to whom the king confided the entire government of
his empire. Moses could not have been honoured
with a more glorious title than that with which the
God of armies invested him, when He called him the
" God of Pharaoh ;" but these titles, these privileges,
admirable as they are, vanish altogether before the
prerogatives of a saint to whom the King of kings
subjected Himself as to His Father and His Lord.

And, doubtless, it is as impossible to find amongst
the multitude of saints one greater than St. Joseph,
as it is to conceive an authority greater than that
which he enjoyed, in virtue of the right which he
had of commanding the Son of God. Let us for a
moment imagine a personage who has been appointed

king over all the kings of the Earth; suppose, also,
that God created ten thousand worlds, that He gives
to each its king on condition that all these kings
should acknowledge as their sovereign one absolute
monarch. Imagine the glory of such a monarch,
receiving the homages of ten thousand great princes;
the sublimity of that throne elevated above so many
thrones; but yet such a monarch would not be so
highly honoured in receiving·allegiance from this
nation of kings, as was St. Joseph by the perfect submission and obedience which was rendered to him
by the Son of God. It was mere boasting on the
part of Hippocrates, that ancient warrior, in order
to flatter his soldiers, and add to his own importance,
when he said, that an honour more precious to him
than an empire was the privilege of commanding
those who were themselves in authority. St. Joseph,
on the contrary, could say with truth : To me alone
belongs the glory of commanding Almighty God, on
whom all creatures depend, to whom all princes
must respectfully submit, and before whom the pillars
of Heaven tremble (*Job*, ix.).

But if the glory of those who exercise authority
over others, consists less in having the power of commanding than in seeing their orders obeyed with
zeal and submission, it follows, that what chiefly constituted St. Joseph's glory, was not so much the
parental authority with which he was invested, as
the perfect obedience of Jesus to his commands. Ye
devout clients of St. Joseph, I shall now endeavour
to gratify your piety by entering still further into
detail, and I shall cite for you a few instances of
that obedience which the Son of God practised in the
" House of Nazareth," with as much simplicity as

if He were quite incapable of acting for Himself. It is true, as I have already stated, that St. Luke has embodied the events of eighteen years of our Saviour's life in these mysterious words, "He was subject to them;" this, however, may not interfere with a fuller development of the meaning of these words, calling in for this purpose the comments of the Holy.Fathers. St. Basil (in the fortieth chapter of his Monastic Constitutions) states, that our Saviour toiled without ceasing in obedience to Mary and Joseph. St. Justin the Martyr (in his Dialogue with Tryphon) assures us that the "Word Incarnate" assisted St. Joseph in his workshop, and laboured at his trade as assiduously as His strength would permit. St. Jerom and St. Bonaventure make a similar statement. But the most irrefragable testimony to this continual exercise of obedience on the part of Jesus to the least wish of St. Joseph, is that which the Blessed Virgin herself gave to St. Bridget, the confidant of her most intimate secrets. These are her words: "So obedient was my Son, that if Joseph said to Him, Do this or that, He instantly did it" (*Rev. of St. Bridget*, b. iv. c. 58).

Whence I behold Joseph and Jesus, one exercising the parental authority by giving his orders, and the other performing the duties of dependence and filial piety by the perfection of obedience. It was necessary that Joseph, in order to maintain a God reduced to a state of poverty, should apply himself to the trade of a carpenter. I hear him saying to Jesus, his adopted son, in the most respectful terms: "Jesus, come and assist me to saw this plank, to carve this block; Jesus, take the hammer and drive in that nail; come and collect this sawdust, and these shavings, and arrange the wood in order. . . . Jesus, take fuel to your mother," &c. &c. The "light" was less prompt in issuing forth from nothing at the command of its Creator, than was Jesus in hearing and quickly executing the orders He received. Hence, it is not surprising that the inhabitants of Nazareth should have looked upon Him as the true son of Joseph. What made them fall into this error, at first innocent, was seeing Him so submissive to this poor artizan. "They said: Is not this the carpenter's son?"

And again, contemplate, with Gerson, this King of Glory, this God of Majesty, who receives the profound homage of millions of angels : behold Him now, not only a partner in trade with Joseph, but also acting as a servant to Mary, in His lowly home at Nazareth ; see how He lays wood on the fire, goes to fetch water at the neighbouring fountain, prepares the frugal repast, and takes part in the most humble and laborious offices of the house. How is it possible that Joseph, on witnessing such unparalleled humility and obedience, was not overwhelmed beyond the power of endurance with mingled feelings of confusion and rapture ? Tobias fell prostrate on the earth, awe-stricken and beside himself, when the angel Raphael, who, under the form of a young man, had served him as a guide, revealed to him the secret of his angelic nature. But had not Joseph, who was so deeply impressed with a sense of the awful majesty and adorable attributes of Jesus, his adopted son, far greater reason to feel profoundly humbled, when he beheld a God made man assume the form of a child, and render to him all those menial services which only a child, or even the lowest servant, would be expected to perform for him?

Oh! tell us, blessed and happy saint, how often, penetrated with the most lively sentiments of respect and humility, you have said to this amiable child, when you beheld Him exhausted and panting from over-exertion and fatigue: "O Jesus! my son, you know what happiness it would afford me, could I have the privilege of obeying rather than that of commanding you. I humbly reverence your obedience; and my authority over you affords me satisfaction only inasmuch as it has pleased you to give to the world the glorious example of the Creator obeying His creature. If you will permit, O my God! we shall exchange places, and you will command as master of this house." But, in order to console Joseph, Jesus may doubtless have said to him what He afterwards said to St. John the Baptist: "Be resigned, cherished guardian of my childhood; be resigned, and refuse not the honour which I render to you: it is fitting that you fulfil in my regard the duty of a father, and that I be subject to you as an obedient and respectful son: it is thus that we shall give to the world an example of all justice."

And is it not reasonable to suppose that, if in this mysterious subjection of our amiable Redeemer to St. Joseph, Origen points out a beautiful lesson on the respect and obedience which children owe to their parents, we may also add, that our Blessed Saviour, by honouring St. Joseph as His father, intended to leave a signal example to His great family, the Church, of the veneration which, in a special manner, it owes to the head of the "Holy Family." Had Jesus Christ passed only one hour submissive to the commands of Joseph, that circumstance alone would have been sufficient to render this holy patriarch of the New Law more venerable than all the saints; how much more so, when Jesus has been pleased to live so long under his directions? Educated and provided with all the necessaries of life by St. Joseph, during five-and-twenty or thirty years, is it not natural that Jesus Christ should desire that all Christians might repay him in some degree, by their fervent and respectful homage, for the long and faithful services which this good father rendered to His adorable person?

Jesus Christ one day declared His wishes on this subject to St. Margaret of Cortona, in an apparition, in which, among other things, He recommended her to be specially devoted to St. Joseph, for the sake of the gratitude which He felt towards him, for having provided for His earthly wants with so much zeal and affection.

Those Christians should reproach themselves with unpardonable ingratitude, who neglect paying a tribute of honour and devotion to St. Joseph for the love of a God-Saviour. As for me, O my Jesus! I will follow Thy example; I will serve those whom Thou hast served; I will honour those whom Thou hast honoured; I will love those whom Thou hast loved with the tenderness of a son. O my sweet Jesus! by that profound humility which made Thee obedient to the smallest wish of St. Joseph, I supplicate Thee to grant to me, Thy unworthy servant, grace to devote myself from this moment for ever to the service of this great saint, in order to please Thee, since Thou Thyself hast given the first example of a tender devotion to him.

CHAPTER II.

Second motive for Devotion to St. Joseph—the Example of the Blessed Virgin.

JOSEPH, the patriarch of old, from his childhood was aware of the glorious career which he was destined one day to pursue. God showed him in a dream the two greatest luminaries in the heavens bowing down and paying him homage. In this respect, the first Joseph may be said to be the type or figure of the second; but, in the latter, the dream was more perfectly realised, when Jesus Christ, the true Sun of Justice, and Mary, that mysterious Moon which communicates her light to the Earth, being herself illumined by that glorious Sun, both most respectfully submitted to him as their chief, and were pleased to commit themselves entirely to his care and direction.

And again, a nearly similar apparition occurred to another prophet (*Hab.* iii.)—the sun and moon appearing stationary. Now, where shall we find this wonderful prodigy realised, if not in the "House of Nazareth"? That was truly the orbit of this Sun and Moon; but of themselves they were motionless: it was the voice of St. Joseph alone that put them in action. We have already seen the Sun—viz., the Son of God—obeying the commands of Joseph as His father: we shall now see the Moon —viz., the Mother of God—subjecting herself to St. Joseph, whom she loved and revered, not only as her husband, but also as her father and protector.

The moon bears a closer resemblance to the sun than any of the stars : Mary, in like manner, has been, of all the saints, the most perfect copy of the virtues and the conduct of the Man-God. Now, among other examples that she left us, we find the respect which she paid to St. Joseph. He was her spouse : as such she deferred to and obeyed him in everything, on every occasion. Yes, holy Virgin! though the conjugal tie had never made you dependant on him, you would, nevertheless, have always rendered him the duties of a most respectful handmaid, were it but to conform to the example of your Divine Son.

It is true that Mary fully appreciated the transcendent gifts which adorned the spouse who had been chosen for her by the Holy Ghost Himself, and this with her was a powerful motive for honouring him ; but when she afterwards witnessed the Son of God respecting him as a father, serving him as His lord, listening to his directions as to a master, who can describe the inconceivable degree of ardour which this new stimulus imparted to the habitual feelings of love, esteem, and veneration which she had always entertained for her dear spouse? She vied as it were with Jesus in rendering him honour and respect ; but not being able to attain to His humility, it being the humility of a God, she found in her very inability itself a motive for confusion, and this holy confusion she offered to St. Joseph, as some faint expression of the desire she felt to render him what she conceived was due to him from a spouse and a handmaid, in imitation of her Divine Son.

Albert the Great bestows a magnificent title upon St. Joseph : he calls him the protector and patron of Mary (patronus Virginis) ; because this saint was

the defender of her honour and her virginity, when, as
yet ignorant of the mystery of the Incarnation, but
anxious to preserve her reputation, he resolved to
leave her secretly, though with feelings of bitter
anguish. And this was certainly the most delicate
mode of proceeding, the most advantageous to Mary;
but he defended her more strenuously still, when an
angel came to inform him of the mysterious conception of the Son of God made man in her chaste
womb : " Joseph, son of David, fear not to take unto
thee Mary thy wife, for that which is conceived in
her is of the Holy Ghost" (*Mat.* i. 20). By these
words, the angel, or rather God Himself, declared
Joseph the protector and guardian of that admirable
purity, which, by a divine privilege, united in the
same person the flower of virginity and the fruit of
maternity : this the Blessed Virgin revealed to St.
Bridget (*Rev.* book vi. chap. 59). Thenceforth, and
throughout all ages, Joseph had become the irrefragable vindicator of Mary's virginity against the
dark calumnies which heresy and the spirit of error
were one day to vomit forth, in order to obscure its
matchless lustre and integrity. The ever-blessed
Virgin, seeing her holy spouse inflamed with a zeal
not inferior to that of the cherub who, armed with
a fiery sword, guarded the terrestrial Paradise,
bestowed upon him herself the title of the glorious
defender of her virginity, as she also intimated to
St. Bridget. And it was but just that she should;
for, although she had conceived by virtue of the
Holy Ghost, it was nevertheless necessary that, on
the accomplishment of the mystery of the Incarnation, she should have the co-operation of St. Joseph,
if we may so speak, in the character of a protector,

in order to preserve both her own and her blessed
Son's reputation in the eyes of the world. As the
heart of Mary is a fountain of grace, and is no less
rich in tenderness, who can conceive the depth of
her gratitude towards her beloved spouse, and her
eagerness to testify it by acts of the most respectful
submission and the tenderest affection? Suffice it to
say, with St. Bernardin of Sienna, that Mary bestowed on Joseph the most precious gifts that a virgin
spouse and a virgin mother could offer him. As a
virgin spouse she gave him her own heart, her immaculate heart, the living sanctuary of the Divinity,
in order that, being enriched with this treasure, he
might thenceforward be entitled to say : "I am the
spouse of Mary, and as such, Mary's heart, the most
tender and amiable of all hearts, is mine." As a virgin
mother, Mary consigns Jesus to the arms of her
spouse—Jesus, the tree of life, the fruitful source of
every blessing. Oh! with what ardent love did not
this Divine Child inflame the heart of Joseph! Oh!
who can conceive the rapture of holy joy which
transported his whole soul at these delicious moments,
during which that God, who constitutes the felicity
of the blessed, smiled on His adopted father as He
reposed in his arms? Was not Joseph then master
of greater treasure than either Heaven or Earth
could boast? In these three words, "Jesus, my
son!" he said infinitely more than St. Thomas, when
he exclaimed, "My Lord and my God!" more than
the seraphic St. Francis, when a thousand times repeating, "My God and my all!"

It is true he was not the father of Jesus according
to the flesh, but this did not lessen his authority
over Him, nor the right to which he was entitled of

calling Him his "Son," for was he not the spouse
of the mother of Jesus? And even independent of
all that, did he not prove himself a father, and more
than a father, by devoting himself to Him with a
love purer and more ardent than ever parent felt for
a child. Accordingly, it was by this beautiful, this
exalted title, that Mary designated him on all occasions. "Your father and I have sought you." It
was not to Jesus only that Joseph proved a tender
and anxious parent, for he acted towards Mary herself more like a father than a spouse or master; and
hence it was that Mary, admiring the virtues of a
spouse so humble, pure, and charitable, considered
it at all times her duty to love, honour, and serve
him with all the deference of a spouse, or rather
with the devoted tenderness of a fond child towards
the best of fathers. She knew that the Eternal
Father was with her spouse, that He directed him
in all his actions, as it is written of the patriarch
Joseph. She knew that he had constituted him His
vicar or representative, the guide and protector not
only of the Man-God, but of His mother also; for
this reason did Mary, like an obedient and respectful
daughter, resign her entire liberty into the hands of
Joseph, that he might dispose of it as he pleased.
Accordingly, when the term of Mary's pregnancy
was accomplished, she immediately set out on her
journey to Bethlehem, in compliance with the wishes
of St. Joseph.; for the same reason did she accompany
him afterwards into Egypt with the new-born Babe,
and pursue her wearisome pilgrimage through bar-
ren wilds and sandy deserts. Joseph remained at
least seven years in that idolatrous land; not even
once did Mary inquire into the cause of so long and

painful an exile. Joseph informs her of the order to return to Judea. Mary follows him as a meek lamb would follow its shepherd; she deems him more worthy than herself to receive the commands of Heaven from angels. In short, Mary was ever more prompt and punctual in the execution of her husband's will, than are the stars in performing their appointed revolutions.

In speaking of an empress, in whose praise he was writing, Pliny the Younger said : "A princess, whose husband is a hero such as Trajan, can do nothing more glorious or more honourable to herself than to obey him." You then, O mighty Empress of Heaven! would you unveil to us, as to your beloved daughter St. Bridget, the secrets of your bosom, oh! might we not hear you repeat to the glory of your spouse those short but comprehensive words : "I did not deem it beneath me to prepare and serve up the repast for my holy spouse; I gloried in rendering him the most trifling and humiliating services" (Rev. b. vii. c. 35). That is to say, O admirable Virgin! that in the house at Nazareth, you, as well as Jesus, placed all your glory and happiness in obeying Joseph in all things : the slightest intimation of his wishes was a command in your estimation, his will was the rule and guide of all your actions, thoughts, and affections. In short, it was your highest ambition to descend to the lowest and most servile offices, in order to testify to Joseph the extent of that affection so justly due to the best of husbands; to show your respect for so zealous and honourable a protector, and your readiness to obey one whom you might well designate the most tender of fathers.

Such was the homage which the Mother of God

rendered when on Earth to this privileged being, whom the same God had chosen to become His adopted father, by making him her spouse. But Mary's devotion to him did not rest here. From the exalted throne which she now occupies in high Heaven, she condescends so far as to continue her services, by the earnest invitations with which she solicits all Christians to declare themselves the servants of St. Joseph. Who is there not acquainted with the facts, that in the sacred house of Nazareth at Loretto, where during his life she had given him so many testimonies of respect and obedience, she recommended F. Balthazar Alvarez, of the Society of Jesus, her devout servant, to take St. Joseph for his special friend and patron (*See Life of this Religious*, c. vi.). She it was also who induced another of her servants, of the Order of Premontré, to change his name of Herman into that of Joseph (*Surius*, April 17). It was our Blessed Lady also who commanded a Moorish slave at Naples, about to be baptized, to take the name of Joseph, in memory of her dear spouse (*Segneri*, c. v.). It is also mentioned in St. Teresa's life, that the Queen of Heaven presented her with a precious gem of inestimable value, as a token of gratitude for the honour which she had procured to St. Joseph, by diffusing so widely the devotion to him throughout the entire Church. She also opened the Heavens, and displayed to the admiring gaze of St. Gertrude, the incomparable brilliancy of the throne which her glorious spouse occupied, and also how reverentially the saints in Paradise bowed down before him in homage (*Rev.* v.).

If Mary has left us such striking examples of respect and obedience to St. Joseph; if now she can

no longer serve him in Heaven where he reigns with
her in glory, and she so clearly intimates her wishes
to her devout servants, that he should be loved and
honoured for her sake, and in imitation of her holy
example on Earth; what Christian can refuse to cultivate a devotion to him? It is true that all Christians, with more or less fervour, profess that, after
Jesus, Mary holds the first place in their heart; but
how can they flatter themselves that this is the case,
when they are so indifferent towards him whom
Jesus and Mary so tenderly loved?

It is to the piety of Anne Kertai that Temore, the
place of her birth, is indebted for the introduction of
the devotion to St. Joseph. It was at the time remarkable for devotion to the Blessed Virgin. What
chiefly contributed to establish the devotion to St.
Joseph, was a chapel which Anne erected in his
honour in the church of the Jesuits. But remark
the consideration that chiefly inflamed her zeal on
this occasion. The love and veneration of the inhabitants towards the Blessed Virgin was in her eyes
a diamond of inestimable value, but which would
require an enchasing in gold in order to heighten
its brilliancy; and with this design did she successfully exert all her zeal in order to inspire the pious
inhabitants with a devotion to St. Joseph, similar to
that which they entertained for the Blessed Virgin.
Some may raise objections to this on the grounds of
its dividing the affections, since what is given to one
is so much taken from the other. Imaginary fear!
Experience proves, that uniting the devotion to St.
Joseph to that of the Blesssd Virgin, far from lessen-
ing, will only serve to increase it. We do not deprive Jesus of our hearts by sharing them with Mary,

and in like manner our affection for Mary does not suffer by sharing it with Joseph. The mutual love which united Jesus, Mary, and Joseph, made this holy family as it were but one heart and one soul: "cor unum et anima una." And thus it is that the devotion to all three will be established in our hearts.

St. Mary Magdalen de Pazzi says, that St. Joseph takes a particular care of those who combat under Mary's standard; and another great spiritualist adds, that it is impossible to have a real devotion to St. Joseph, without having the same for Mary, his immaculate spouse; so true it is that these two amiable spouses bear a resemblance to two lyres, which, being tuned in unison, produce the most perfect harmony. Honour St. Joseph, then, dear reader, and fear not to do too much for him, since the respect testified for the husband does honour to the wife in virtue of their mutual affection; and also, according to human laws, there exists between husband and wife a community of goods and of honours.

CHAPTER III.

Third Motive for this Devotion—the Example of the Holy Angels.

WHEN the holy patriarch Jacob became an ocular witness of the glory of his beloved son, he forgot that he was his father, and prostrating himself before Joseph's sceptre, paid him the most respectful homage (*Heb.* xii.). Oh! what sentiments of respect and veneration must not the father's example have awakened in the breasts of his other children towards a brother become so truly great—so worthy of being revered. Perhaps, pious reader, after contemplating the Son of God and the Mother of God at the feet of Joseph, you will deem it superfluous that you should be asked to witness the honours and the services which he also received from the angels. You will naturally say : What wonder is it that the lords and princes of a great court should honour a personage on whom their sovereign had conferred even regal favours? I agree with you perfectly. However, if what I am going to say will add nothing to the praise or merit of our saint, and may so far be judged superfluous, yet surely, as far as your devotion is concerned, it cannot be considered so; since the example of the holy angels—those faithful servants of Jesus and Mary—will be a further stimulus to your exertions in the service of this great saint.

The blessed spirits were influenced by two powerful motives in the honour which they rendered to St. Joseph : the first, that he equalled them in purity and other virtues; the second, that he surpassed them in dignity. Our Divine Master, in speaking of virgins, compares them to angels : " Erunt sicut angeli Dei in cœlo " (*Mat.* xxviii.). And most true it is that virgins, though enveloped by the corruption of the flesh, are nevertheless happily enabled to preserve, in all its pristine beauty and perfection, a flower which, though a native of Heaven, has become naturalized to our earthly soil, where it flourishes with unfading brilliancy, and wafts its delicious fragrance to the throne of the Most High. Hence it is that an appellation is so often appropriated to virgins, which, properly speaking, belongs only to the blessed spirits. Thus the title of "Angel" is given to an Aloysius Gonzaga, to a Stanislaus Kostka, to an Alexis, a Casimir, an Eleazar, and many others. But with far greater justice may St. Joseph be compared to the angels, or even styled an angel, he being a saint, the perfection of whose virginal purity as far surpasses that of all the other saints, as does the lily, the king of flowers, surpass the pink, the ranunculus, or the violet.

It is worthy of remark, that the virginity of St. Joseph was considered, at the period in which he lived, as an inconceivable and unheard-of circumstance, since he it was who first made it compatible with the state of marriage. From the union of these two virginal hearts, that super-angelic purity, which constituted the principal merit and glory of Mary and Joseph, received an additional degree of lustre.

Permit me to say it, O ye blessed spirits! yes, forbid me not to say, that the purity of St. Joseph was far superior to yours. The vision of the angel Gabriel in human form, and the words of his salutation, made the Queen of Heaven fearful (says St. Ambrose). Never did the aspect of her holy spouse produce this fear—this agitation; she lived and conversed with him in the most perfect confidence. I hesitate not, then, to say, with St. Francis de Sales, that St. Joseph surpassed in purity the most exalted order of spirits, during the twenty or thirty years that he spent in the society of the Mother of God. Could it be otherwise, when so intimately connected with this virgin mother, who was purity itself?

The eyes of Mary (says Gerson) distilled a sort of virginal dew, which purified the hearts of those on whom it fell: "Quidem ex oculis virgineus vos spirabat."

And as this celestial dew fell abundantly every day on the heart of Joseph, open to all its sweet influence, every day added new lustre to the purity of the holy patriarch. It is not, then, astonishing that Joseph became, so to speak, a pure spirit, and that he merited to be numbered among angels rather than men, as a celebrated interpreter of Holy Scripture says : "Fuit ipse angelus potiùs quam homo" (*Cornel à L. in S. Mat.*).

If, as it appears, St. Joseph, in virtue of his virginal purity, does not rank inferior to the angels, neither does he for the prerogatives to which his inconceivable sanctity has entitled him. It befits not my feeble pen to transport you to the Heavenly Jerusalem, there to behold Joseph in possession of the power and functions of each of the celestial hierarchies : other pens have undertaken the task, and, penetrating the Heavens, we behold Joseph equal to the angels-guardian of the first order, having no less a charge than an Infant-God; equal to the archangels in communicating to Mary the orders of Heaven; equal to the powers in manifesting to the Egyptians the omnipotence of the Word Incarnate, who overturned their idols; equal to the virtues as ruler of the Holy Family; equal to the principalities and the dominations in commanding the King and Queen of Heaven; equal to the thrones as having himself served as a throne to the child Jesus when he held Him in his arms; equal to the cherubim in penetrating the most profound mysteries of Incarnate Wisdom; equal to the seraphim in elevating himself upon the wings of love to the highest degree of contemplation, in order to repose sweetly in the bosom of this Divine Master, whom the blessed spirits incessantly behold with ever-increasing rapture : "In quem desiderant angeli prospicere" (*l'et.* i.).

As resemblance is said to produce love, is it, then, surprising that the angels should so highly venerate and esteem one who, though born of Earth, has, by a special privilege of grace, been raised to an equality with them in purity and holiness? Wherefore it was not without a mysterious signification that the angel, in his first apparition to St. Joseph, called upon him by name, "Joseph, Son of David." We see in Holy Writ, that it was not usual with the angels to act thus when announcing the decrees of Heaven to men. "Son of man, stand upon your feet," said the angel to Ezechiel; "Rise quickly," said he to St. Peter; and to St. John the Evangelist, "Write what you see." The angels seem to make no account, or else to be unacquainted with the names of these illustrious personages. But how differently do they act with regard to St. Joseph; they call him by his own name, and greet him as a prince of the royal house of David : "Joseph, Son of David." This magnificent title belonged to him, and was given him by the angels as a mark of distinction justly due to one who, for sanctity alone, stands unrivalled among the children of men. Again, they were proud to claim him as a fellow-citizen, even while he yet dwelt in this land of exile; and it might truly be said that St. Joseph, though dwelling corporeally upon Earth, was in spirit an inhabitant of Heaven, and enjoyed a foretaste of its inconceivable bliss. This is the sentiment of our holy mother the Church, who thus apostrophises St. Joseph : "Admirable destiny!—even in this life equal to the angels—you participate in their happiness—you enjoy the intimate presence of God"

(*Hymn to St. Joseph*),   Do we find in the books of
the New Testament a man so frequently honoured
with the visits of angels as St. Joseph? According
to the Gospel he received at least four. Speaking of
this, a celebrated interpreter of the Sacred Scriptures
proposes the question—why our Lord, who had Himself warned the Magi not to return to Herod, should
employ the ministry of an angel in order to apprize
Joseph of that wicked prince's evil designs regarding
the Divine Infant.   In answer to this, he (Sylveira)
says that our Divine Lord, though actually living
with St. Joseph, was pleased to make known His will
to him by angels, in order to afford the latter an opportunity of conversing with a saint for whom they
entertained so profound a respect, and who was the
object of their sincere affection.   It may also appear
strange that the angel, in revealing to St. Joseph the
cruel projects of Herod, should have merely given
him an order to fly into Egypt, without specifying
the duration of his sojourn there; and when appearing to him again, after the lapse of seven years, he
tells him simply to return to Judea, without direct-
ing him to any particular place where he might dwell
in security with the Holy Family.   Why three visits,
when one would have been sufficient?   Why abandon
Joseph to a state of such painful anxiety?   The same
interpreter will inform us: "So desirous was the angel
to repeat his visits in order to admire the greatness
of St. Joseph's faith regarding such profound mysteries, and the perfect tranquillity of his soul amidst
such perplexing occurrences, that he preferred the
satisfaction of seeing him more frequently to the
glory of fully enlightening him in a single apparition."

We may also remark with St. Chrysostom, that the angels always visit St. Joseph in his sleep. And why, he inquires, do they not present themselves before him in public, and while awake, as to Zachary and the shepherds? If they wished to honour Joseph, would it not be more glorious to him, that they should visit him with a pomp and retinue worthy of the celestial court? In the eyes of the world, those visits are always considered the most flattering and honourable, which are attended with the greatest pomp and display. Yet who will believe it? the angels honoured St. Joseph infinitely more by appearing to him and disclosing to him the secrets of God in the obscurity of a dream, than they could have done by the most brilliant and imposing demonstrations of respect; for thus they proved how fully convinced they were of the firm and lively faith of a man who, in order to believe the mysteries which they announced to him, needed not to behold with his corporeal eyes those heavenly ambassadors, all radiant with light and glory. Thus speaks St. John Chrysostom, as also Theophylactus.

The learned and pious Cardinal of Cambray, in ecstatic admiration of St. Joseph's great faith, thus apostrophises him: " O Joseph! O the most just of men! How couldst thou have believed so promptly, so firmly, a mystery so new, so profound, and hitherto unexampled?" But for my part, I am even more astonished at the promptitude with which he executed the orders thus intimated to him, difficult though they were; and I will say to him, with another interpreter: " Be pleased, O glorious saint! to inform me why the angels, who make it a duty to honour your virtues and prerogatives, should not

render you some exterior demonstrations of respect,
in the intimation of their orders? Why not give
you time to make preparation for your flight and
long exile?" "Take the child and its mother;"
thus was the command given. "Fly into Egypt;"
thus was announced the manner of performing it.
"Remain there until you receive further orders;"
thus was intimated to him the duration, or rather
the uncertainty of the duration, of his exile, which
he had no time either to think of or prepare for.
Why not give St. Joseph even a few days' notice?
While awaiting an answer, behold! St. Joseph is
already on his road, as prompt in obeying the angel's
order as was the latter in executing the commands
of the Almighty.

It may be asked, what respect did the angel here
testify for St. Joseph? for is it not more honourable
to command than to obey? To this question I reply,
that on this occasion the obedience which St. Joseph
practised, is more worthy of admiration than the
authority with which the angel was invested; and
it was with a view to his exaltation that the latter
commanded him, for he knew how superior Joseph
was to the weaknesses and pride of human nature,
and what a brilliant example of angelic obedience
he was about to exhibit to the world : for, as the
angels obey God with promptitude and decided love,
so did St. Joseph ; he hears the order, rises up, and
departs. Oh! what a subject of joy to the angel,
to witness this miracle of obedience! In former
days, the angels were constrained to use violence
with Lot in order to oblige him to quit Sodom—they
were obliged to take him by the arm and put him
forcibly outside that sinful city. With Joseph it

was quite the reverse—a word, a mere sign, was sufficient to make him quit his native land : he neither delays nor deliberates, but obeys in silence (*Hom. St. J. Chrys. Octave H. Innocents*).

If the angels so highly honoured St. Joseph, whom they esteemed their equal in purity, fidelity, and obedience, what must not their reverence for him have been when they saw him raised to a dignity far above that of all the celestial hierarchies? Which, I do not say of the angels, but even of the seraphim, have been ever invested by the Almighty with His paternity? To which of them has He ever said, "You are my son" (*Heb.* i.); or what is yet more wonderful, "You are my father"? Joseph alone was deemed more worthy than all the blessed spirits to bear a name which seemed incommunicable. The angels were commanded to adore on Earth the Son of God incarnate. Joseph was the only one entitled to say to the angels, when uniting his adorations of the Divine Infant to theirs : "To you it belongs, ye holy angels, to adore and praise Him; He is your Lord, your Creator, and your God; but I can do more, for it is my happy privilege to caress Him, to kiss Him, to hold Him in my arms, because He is my son" (*St. Cyprian*). Were the angels filled with envy on beholding St. Joseph invested with so sublime a dignity? No, for they are not capable of so base a passion; but their sole ambition was, if possible, to outdo one another in testimonies of esteem, respect, and affection for a *father* so highly favoured by God.

How many saints have there been who were honoured and served by angels, merely because they were considered by them in the light of "servants

of God." Père Segneri informs us that they acted
as infirmarians during seven days to a holy hermit
in his last sickness; as physicians to Thimatheus;
as couriers to Anthony; as labourers to Isidore; as
sailors to Basilides; as pilots to the old man whose
marvellous history has been transmitted to us by St.
Paulinus. What multiplied attentions and services,
then, must they not have lavished upon one who
was not only the friend of God, but the prince of
the friends of God; on one who was not only a
saint, but who holds the first rank among the saints;
on one whom an Infant-God so often called by the
sacred name of "father"! When the angels beheld
Joseph wearied and exhausted with manual labour,
to which he was obliged to apply himself in order
to provide for the wants of a God hidden and
despised, humbled and utterly destitute—who had
not even whereon to rest His sacred head—did they
not esteem it a duty, as well as a personal consolation, to testify their respect for him by descending
in multitudes from Heaven, in order to assist him in
his workshop in carving the wood, or else to aid
him in the performance of his domestic duties in the
"House of Nazareth"? They would also attend him
on his journeys. to serve as guides, or perhaps solely
for the pleasure of enjoying his society, and of witnessing his affectionate solicitude for the "Incarnate
Word" (*Sylveira*).

A religious who was favoured with revelations on
the mysteries of the "Divine Infancy," the venerable sister Margaret of the Most Holy Sacrament,
was one day asked by her superior whether she had
received any lights relative to St. Joseph? In reply,
she mentioned, among other things, that St. Joseph

frequently worked as a journeyman, Providence always providing for him that description of work which was best suited to his peaceful disposition, his spirit of silence and prayer; and that the angels, who everywhere accompanied him, considered it their duty to labour with him; but that his whole attention was too much engrossed by the adorable child Jesus from the moment he first beheld Him, as likewise with His blessed mother, to admit of his taking particular notice of the presence of the angelic band.

It may be easily conceived that the humble Joseph was not without some concern on seeing angels ministering to him, and sharing in his labours; he would have preferred conforming himself in all things to the Divine Child, who, though the King of Angels, nevertheless came on Earth, not to be served, but to serve, and to devote Himself to every species of labour and fatigue. However it may be, it is sufficient for the glory of our saint to have shown, that from his resemblance to the angels in his functions and his virtues, he merited their respect and services; but his glorious title of the "Father of Jesus," rendered him still more worthy of them. "Being made so much better than the angels, as he hath inherited a more excellent name above them" (*Heb.* i.).

Permit me to say, O glorious St. Joseph! that, so convinced am I of your pre-eminence above all the celestial spirits, that, in order to render you due praise, I desire, with one of your devout panegyrists, that all the members of my body were converted into so many tongues. Ah! at least I wish to love and serve you in union with Jesus and Mary, and to render you a tribute of praise and homage with the angels.

CHAPTER IV.

Fourth Motive for the Devotion—the Example of the Church.

THE chaste Joseph, when at Pharaoh's court, had fallen a victim to the perfidy and passion of a base calumniator: he was condemned, and cast into a darksome dungeon, where he passed many tedious years. But at length he was liberated, and attained the highest pinnacle of glory at the palace of the Egyptian monarch; like the sun, which, lost to our vision for a moment by the intervention of a transient cloud, bursts forth again with redoubled splendour.

Somewhat similar was the position in which the glorious spouse of Mary was placed. For the lapse of several ages, his existence seems to have been forgotten and almost unknown to Christianity; but the thick mist in which the efforts of heresy had enveloped him has at length been dissipated, and, like another sun, he has issued forth with a brighter lustre to illuminate the ecclesiastical firmament.

And true it is that our holy mother the Church seems in these latter ages anxious to indemnify him, by the most solemn homages, for those which she has hitherto been compelled to withhold from him. Coincident with her birth was her conviction that St. Joseph was a just man—a perfect man—the true spouse of the Mother of God, and the father of Jesus Christ by his love and solicitude for that blessed Child: but as too brilliant a light is only calculated to dazzle persons of weak sight, so the Church, by a wise disposition of Providence, judged it expedient, during a certain period, to throw a veil as it were over the illustrious sanctity of the blessed St. Joseph. It was not without deep regret that she witnessed how the heresiarch Cerinthus, having had the temerity to fix his feeble eyes upon this beauteous sun, was so dazzled and blinded by it, as to fall into a mortal error against faith. He took upon him to elevate St. Joseph to such a height as to make him the natural father of Jesus Christ, whilst an infallible revelation attests, that he is only the reputed father. But by this proposition the innovator derogated from the personal dignity of Jesus Christ, as also of His blessed Mother. He deprived the latter of one of the most brilliant gems in her diadem, namely, her immaculate virginity, and her Divine Son of the glory of having been miraculously conceived immaculate by the operation of the Holy Ghost. However, the Church, anxious to eradicate this poison, the effects of which might have proved so fatal to the faith of her children, took the precaution, among others, of not favouring at that particular period the devotion to St. Joseph, fearing it might only increase the evil.

This is the opinion of a learned theologian. A celebrated modern writer—Father Paul Segneri—adds, that it was for this reason that the Church affected to forget St. Joseph, to place him with the crowd, and even apparently to give a preference to several other saints, who assuredly did not equal him in merit. Such was the prudent reserve which the Church found it expedient to adopt, in order to preserve the real dignity of the sacred person of the Man-God from being again impugned.

Another author, who quotes the authority of St. Gregory of Nazianzen, directs our attention to the fact, that, as the early Church refrained from developing fully all the points of its faith concerning the adorable perfections of the Holy Ghost, the invisible spouse of the Blessed Virgin, until the belief in the divinity of our Lord had previously taken deep root in the breasts of the faithful; neither in like manner did she judge it necessary to direct their piety to the devotion to St. Joseph, the visible spouse of Mary, until the virginity of that blessed Mother had been fully acknowledged and reverenced by the whole universe.

But now, that the darkness of past errors has been dissipated, and that the opposite truths shine out with all their lustre in the broad daylight of Christianity, the holy Church makes it an essential duty, as I have remarked above, to render to St. Joseph the most solemn homages and every possible mark of respect and veneration : thus as it were to indemnify him for those which she withheld from him in the early ages of faith. Not content with erecting altars, oratories, and temples in his name—with forming confraternities and religious orders under his patronage—establishing several feasts in his honour—giving him a Mass and Office, inserting in this Office new hymns, in which his praises are resounded in a strain so sublime, so exalted, that in the absence of aught else, they would of themselves be sufficient to give an adequate idea of the many virtues and privileges which entitle him to a rank far above all the other saints; but remark, moreover, that by appropriating one of the days of Lent for the celebration of his principal festival, she has imposed on innume-

rable preachers the pleasing duty of solemnly setting
forth every year the glories and privileges of St.
Joseph throughout the Universal Church : so that on
this day, and nearly at the same hour, his praises
may be heard to resound from every pulpit in
Christendom !

Can this be said of any other saint? No. It is
true that the panegyric of any other saint may be
heard on the day appointed for keeping his festival ;
but only in some particular town, and in a certain
particular church. It is not so with the feast of St.
Joseph, for it is the feast of every city, town, village,
and church ; and wherever a Lent-preacher is to be
met with (and remark that in one city alone may be
found thirty or forty), will also be heard a panegyric
pronounced upon St. Joseph; so that from the East
unto the West, wherever the Redeemer's name has
been made known, there will also be celebrated the
name of His beloved guardian, thus verifying the
words of Ecclesiasticus, " He who watches over the
safety of his Lord, shall be glorified."—" Qui custos
est Domini sui glorificabitur." The intention of the
Church clearly manifests itself by the singular favours
she has conferred in our days to those practices
calculated to inspire devotion to St. Joseph, and by
the encouragement she gives to the associations enrolled under the banner of the glorious patriarch.
After the practices whose special end is to honour
our Lord and His Holy Mother, we shall find none
more powerfully patronised than those which relate
to St. Joseph. It is not too much to say, that every
class of society, clergy as well as laity, vie with
each other in extending devotion to this illustrious
saint.

But in the honours which the Church now-a-days
renders to this great saint, she is not alone actuated
with a view of indemnifying him for having been
deprived at an earlier period of those public tributes
of veneration which he has since received at her
hands; she wishes also to evince her gratitude towards him for the many signal favours for which she
feels herself indebted to him.

She well knew that, as St. Bernard says, St.
Joseph had co-operated more fully, by the sanctity of
his life, in the ineffable mystery of the Incarnation of
the Word, than had all the ancient patriarchs by
their sighs, tears, and merits; she knew that, in one
sense, his virginity had proved more fruitful, than
had the numerous posterity of our Saviour's ancestors; she knew that great saint had been in a certain
sense necessary to the accomplishment of the greatest
of our mysteries, not only to shield our Divine Lord
from dishonour on coming into the world, but likewise (as St. Thomas concludes) in order to establish
throughout the Universe the belief in the Incarnation
of the Son of God, and in the Virginity of Mary;
she felt that if the family of Tobias had reason to be
so grateful to the angel Raphael, who had been a
guide and protector to that dear son on his journey,
the holy family of all Christian nations owes, with
much greater reason, a far deeper debt of gratitude
to St. Joseph, who had been the guardian of the
infancy of the Incarnate God, its father and its
saviour. The Church knew that our Joseph had not,
like the viceroy of Egypt, amassed provisions of
material corn to support the subjects of an idolatrous
monarch, but that he had prepared and preserved to
the faithful of Christ the wheat of the Elect, the true

bread of children, the living and vivifying bread, the food of immortality, the germ of salvation. She knew that if St. Thomas's incredulity had contributed to establish that fundamental principle of our faith, the resurrection, on a more solid basis than before, so also should St. Joseph's reasonable doubt, on seeing Mary's mysterious maternity, serve to confirm the early Christians in their belief in the mystery of the Incarnation, which is the source and principle of all the other mysteries. Was she not also fully sensible that the functions of guardian and foster-father to the child Jesus, and of protector of both mother and Son, must have cost St. Joseph many an anxious hour, much toil and labour, which he endured with the most devoted love and constancy?

In acknowledgment of so many invaluable services, she feels bound to make a due return of gratitude to so munificent a benefactor, and therefore invites all her children to unite with her in rendering him all those testimonies of honour, veneration, and affection, to which he is so justly entitled. When Pharaoh wished to testify his gratitude to Joseph, the patriarch of old, he not only elevated him above all the lords and nobles of his court, he moreover invested him with supreme authority throughout his dominion. Our holy mother the Church has not acted less nobly towards Joseph, the foster-father of the Redeemer. "O Joseph!" she exclaimed, "behold, I place in your hands my entire family, and the authority with which I have been invested : with what perfect security may it not repose under the guardianship of him, to whom the Eternal Father had confided His well-beloved Son! Jesus, your adopted Son, is my spouse; Mary, your immaculate spouse, is my mother and my

queen; and you, O great saint! will ever be my
father and protector. In adopting the Saviour of
the world as your Son, you have likewise adopted all
His brethren, viz., all the faithful who are my children. All the services which you have rendered to
Jesus Christ, you have also rendered to His brethren.
Surely no homage that I can present to you will ever
be worthy of your merits, and of the great benefits
you have conferred on me. I shall proclaim to the
whole world that you are the glory of the angels
and saints, the invincible shield of Christianity, the
glorious conqueror of Hell, the chief negociator of our
salvation, the advocate of sinners, the refuge of the
afflicted, the help and comforter of the dying; in short,
to name all your titles, prerogatives, and praises, in
two words, I have only to say, that you are the
father of Jesus and the spouse of Mary!

"O blessed father of Jesus! be thou also the father
of the Church. Unite with your chaste spouse in
protecting my children, and in defending them against
the impiety of those Herods who use their utmost
efforts to destroy in their souls the faith and love of
Jesus. What a subject of exultation is it not to me,
to hear your august name, O glorious Joseph! re-
sounding throughout the Universe in unison with
those of Jesus and Mary! What an enchanting concert will not the Churches militant and triumphant
form, when with united voices they shall celebrate
the virtues which have entitled you to the supreme
bliss of being the worthy spouse of the 'Queen of
Virgins.'" "Te Joseph, celebrent agmina Cœlitum,
Te cuncti resonant Christiadum chori; Qui, clarus
meritis, junctus est inclytæ Casto fœdere Virgini"
(*Brev. Rom. Feast St. Joseph*).

CHAPTER V.

Fifth Motive—the Devotion to St. Joseph is a Source of Benedictions to the entire Universe.

It is a remark of St. Bernard, that no sooner had the real greatness and the many admirable qualities of the patriarch Joseph rivetted the attention of the Egyptians, than all, as if by a stroke of magic, hastened to him, as to a friend and father. The second Joseph, whose goodness so far exceeds that of the former, has obtained even greater influence with, and is paid infinitely more respect by, the subjects of the King of Heaven, especially in these latter ages, when at length the lustre of his virtues shines forth so brilliantly, and his extraordinary merits and prerogatives receive their due tribute of admiration and praise; there is no heart now, not even the most savage, which does not acknowledge his empire. The devotion to St. Joseph is not merely confined to Europe, which is the centre of religion; it has also been diffused throughout Asia, Africa, and America. In Turkey, we find that the Latins and Greek Catholics have signalized themselves by their devotion to St. Joseph. If we penetrate into the deepest recesses of the forests of North America, we shall hear the first among the Iroquois who there received baptism, proclaiming joyfully, that he has the honour of being called by the name of Joseph. Let us cross the seas, and enter upon the burning sands of Paraguay: we shall there meet a multitude of newly-made Chris-

tians, who have all assumed the name of the spouse
of the Mother of God; and we shall be filled with
admiration on beholding the devotion to this great
saint wafted so prosperously by the breath of the
Holy Spirit over the ocean, and even passing beyond
those boundaries almost inaccessible to the bravest
conquerors, in order to take possession of the hearts
of this hitherto barbarous people.   Following the
Apostolical Missionaries into Tonquin, we may fearlessly enter its harbours, for they are all under the
protection of St. Joseph; his name was taken by the
first of the Tonquinese who received baptism.   But
let us still proceed farther, and even to the most remote parts of India, and everywhere, in the East as
in the West, our hearts will exult with joy, because
everywhere we shall hear the name of Joseph.

Should we now wish to ascertain why the devotion
to this great saint should have made so many conquests in so short a space of time, in those countries
where idolatry before reigned, we may easily do so,
by the reflection, that as our Lord would in infancy
be conducted into Egypt by St. Joseph, so it would
also appear that St. Joseph's powerful intercession
was requisite in order to introduce the faith of the
Redeemer into all infidel nations, and as the "child
Jesus," while travelling under St. Joseph's protection, once overturned the Egyptian idols, He still
continues, in our days, to employ the arm of His beloved father in order to achieve their destruction.

And may it not have been in order to reward St.
Joseph for all the privations and hardships which he
had to suffer in a barbarous country, that God has
rendered his name so glorious amongst idolatrous
nations?   And was it not also for the purpose of

manifesting to the world this saint's ardent zeal for
the salvation of the Egyptians, who once offered an
asylum to Mary and her Son, that the Eternal Father
has placed in his hands the conversion of several infidel nations? In St. Joseph's journey from Judea
into Egypt, with the Infant-God in his arms, St.
Hilary sees a type of the zeal and fervour of the
holy apostles, who, for the instruction and regeneration of mankind, have carried into all parts of the
Universe the Divine Gospel and the precious blood
of their Divine Master. St. Anselm likewise observes, that St. Joseph, whose heart burned with holy
zeal to see the entire Universe subjugated to the
amiable yoke of our Blessed Saviour, represented
those preachers who, like valiant captains, cease not
to recruit and enlist new soldiers in the service of
Jesus Christ. God was pleased then, it appears, to
do greater things for our saint than the king of Egypt
had done for the ancient patriarch: the reward of
his zeal and of his labours was, first, the conversion
of a great number of idolatrous ñations, such as the
Egyptians, effected by his special intercession, and
finally, their perseverance in following the light of
faith, owing chiefly to the efficacy of his powerful
protection.

It is, however, a subject of great joy to the Church,
to see the success of her project, which was, to
diffuse the devotion to St. Joseph throughout the
Universe, in order that in him she might find a patron
filled with zeal for the propagation of the faith. It
is natural to suppose that none should be more zealous
for the preservation of the laws than those who make
them: if, then, our holy religion, while yet in its
infancy, in the person of our Lord, was entrusted to

the care and guardianship of St. Joseph, is it not
reasonable to believe, that according to the different
states in which it has been since found, Divine Providence specially designs that it should rise, increase,
continue, and flourish, in virtue of the merits of the
saint who, according to St. Bernardin of Sienna, had
the keys in his hands to open the doors of the New
Law, and to close those of the Mosaic ?

There is nothing of which the Church is so jealous
as her faith : she considers it as the bulwark or
fortress which sustains the kingdom of her Divine
Spouse. It is not that she fears that the powers of
Earth or Hell shall ever prevail against her, supported as she is by the infallible promises of Jesus
Christ; but she fears the snares which are laid for
her beloved children, and wishes to make use of all
her energies, in order to shield them from the enemies
by whom they are surrounded. For this reason it is
that she has recourse to the patronage of those saints
who have most successfully defended or propagated
her faith, such as the princes of the apostles, Saints
Peter and Paul. According to Gerson, the devotion
to St. Joseph chiefly dates its rise from a period in
which the afflicted Church beheld with painful solicitude an awful schism forming in the West, which,
like a furious tempest, shook and tore it to pieces
from all quarters. A council was held at Constance,
for the purpose of counteracting its baneful influence.* In a discourse pronounced by Gerson, in

---

* The Council of Constance, convoked by John XXIII., was
opened on the 5th of November, 1414 : it lasted till the month of
April, 1418. The schism, caused by several pretenders to the
Papacy, had already desolated the Church for a long time. It
was on the 8th of September, 1416, that Gerson, deputy and

presence of that august assembly, among other means
calculated to calm the tempest, and effect a total reformation of morals, he proposed that of a special invocation of St. Joseph, and of promoting as much as
possible the practice of devotion to him, hoping that
this new devotion might prove a beacon-light to
guide all hearts to peace and holiness. He proceeded
to state that this great saint, having been the guardian
and instructor of Jesus Christ, acts in the same capa-
city towards all Christians: he then dilated with
much zeal upon the glorious prerogatives of St.
Joseph. His discourse was heard with the deepest
interest, and applauded by the entire Council. But,
had it not also the sanction of the Holy Ghost Himself? It was Gerson who inspired the people of the

Chancellor of the University of Paris, as well as envoy-extraordi-
nary to the Council of the King of France, pronounced the discourse of which mention has been made. He took for his text
this passage of St. Matthew: "Jacob genuit Joseph virum
Mariæ; de quâ natus est Jesus, qui vocatur Christus." To the
praises of Mary he joined those of St. Joseph, and exhorted the
Fathers of the Council to have recourse to them both, in order
to obtain, by their intercession, the peace of the whole Church.
" Ita Mariæ meritis et intercessione tanti tamque potentis impe-
riosi Josephi et si fas est dicere; quodam jure jubentis ; Ecclesia
reddatur unico viro et certo summo Pontifici ; Sponso suo vice
Christi." Gerson, in the same discourse, puts forth a remarkable
opinion about the Blessed Virgin and St. Joseph. Although he
acknowledges that the Immaculate Conception of Mary is not
formally declared in the Scriptures, nevertheless he proposes to
the Council to examine whether this privilege ought not to be
made an article of faith. Then extolling the prerogatives and
dignity of St. Joseph, he speaks of his sanctification from the
womb of his mother, of his perpetual virginity, of his assumption
into heaven, of the place he there occupies above the other saints,
though below Mary. He even goes so far as to propose the

West with the desire of honouring St. Joseph by a
particular devotion, and with a firm conviction that
his prayers and merits would avert all the evils with
which the Catholic faith was threatened, and would
likewise draw down a multitude of graces and favours
upon the faithful. Thus speaks Isidore de Lille, a
pious and learned Dominican.

Since the Church has had so many remarkable
instances of the efficacy of St. Joseph's protection,
especially in what regards faith, which holds the first
place among her best treasures, she uses all her influence to extend and establish the devotion to this
great saint, as being a powerful instrument either to
prosecute the propagation of that faith, or to maintain it in all its purity.   In this she is also actuated

institution of a feast in honour of his immaculate Birth.   We
do not venture to pronounce upon the doctrine of Gerson; we will
only say, that it certainly merits consideration from the circumstances under which he spoke.   The legates of the Holy See, more
than twenty cardinals, two hundred bishops, and an immense
number of doctors, were there present; far from contradicting
this learned theologian, they listened to him with respectful attention, and applauded the proposition he made of invoking the
aid of St. Joseph.   A year had hardly elapsed before peace was
restored to the Church; the whole Catholic body were reunited
under Martin V., who was elected in the place of Gregory XII.,
Benedict XIII., and John XXIII., at the forty-first session, November 8th, 1417.   The celebrated Cardinal Peter d'Ailly, Arch-
bishop of Cambray, assisted at this Council. He, as is well
known, vied with Gerson, his former disciple, in devotion to St.
Joseph.   He had been Chancellor of the University of Paris, and
became later legate to Martin V.   If it be true what several
authors affirm, that the progress of the devotion to St. Joseph
dates from this Council, we shall recognise with pleasure the
part these two illustrious children of France took in a cause so
gloriously maintained afterwards by such a number of celebrated
personages.

by another motive not less noble, viz., the particular
advantage it is so well calculated to afford each of
the faithful individually.   Accordingly, she seems to
look upon St. Joseph as the universal protector of all
Christians, and entitled as such to the confidence and
imitation of all, without exception, whatever be their
age or condition.

It is no wonder, then, that Isidore should style
him the "Patron of the Church militant."   But this
subject deserves to be treated of separately and more
at length in the following chapter.

CHAPTER VI.

Sixth Motive—St. Joseph is a Powerful and Beneficent Patron
to all Christians.

THE Angelical Doctor teaches, that God has been
pleased to give some saints a special power to protect
under certain peculiar necessities, and others he has
endowed with gifts of various kinds; but to St.
Joseph He has been more generous—He has made
Him as it were His plenipotentiary, His treasurer-
general, that he may have it in his power to assist
and relieve every description of person, whatever
may be his necessity.   Thus it is that St. Theresa
speaks, and her testimony is worth a thousand others,
because it is founded upon her daily experience of
the power of this glorious saint.   This is likewise
the sentiment of the Church, since she asks through
his intercession what she cannot of herself obtain—

" That what we cannot obtain may be granted to us
through his intercession," &c.

King Pharaoh, on being presented with the peti-
tions of his subjects, referred them to Joseph of old,
whom he hath invested with absolute authority over
his court and kingdom. " Go to Joseph, and do all
that he shall say to you." (*Gen.* xli.). The King of
Heaven has invested St. Joseph with an authority no
less unbounded. The other saints, it is true, have
great power, but only to a certain extent. They intercede and supplicate as dependants, but they do not
rule as masters; whereas St. Joseph, to whom at
Nazareth Jesus and Mary had lived submissive, as
being the father of one and husband to the other,
now that he dwells in the House of God, where his
titles, far from being obscured, shine out with incomparable brilliancy, may doubtless obtain all he
desires from the King his Son and the Queen his
spouse. His influence with both is unbounded, and
as Gerson says, " he rather commands than suppli-
cates." Hence it may be seen, how powerful is the
intercession of St. Joseph !

But can anything contribute more powerfully to
render St. Joseph's intercession infallible, than the
goodness of his own heart, and the paternal love and
interest which he feels for all those who ask his
prayers ? Jesus Christ Himself, in becoming his Son,
filled his heart with a love infinitely more tender
than that of any ordinary parent, and in doing so,
His views were not confined to Himself alone, but it
was also His design that this love should be extended to all mankind, who are the adopted children
of St. Joseph. It is also in allusion to this truly
paternal love, that the venerable Mother St. Joseph,

the first French Carmelite, says, that God, in appointing our glorious saint to be a father to His only Son, desired that he should also be a father to His adopted brethren, to the mystical members of the Divine Child; and that with this intent He communicated to him, as a special favour, an extraordinary degree of tenderness in their regard, which engages him to watch over their interests with more devotion and solicitude than an affectionate parent over the interests of his own children (*See her life*). And surely is not St. Joseph's family a numerous one? yes, even as great as that of Jesus Christ Himself, for it comprehends all the children of the Catholic Church. Yes, my divine Jesus! You who have so often reposed upon Joseph's bosom, therein to enkindle a furnace of love proportioned to his paternal obligations, have you not also given him a heart far greater and more capacious, than was that which you gave to Solomon, the wisest of kings? For this reason, then, let all the children of the Holy Church hasten to have recourse to the paternal heart of St. Joseph; they may depend on finding it large enough for the reception of all, and sufficiently tender to impart to each an abundant share of its choicest favours. As the wide vault of the Heavens encompasses all parts of the Earth, so is the beneficent influence of St. Joseph's heart felt by all without exception, for it is generous enough to embrace the whole world in its affections.

But now, previous to inviting the faithful individually to place themselves under the protection of a patron, at once so powerful and so benign, I will have recourse to yourself, blessed St. Joseph! father full of goodness! Deign to purify my tongue and my heart, give me not a mere scholastic eloquence, but impart to my words a grace and an unction that will persuade, even by their very simplicity, persons of every age, rank, and condition, to choose you as a father and protector.

CHAPTER VII.

Seventh Motive—the Interest Virgins, Interior Souls, Religious, Artizans, Married Persons, those engaged in the Instruction of Youth, Priests, and even Sinners, have in taking St. Joseph for their Patron.

IF, according to St. Cyprian, virgins be the most honourable, as well as the favourite portion of the family of Jesus Christ, it follows that this tender parent watches over them with a peculiar love and attention to their minutest interest. You then, Christian virgins, are those whom I would, in the first place, exhort to make choice of the glorious St. Joseph as your father and protector, for to his care was entrusted the divine innocence of the Infant Saviour, and the integrity of the Queen of Virgins. The latter, as above-mentioned, found in St. Joseph a zealous defender of her virginity against the poisonous blast of heresy, which strove to tarnish it. "He is my most zealous champion against those who question my virginity," said she to St. Bridget (*Rev.*). St. Francis de Sales assures us, that St. Joseph's purity surpassed that of the angels of the first hierarchy; for, as he says, if the material Sun can perfect the dazzling whiteness of the lily in a few days, who can conceive the admirable degree of perfection to which St. Joseph's purity was raised, when it was exposed, not for a few days only, but for the space of thirty years, to the rays of the Sun of Justice and of the mystical Moon, which derived from that Sun all her splendour? Does not all this, ye Christian virgins, teach you to appreciate the power of the great patron, to whom I now recommend you? Imitate those young virgins of the town of N., who make an annual offering of a bouquet, composed of those flowers which are considered to be the emblems of purity, to St. Joseph, in order to obtain through his prayers the grace of preservation from whatever might in the least endanger that precious treasure.

And all you who are anxious to lead an interior life, do you seek a prudent guide, an enlightened spiritual father? Place yourselves with perfect confidence under the direction of a saint who, even during his mortal life, enjoyed, like the angels themselves, the most intimate communication with God in holy prayer and contemplation, according to the Church Office (*Hymn to St. Joseph*). For this reason it is, that retreat-houses are usually placed under the protection of St. Joseph; and likewise St. Theresa assures us, that never was there known a person truly devoted to St. Joseph, who did not make great progress in the spiritual life. It is a well-known fact, that the venerable father Claudius de la Colombiere, and Louis Lallemant (Society of Jesus), who were specially devoted to St. Joseph, and had chosen him as their model and patron, attained a high degree of prayer and union with God. With the help of so powerful and zealous a friend, who may not hope to advance, and make new progress daily in the paths of perfection?

The world may be compared to a vast ocean, agitated by a tempest, and the most dangerous rock within its bosom is the marriage state, for scarcely a day passes on which we do not therein witness some new wreck; whence it follows, that those who are exposed to such a danger, would require a good pilot to conduct them safely into port; and where meet a more experienced one than our glorious saint, who, in accordance with the designs of God, embraced that state, and is a model for those who desire to render it conducive both to their temporal and eternal welfare? Scripture informs us that the patriarch Joseph brought down the benediction of Heaven not only on Potiphar's household, but also on Pharaoh's court and the entire kingdom. This prosperity continued as long as the king followed the advice of Joseph, his prime-minister; but when, on the accession of a new sovereign, Joseph was dismissed from office, how changed was the scene! "A new king over Egypt that knew not Joseph," (*Exod.* i.).

Does not this metaphor clearly indicate to all Christian families, that God will give a special blessing to those who duly honour the second Joseph, who is as superior to the former, as the substance is to the shadow? You then, heads of families, if you wish your children to be well brought up, if you wish to ensure peace in your married state, fidelity in your servants, patience in tribulations, in a word, if you desire that your household should be well regulated, and live in peace and tranquillity, place it under the protection of him whom God has constituted head of the Holy Family : "Quem constituit Dominus super familiam suam." Let Joseph be your counsellor, your steward, your example; God Himself has appointed him such for those who are engaged in the married state.

The motives which should induce religious families to choose St. Joseph for their patron, are not less urgent than those which oblige seculars to do so. And, in truth, where do we meet the founder of any religious order, whose example stands forth with greater lustre than that of St. Joseph, as an adept in all the virtues to which religious persons are bound by vow, and as an excellent master of holy poverty, chastity, and obedience. The humble homestead of Nazareth furnishes a complete model of the monastic or common life, and a living rule of the active and contemplative. Many religious houses, as we can prove by authentic facts, have experienced the efficacy of St. Joseph's protection, either when in want of subjects, or in time of scarcity. Religious houses will be always dear to a saint who sees in them a lively representation of the life which Jesus led during thirty years at Nazareth, in obscurity, and under the yoke of obedience.

St. Joseph exercised the trade of a carpenter, according to the opinion of the Holy Fathers : he is, therefore, considered not only as the patron of all the members of that profession, but likewise of artizans in general, who should take him as a model of all the virtues which should adorn their state of life. Whom will they find more holy than him, whom the Son of God was pleased to call by the endearing name of father ? Let them reflect for a moment on the manner in which he sanctified his laborious occupations. He lived a life of faith, and therefore the love of riches and a thirst for gain held no sway in his heart; he deemed his labour sufficiently repaid, when they procured him the means of providing for his family. What admirable honesty and integrity he displays in all his dealings! How indefatigably assiduous at his work, but yet without for an instant losing sight of Jesus, his divine pupil; like the angels, who, while watching over us with the tenderest vigilance, cease not to contemplate that infinite and adorable Being, in whom all their beatitude consists! Ah! if they, whose avocations resemble those to which St. Joseph devoted his time when on earth, would only learn from him the precious art of uniting prayer with labour, they would make a twofold acquisition; for a blessing would accompany their exertions, even in this life, and a happy eternity would be their reward, exceeding great, in a better world. All artizans, then, have a particular claim on his protection, which they should daily invoke, and insure for themselves and families, by a faithful imitation of the virtues which are suitable to their state, and of which he has given them so illustrious an example.

Those who are charged with the instruction and education of youth, are particularly called upon to choose St. Joseph as their guide and patron in an employment so useful to religion; since having been the master and guardian of the Most High, he has received from Him peculiar graces and favours for the protection of youth. The young Tobias had an angel as his guardian, but Jesus would have no other guardian than St. Joseph. Hence, the brothers of the Christian schools, and many other societies, have placed their schools, especially those for young children, under the special protection of St. Joseph. The interpreters of Scripture and ecclesiastical writers, have given him various names, as those of father, foster-father, guardian, guide of Jesus Christ. All these functions which he fulfilled towards an Infant-God, he still continues to exercise in favour of those colleges and seminaries which are entrusted to his paternal vigilance. Superiors and masters may learn of him the charity, prudence, vigilance, and the other virtues, requisite for governing well. On their side, likewise, the pupils may receive from the Child Jesus the most perfect examples of docility, respect, and love, towards their masters and superiors.

Our saint may also be considered the model and patron of prelates, and of all ecclesiastics in general. And we, priests of the Most High God, we, who so often, though unworthy, touch the body of Jesus Christ! should we not singularly love and venerate the privileged being, who, as representative of the entire human race in general, and of the ministers of the altar more particularly, was the first who received the Redeemer into his arms, and who offered up to the Eternal Father, at the circumcision of the Divine Infant, the first effusions of that most precious blood which was afterwards so profusely shed on Calvary, to wash away the sins of the world, and which is daily offered by the hands of God's sacred ministers for the living and the dead? The real presence of Jesus upon our altars, should inspire us with the same sentiments with which St. Joseph was animated on beholding Him, a helpless little babe, lying on straw in the manger. On these occasions, when it becomes our awful duty to convey to the house of mourning the

God of all glory, the glorious conqueror of sin and
death, the joy of the angels, the beauty and the bliss
of Paradise, not concealed beneath the humiliating
garb of human nature as He appeared when on Earth,
not in the effulgence of His glorified humanity as He
now appears in Heaven, but disguised beneath the
Sacramental veils, to which His own infinite love has
reduced Him—when we pass through streets, and
towns, and districts, with our mysterious charge, do
our interior sentiments correspond with those of holy
Joseph? are we animated with the same piety, love,
and reverence, with which he carried his Infant
Saviour into Egypt? And yet, faith tells us, that
the dignity of the priesthood is greater still than that
with which Joseph was invested.

O glorious saint! Jesus was subject to you in all
things; He now obeys the voice of the priest, whoever he may be! Whilst He reposed like a gentle
lamb in the crib, you presented Him to the shepherds,
that they might adore Him; and the priest offers up
to the Eternal Father the flesh and blood of the Lamb
that was slain, the Lamb of God who takes away the
sins of the world. You nourished Jesus with that
bread which was necessary to sustain His mortal existence; but the priest nourishes the faithful soul
with an incorruptible food, even Jesus Christ Himself, under the appearance of bread, that he who eats
thereof with faith and love, may live for ever.
Happy saint! you were permitted to caress, and
receive in return the caresses of the Divine Child;
but yet the priest need not envy you, nor even the
laity themselves, for do they not often enjoy the inestimable happiness of receiving Jesus Himself as
their food? But that which should principally

excite our admiration and holy envy, is that admirable purity of heart, by which St. Joseph was habitually disposed to receive new stores of grace and sanctity. Jesus was his treasure. From the hands of Jesus he received the grace of performing all his actions for Him alone; the eyes of Jesus so enlightened his mind, as to enable him to understand perfectly the divine mysteries; the flames of divine love which issued from the adorable heart of Jesus, consumed him with the most lively and ardent charity, with love to God and benevolence to man. In order to produce similar effects in our souls, our Blessed Lord has delivered Himself unreservedly into our hands. Let us, who are priests of the Most High God, earnestly implore St. Joseph for all those graces we stand in need of, in order that we may be worthy ministers of a Sacrament which he never enjoyed the privilege of administering or receiving.

But the wish nearest to my heart is, that all unfortunate sinners would have recourse to St. Joseph, that he may rise them up speedily from the abyss in which they are immersed; let them call on him with the same vehemence and ardour, as they doubtless would cry for help on accidentally falling into a dark pit. The patriarch Joseph of old did not surely possess a more tender and compassionate heart than our saint. He could not refrain from weeping, on beholding his brethren penetrated with horror, remorse, and anguish, at the recollection of the fratricide they had committed. If the second Joseph sheds no tears, he will do something more; he will draw tears of sincere contrition from the eyes of unhappy sinners. If Mary be the refuge of sinners, Joseph is their refuge on the same grounds. It was compassion

for sinners that brought the Son of God down from
Heaven. "O felix culpa!" exclaims the Church in
its Office for Holy Saturday. Had this not been the
case, would Mary have been the mother, and Joseph
the guardian and adopted father of Jesus? In Jesus
only can true and solid happiness be found, even on
Earth; Joseph knew this well; he also knows that
the sinner's misery springs from the misfortune of
having lost Jesus! Joseph himself experienced that
grievous torment; his anguish was great on that
occasion, though his own conduct was irreproachable;
he can, therefore, more feelingly sympathise with
poor sinners, he is more alive to the misery of their
condition, and consequently a more strenuous advocate in their behalf: in the company of Mary he will
conduct them to the Temple, where, after three days'
careful research and heartfelt grief, they will have
the happiness of finding Him! "If you seek Him,
you will find Him with Joseph and Mary," says
Origen. Alas! my brethren, we are all sinners; let
us, therefore, go with confidence to Joseph, and let
us address him in the words of those Gentiles, who,
desirous of being presented to our Lord, said to the
apostle St. Philip: "We wish to see Jesus." Ah!
most powerful and compassionate father! do bring us
to Jesus; it is by you we would be introduced into
His divine presence: rebels and sinners, we have not
courage to present ourselves; but we now appeal to
your goodness in the words of the Egyptians to your
representative of old: "Our salvation is in your
hands." It is our firm conviction, that in virtue of
the authority which you exercised over Jesus here
below, we shall the more easily be restored to His
grace and friendship.

The invitation which the learned and pious Gerson once gave a distinguished personage (the Duke de Berri), I now address to all Christians in general, as an appropriate conclusion to this chapter : " My lord," said he, " take St. Joseph for your special patron, your most powerful mediator, and best friend." Beloved brethren in Christ, I conjure you, by your love for Jesus and Mary—by your respect and attachment for your holy mother the Church—and by that yearning after happiness which nothing merely transitory can ever content, that you choose St. Joseph for your protector, advocate, and friend. Remember that you must ere long make your exit from this scene. Be not so foolish as to neglect making interest, while time yet remains, with one who is considered the particular patron of dying Christians.

CHAPTER VIII.

Eighth Motive—the Example of Religious Orders.

RELIGIOUS ORDERS have at all times been remarkable for devotion to a saint, who is regarded as the most perfect model of religious perfection after Jesus and Mary ; but in this respect it must be acknowledged, that Carmel has far surpassed all other orders. It was this order which first established an office in his honour, and from Syria introduced it afterwards into Europe. But, as the impress of change is on everything human, so, in the lapse of time, the devotion to St. Joseph gradually declined in this order, and even his office was neglected or forgotten. However, the illustrious Theresa, who was the instrument made use of by Providence for the reformation of Carmel, re-established there the devotion to its former patron, when once more it flourished in all its primeval fervour. This extraordinary personage was the foundress of innumerable religious houses, and, with hardly an exception, placed them all under the special patronage of St. Joseph.

In order to complete the good work so happily commenced by the august reformer of Carmel, the general chapter of the order, which was convoked in the year 1621, solemnly acknowledged St. Joseph to be their special patron and spiritual father. The decree was published, and received with universal joy. In 1680, they obtained from the Congregation of Rites authority to establish the feast in honour of the Patronage of St. Joseph, as a double of the second class, with a proper office, composed by Father John of the Conception. The Congregation of Rites has fixed this feast on the third Sunday after Easter, and his Holiness Pius IX., by a decree of the 10th of September, 1847, has rendered it obligatory on the whole Church.

The order of St. Francis has been remarkable, from its very infancy, for devotion to St. Joseph. A general chapter, held in 1399, established a feast in his honour; and other chapters, which were held subsequently, added considerably to the solemnity of its celebration.

Without entering into the details of that remote period, we may form a true estimate of the veneration in which he was held by the Friars Minor, if we peruse that affecting and most interesting document, written by St. Bernardin of Sienna, on the subject.

St. Peter of Alcantara, who was the reformer of the Franciscan order, with permission from the Holy See, convoked a chapter, in which the nine recently-reformed houses of the order were erected into a particular province. He also placed this yet feeble plant in the hands of St. Joseph, that under his fostering care it might grow and increase unto the measure of a mighty tree, in which the birds of the air might dwell; he bade his religious cultivate a particular devotion to the saint, and likewise gave orders that a seal should be struck for the newly-established province, to represent St. Joseph carrying the Divine Infant in his arms.

The order of St. Dominick proved no less zealous in procuring the glory of our holy patriarch. So early as the fourteenth century, we find that Albert the Great composed an office in his honour, in compliance with the pious wishes of the saint's devout clients. At a more recent period, the Father-General ordered that a new office should be composed in his honour; and so replete with unction and piety is this little formula, that its author, Isidore de Lille, has a just claim on the gratitude of St. Joseph's devoted children. This venerable writer was one of the first who made use of his pen in order to draw forth the name of our saint from that obscurity which concealed it from the eyes of the world. Looking into futurity, he beholds all the glory that is in reserve for St. Joseph, and invites a host of accomplished penmen, who were to come after him, to make the life of that glorious saint the subject of their most assiduous meditation, in order to discern and bring to light the inestimable treasures of merits therein contained. His words were prophetic, for we now see them verified. "Men," says he, "eminently wise and virtuous, shall study to become intimately acquainted with the great St. Joseph, and they shall find him possessed of hidden treasures far more precious and beautiful, than any of which the ancient patriarchs could boast."—"Viri magni scrutabuntur interiora Dei dona abscondita in Josepho, et invenient thesaurum qualem apud sanctos Patres Veteris Testamenti non invenerunt." All the honours which the Church renders to St. Joseph on the festival of his espousals with the Mother of God, must, in a great measure, be attributed to the Dominicans; for though this feast was first established by the Franciscans, yet it was the Dominicans who established a particular office for that day, and obtained from Pope Paul III. that it should be celebrated on the 23rd of January, with the greatest solemnity.

St. Joseph was held in no less veneration by the Augustinians. In 1632, a general chapter, held at Rome, decreed, that all their houses, both in Italy and Germany, should have St. Joseph as their special patron; and consequently all the novitiate houses and colleges of the order were, in a special manner, dedicated to the Holy Family; the vespers of the saint are therein recited on all Fridays throughout the year; and, in 1700, it was decreed, that a commemoration of this saint should be made in all the semi-double offices, and that permission be obtained from the Congregation of Rites, for the solemn observance in their houses of the Feast of the Patronage, as celebrated in the order of the reformed Carmelites.

And finally, the children of St. Ignatius would not be fully entitled to be called members of the "Society of Jesus," were they not devoted to a saint who had been the nursing father of the child Jesus. It was by the Jesuits he was instituted patron of the spiritual exercise called the "Bona Mors," in order that all those who use this holy practice may call upon him with confidence in their last moments, in virtue of his own precious death in the arms of Jesus and Mary. They also, with permission, inserted among the Votive Masses in the Roman Missal, one for the special purpose of obtaining a happy death. St. Joseph being justly regarded as a perfect model of humility, recollection, and the interior life, the Society has placed under his special protection those houses in which the junior members make it their special object to perfect themselves in the science of the saints, after having previously gone through their course of humanities. Bollandus remarks, that in Spain, France, and the Netherlands, all the churches belonging to the colleges of the Society are dedicated to St. Joseph. We may also remark, that it was the Jesuits of Lyons who first erected a church in his honour in France, and that he has been singularly favourable to those who invoked his name within that privileged sanctuary. Not content with seeing him honoured in our own hemisphere, the Jesuits have carried his name, and infused a devotion to him, among the savage tribes of the New World, or rather, from one extremity of the vast continent of America to the other; and among the numerous reductions of Paraguay, that of "St. Joseph," was hardly established, when, through the interest of its powerful patron, it obtained the glory of drawing, by its good example, six neigh-bouring tribes to Christianity. This filial affection of the Fathers of the Company of Jesus has only in-creased with time; at the present moment several of its missions and colleges are placed under his protec-tion. The Congregation of the Bona Mors and of the Pious Workmen, established in every town where the Fathers themselves have obtained a footing, are so many proofs of their devotion to St. Joseph. In 1859, the Father-General asked, as a special favour, that the Society of Jesus should be allowed to celebrate the Feast of the Patronage as a double of the first class, with an octave.

CHAPTER IX.

Ninth Motive—The Example of Princes, Kingdoms, and Cities.

SINCE Heaven has revealed to the Christian world the glory of a saint so little known in former ages, the emphatic words addressed by Assuerus to Morde-chai may be far more aptly applied to him : "This honour is he worthy of, whom the king hath a mind to honour" (*Esther*, vi.). And was it not worthy of His divine magnificence, that our Lord in these latter times, after proclaiming the glorious name of St. Joseph from the rising to the setting of the Sun, should have brought monarchs and empires to pay a tribute of respect and love to the saint, whom He acknowledges to be His favourite, His guardian, and His father?

Whatever practices of piety are favoured and adopted by princes, will soon become popular with their subjects; the devotion to St. Joseph has had this advantage. Almost incredible was the rapidity of its growth in Germany at that period, when the pious Emperor, Leopold I., of glorious memory, so zealously laboured to inspire all his subjects with that confidence and veneration towards this great saint, which he himself possessed in a eminent degree. On occasion of the consecration of Bohemia to St. Joseph, that country gave him the title of the "Guardian of the Peace;" the entire kingdom acknowledged and invoked him as its special patron, on seeing its pious sovereign lay Hungary at his feet, immediately after having rescued its capital from the yoke of the Turks, beneath which it had groaned. Leopold, under the conviction that so glorious a victory was the fruit of the joint intercession of Mary and Joseph, and wishing to give them a public mark of gratitude, obtained from Rome the privilege of keeping the festival of St. Joseph's espousals a strict holiday throughout his dominions. But it must be acknowledged, that the devotion to this saint never shone forth with greater lustre in Germany, than on the memorable occasion of which we are about to speak. The imperial family was much affected on seeing no prospect of an heir, who might one day fill the throne of the Cæsars, as successor to the reigning sovereign. In this painful situation, Leopold had recourse to St. Joseph's intercession. In order to propitiate the saint in his favour, his first act was to publish a solemn declaration, whereby he acknowledged St. Joseph to be the special patron of the House of Austria; he then erected a large statue of the saint in massive silver, and ordered that, during eight successive days, processions should be made in eight different churches, and a panegyric of the saint preached in each church. St. Joseph heard the prayers of this religious family, of which he soon gave convincing proof; for, after the nine following months had elapsed, the empress gave birth to the prince who had been so ardently desired. On the news of this great event, St. Joseph was honoured by all Germany and Austria, with a simultaneous tribute of praise, and the air resounded with heartfelt expressions of joy and gratitude. The Emperor, in the transports of his thankfulness, gave the name of Joseph to the new-born prince, who was the first of his family called by that name; and, in order to give his glorious benefactor a new pledge of his devoted affection, Leopold made a vow to erect a second statue to him, on one of the public squares at Vienna: death prevented him from fulfilling this pious engagement; but Joseph, who was not only heir to his throne, but who also inherited his father's devotion to our saint, had this statue erected, on the feast of him to whom he was indebted for existence, the 19th of March, 1709. He assisted in person at this august ceremony, surrounded by all his courtiers and the inhabitants of Vienna.

Spain has, at all times, been remarkable for its piety, and the glorious spouse of the Mother of God has ever been the first and most cherished object of veneration in that country, after Jésus and Mary. The lively devotion to our saint, which the burning zeal of St. Theresa had established throughout the

entire kingdom, was much increased by the good
example of the court, which procured the introduction of the feast of his espousals into that kingdom.
Spain soon communicated its fervour to other countries, especially to the Netherlands, by means of the
Archduchess Isabella-Clare-Eugenia, who was regent
for His Catholic Majesty. Almost immediately on
her arrival at Brussels, this pious princess gave such
edifying examples of devotion to St. Joseph, and
made such an impression on the people, that even
previous to the decree of Urban VIII., appointing
his feast to be kept holy, all manual labour was suspended, the shops were closed, and his feast was
celebrated by the citizens with the utmost devotion
and solemnity. But Antwerp is more remarkable
for devotion to him than any other city in the
Netherlands. The Romer family in that city erected
two magnificent chapels in his honour, one in the
Church of the Augustinians, the other in that of the
Jesuits. The latter is a masterpiece, on which art
seems to have lavished all her attractions; but what
is yet more worthy of admiration is, that within the
lapse of six years, St. Joseph was pleased to favour
it with so many miraculous pledges of his benign
patronage, as would require volumes to enumerate.
You will find in Bollandus a detailed account of
these graces, and of the honours paid to the saint in
that city : it remains for us now only to say, that in
the chapel of which we speak, three Masses are
offered up every Friday, to obtain the grace of a
happy death, through the merits of St. Joseph's precious death; after each Mass, there is exposition and
benediction of the Most Holy Sacrament; and the concourse of people is so great, at first Mass especially,

which is celebrated at break of day, that the church, spacious though it be, can scarcely accommodate the immense congregation.*

The illustrious chancellor, John Gerson, sowed the first seeds of devotions to St. Joseph in France, at a period when, in other countries, his name, had been unknown, or rather forgotten, for ages. This precious seed did not bring forth fruit for some time, like the grain of wheat, which during winter lies buried in the earth, but at the return of spring, makes a rapid growth, and shoots forth vigorously. The first chapels erected in France in honour of our saint, were those at Avignon, by Gregory XI.; here was likewise established a sodality of young girls, who were called Josephines. The pious Queen of France, Anna-Theresa of Austria, contributed much

---

* The Bollandists, from whom our author borrows these details, published their Life of St. Joseph in 1668. Since that period, the chapel erected by the brothers Romer, in the Church of the Company of Jesus, continues to be frequented; but the one which they built in the Church of the Augustinians has entirely disappeared. The numerous Confraternity of St. Joseph, which used to meet at the Carmelites, has shared the same fate; but the archives of these two churches have been carefully preserved, and afford us, by the illustrious names inscribed on their registers, abundant proofs of the predilection of St. Joseph for Antwerp. At the present day, the devotion to the holy patriarch is more flourishing than ever. The Confraternity of the Perpetual Devotion, commenced three years ago, in the Church of the Augustinians, already numbers six thousand. Other and not less flourishing Confraternities are aggregated to the Church of Notre Dame, and to that of St. Paul. St. Joseph, sensible of so many homages, continues to shower upon the inhabitants of Antwerp the graces which he so abundantly shed upon their ancestors. [These details are taken from a letter, dated March 9th, 1860.]

to the increase of this devotion, by inviting into her
kingdom the daughters of that admirable virgin who
had done so much for St. Joseph in Spain. The
name of Theresa, which she bore, was an additional
motive with the queen for imitating the zeal of
her holy patroness, by endeavouring to propagate a
devotion to this saint; it also induced her to add the
name of Joseph to that of her eldest son Louis.

It would be tedious to enumerate the many religious orders of both sexes which have devoted themselves in this country to the service of youth, under
the special protection of St. Joseph, and have been
called after his name; their beneficial influence on
society, even at the present day, makes them sufficiently conspicuous. Neither shall we here cite the
vast number of authors who, since Gerson, have
employed their talents in the composition of works in
honour of St. Joseph, which have been translated
into every language; their multitude is in itself a
sufficient proof of the tender devotion of the French
nation towards the worthy spouse of Mary.

We shall now glance at Italy. This country has
not been outdone by any other in its love and veneration for this great saint. To begin with the town
of Florence, where I now write: The Florentines
prepare for the feast of St. Joseph by two novenas,
and the feast itself may be deemed a real triumph of
Christian charity. It is usual with families to invite
three poor persons to dinner on this day—an old
man, a woman, and her child. This was a practice
which the pious merchant of Valencia made a vow
to observe, as cited by St. Vincent Ferrer. Those
families who cannot do so, give alms to three poor
persons. In addition to the solemn feast of the 19th

of March, which is celebrated all over the world, the
Florentines keep three others, to satisfy their devotion,
viz., the first Sunday after the Epiphany is the feast
of the hidden life which Joseph led with Jesus and
Mary; the 23rd of January, the feast of his marriage
with the Blessed Virgin; and the 20th of June, that
of his holy death in the arms of Jesus and Mary.
Here are likewise established several congregations
of both sexes in honour of St. Joseph; but we have
said quite sufficient to give an idea of the genuine
attachment of the Florentines to St. Joseph.*

The city of Naples prepares for the feast of St.
Joseph by various practices of piety in his honour,
which are performed on the seven Wednesdays immediately preceding the 19th of March.   In Venice,
novenas are offered up, with great devotion, in all
the churches at the same hour : this devotion is not
confined merely to the city; the entire Republic of
Venice glories in paying homage to this great saint;
and here it was that the feast of his patronage was
first generally established, the feast of his espousals
having been previously kept there as a strict holiday.
It was from Rome, the centre of Catholicity, that
as from its source, the devotion to St. Joseph diffused
itself, in its present form, throughout the whole
Christian world.   Since Pope Clement X. made his
feast one of first-class solemnity, and gave him a
particular office, the devotion of the faithful towards
the head of the Holy Family has wonderfully in-

---

* The author was residing at Florence when he wrote this.
Whether the inhabitants of this city are justified in keeping the
feast of the death of St. Joseph on the 20th of July, is a question
he does not enter into, and which we will not decide.   Several
churches have had this custom (*See the Bollandists*, March 19).

creased. Shortly after that epoch, churches, chapels, and oratories, in his honour, sprung up within the precincts of Rome; various confraternities, still subsisting, were established in his honour; and the example of the capital created a pious emulation throughout all the towns of Italy. The States of the Church, so zealous in propagating this devotion, received greater favours from St. Joseph than any other part of the world; and even that precious relic, his nuptial ring, is deposited in the town of Perugia; his mantle and staff are venerated at the Church of St. Anastasia, at Rome; and in union with his immaculate spouse, has he enriched Loretto with that singular treasure, that terrestrial Paradise, into which the infernal serpent never dared to penetrate—that secure asylum and refuge of poor sinners—that propitiatory; always overflowing with graces for all the faithful—that sanctuary where Mary was conceived without sin, where the "Word" was made flesh, where He spent almost all the years of His mortal life, in the society of Mary and Joseph, the lowly hut of Nazareth.*

* The House of Nazareth was converted into a chapel during the early ages of Christianity, and at a later period a church was erected over it by St. Helena, mother of Constantine the Great; since that time it became the favourite resort of pilgrims, who used to come thither from all parts of Christendom. We have evidence of this fact in the writings of St. Gregory of Nyssa, St. Jerome, St. Epiphanius, Nicephorus, Evodius, St. John of Damascen, Ven. Bede, &c.

The first Christians whom the Crusades had attracted to the East, always considered it a duty to visit this church, in order to offer their homage to the Man-God and the Virgin-Mother who once honoured it by their sacred presence. There Cardinal Vitry celebrated the holy Sacrifice, and the good King St. Louis

CHAPTER X.

Tenth Motive—the Example of many Holy Authors.

FROM the very infancy of the Church, our Lord has made the Christian's pen instrumental in publishing to all nations the glories of Mary, His Blessed Mother, in order that all nations should exult in her

received holy Communion. These facts are incontrovertible. Another incontestible fact is, that the House of Nazareth is the only sacred monument in Palestine which has disappeared from it, all the other ancient monuments remaining to this day; but the House of Nazareth was no longer to be seen there after the conquest of the Holy Land by Saladin, in 1291. There is also a tradition, founded upon historical facts, which attests that, at this precise period, it appeared near Tersata, in Dalmatia, then at two places in the neighbourhood of Loretto, and finally on the exact site upon which, shortly after its appearance there, the town of Loretto arose under the auspices of Mary. We are aware that this miraculous translation is a matter of ridicule with heretics and modern sophists; but the arguments which they make use of to destroy it, are those which only serve to prove more fully its authenticity. We here give the principal objection urged against it, and this will enable us to estimate the futility of all others. One person who will not admit the translation, supposes that Pope Boniface VIII. had a house built in one night, and that he published on the following day that this was the House of Nazareth! but it only requires a moment's reflection to perceive the absurdity of such a supposition.

In the first place, the author of this fabrication, if such a being ever did exist, would more probably be Celestine V. than Boniface VIII., since it was during the reign of the former (1294) that the Santa Casa quitted Dalmatia, and appeared in Italy. Now, remark that Celestine V. is honoured by the Catholic Church with the title of St. Peter Celestine; it would, therefore, be a

happiness, according to her own prediction: "All generations shall call me blessed" (generationes) (*Luke*, i.); and in like manner, for many ages past, He has provided various writers, whose aim it has

difficult task to introduce a false statement of facts into the life of a saint so well known; it were even better to disturb the order of the history, and incur the charge of anachronism.

In the second place, were it even possible to begin and finish the building of a house in the same night, the new and fresh appearance of the building would suffice to expose the imposture.

Thirdly, the walls of the Santa Casa massive, and much thicker than those of most modern buildings: therefore, one night would not afford sufficient time for their construction.

Fourthly, either the necessary materials for the building had been collected beforehand, or they had not: if they had been previously prepared, why then the illusion must have been at once destroyed by seeing them employed in the building; but were not this the case, what an Herculean undertaking in so short a space of time! What a multitude of men must have been employed to perpetrate this sacrilegious fraud; and how could the secret avoid being divulged when such a multitude of persons were entrusted with it! An infidel of the last century being urged to decide this point, replied that the Pope had ordered all the masons to be thrown into the sea; but then, in order to drown a hundred men, another hundred would have been requisite: and here again is another difficulty! Who, then, can undertake to explain, in like manner, the successive appearance and disappearance of the Santa Casa in three different places, before it finally rested in its present locality? Three edifices, each of which was built and destroyed in one night; and, doubtless, after each operation, the workmen were either drowned or buried alive, in order to avoid the consequences of any indiscretion on their part! We are not informed as to the fate of the perpetrators of these crimes. But really these objections are rather too absurd to deserve attention, and all brought forward merely with a view of not being under the disagreeable necessity of acknowledging the divinity of a religion which does not coincide with the passions, and which requires of those who

been to exalt the incomparable privileges of the
spouse of Mary, of the guardian and the adopted
father of our Lord; and thus has been accomplished

profess it not a mere speculative belief in its teaching, but that
its doctrine be reduced to practice, and shine forth in their
conduct.

This is the opinion of Geuranger on this fact. The learned
religious, in his life of M. Olier, after having related to Mr. Gos-
selin the history of the translation, adds: "Considered in the
light of mere criticism, this prodigy is attested not only by the
annalists of the Church, Baronius and Rainaldi, and by Tursel-
lini and Martorelli, historians of Loretto, but also by the learned
of the first class, among whom we will cite Papebroek, Noël,
Alexandre, Benedict XIV., Trombelli, &c." What impartial
man will dare to advance vague objections in presence of these
oracles of science, whose authority is universally admitted on
every other subject?

Considered in the light of Catholic piety, it cannot be denied
that they who make no account of the innumerable prodigies
wrought in the House of Loretto, render themselves guilty of
extreme rashness, as if God could authorize by miracles what
would be the grossest of impositions. They would not deserve
the less this censure for the insult they would offer to the
authority of the Apostolic See, which has, during several centuries, been zealously employed in studying this prodigy, and
proposing it to the faithful as a powerful means of giving glory
to the Incarnate Word and His most Holy Mother. We will
cite as explicit acts of the Holy See upon the miracle of Loretto,
the bulls of Paul II., Leo X., Paul III., Paul IV., and Sixtus
V. the decree of Urban VIII., in 1632, to establish the feast
of it in the Marches of Ancona; that of Innocent XI., in 1699,
to approve the office; and lastly, the indults of Benedict XIII.
and his successors, to extend this feast to most of the provinces
of Catholicity.

The authority of Montaigne will not be suspected by any one:
we find in his Memoirs an account of a miraculous cure which
he himself inquired into with the greatest care, during a pilgrimage which he made to Loretto, where he left a rich offering for
himself and his family.

the oracle: "He that is the keeper of his master shall be glorified."—"Qui custos est Domini sui glorificabitur"(*Prov.* xxvii.). That this oracle of the Holy Ghost has been fully verified in the person of St. Joseph, is quite evident from the strain of joy and congratulation in which the Church addresses him, and which resounds from pole to pole: "Let all Christian nations sing canticles in your praise."

Great examples are the most powerful means of making converts to any cause: I shall, therefore, cite some of those authors who have signalised their devotion and zeal by the eulogies which they have written upon St. Joseph. The Holy Ghost Himself was his earliest panegyrist, as may be seen by the writings of the Evangelists. If His notice of the Blessed Virgin be so very brief, we cannot wonder that He should have said but little respecting her holy spouse; but the little that He has dictated concerning him to the sacred penman, is a mine of inexhaustible riches, and might furnish materials sufficient to fill many volumes. What He says is as follows: "Joseph, Spouse of Mary, the Mother of Jesus." "Joseph, her spouse, was a just man." "Joseph, son of David, fear not." "You shall give him the name of Jesus." "Your father and I have sought you sorrowing." "He was subject to them." These words, each of which seems only like the careless stroke of a pen, are, nevertheless, to those who can penetrate their mysterious signification, like the stars which, by ignorant persons, are considered only as luminous specks, but which appear to the eyes of the astronomer as so many suns of immense magnitude. I shall be content to adore in silence the words of the Spirit of God, and will leave to others the task of developing their hidden meaning, not with the pen, but, if possible, with the rays of the sun. St. Gregory of Nazianzen, struck with admiration of the extraordinary virtue and pre- rogatives of our saint, cries out: "Yes, the Almighty has concentrated in St. Joseph, as in a sun of un- rivalled lustre, the combined light and splendour of all the other saints."

Among the panegyrists of St. Joseph, is Mary herself, his immaculate spouse : she has been pleased to dictate her praises of him to her servant St. Bridget, who, on this occasion, acts as secretary to the Mother of God. I shall here mention only a few of the most remarkable passages. "Be assured," says she to this saint, "that, previous to our mar- riage, St. Joseph had been informed by the Holy Ghost of my having consecrated myself to God by a vow of virginity, and of the angelic purity of my thoughts, affections, and actions ; he, therefore, determined ever to consider himself my servant, and to look up to me as to his queen and sovereign. By the light of the same Holy Spirit, I foresaw that my virginity should ever remain pure and stainless, although, by a mysterious dispensation of Provi- dence, I consented to take a spouse. St. Joseph's astonishment is not to be described, when he saw that I was about to become a mother ; nevertheless, not the shade of any reflection, in the slightest degree derogatory to me, crossed his mind for a moment; but, on the contrary, remembering the prediction that the Son of God was to be born of a virgin, he deemed himself unworthy to serve the mother of such a Son : however, as he knew nothing certain as to the matter, and undecided as to what part he ought to take, he judged it might be expedient to leave me secretly. But an angel of the Lord appeared to him in a dream, saying : ' Do not abandon this virgin, who has been confided to your care; it is by virtue of the Holy Ghost that she has conceived, and she shall soon give birth to the Saviour of the world.' From that time forward, St. Joseph rendered me all the homage and respect due to a queen; nevertheless, I always continued to serve him as his humble and devoted handmaid (*Rev.*). In the performance of the mutual services we rendered each other, I never knew a complaint or an impatient word to escape him. He endured the labours and privations attached to poverty, with admirable resignation : in order to supply our necessities, he applied himself unsparingly to the hardest labour; and when reviled or ill-treated, the most angelic meekness was his only revenge. Towards myself he discharged all the duties of the most devoted spouse ; he served me with the utmost reverence and affection ; he was the faithful guardian of my virginity, and the irrefutable witness of the wonders that God wrought in me. Moreover, St. Joseph was perfectly dead to the world and the flesh; all his aspirations were after heavenly things. So great was his confidence in the divine promises, that I frequently heard him exclaim: ' Ah! if anything could make me anxious to prolong my life, it would be my ardent desire to see the great designs of God accomplished !' His only aim was to accomplish this adorable will ; and to the conformity of his will with the will of God, must be attributed the greatness of his glory in Heaven." Such is the sketch of St. Joseph's life, for which we are indebted to his

blessed spouse. It is brief and simple, and, in this
respect, may be aptly compared to pearls and dia-
monds, which, though scarce and small, are, nevertheless, of immense value ; so much does it comprise,
that it would furnish matter for as many panegyrists
as it attributes virtues to St. Joseph.

All the Greek and Latin Fathers have spoken
more or less of the prerogatives of St. Joseph; but
of all modern authors who make mention of him,
the palm must be awarded to Gerson, who is superior to any in purity of doctrine, and in the tenderness and fervour of his devotion towards St. Joseph.
He is well entitled to hold the first rank among his
panegyrists ; and a modern author observes, that
those who subsequently undertook to write the
praises of this saint, have mentioned nothing of
which Gerson had not previously spoken. Among
the authors alluded to were :—

The learned Cardinal D'Ailly, cotemporary with
Gerson.

The pious Isidore de L'Isle, a Dominican, of
whom we have already spoken : he wrote in 1522.

Pere Barri, a Jesuit, whose work has gone through
twenty-six editions. He published it in 1639, and
dedicated it to St. Joseph himself, as a tribute of
gratitude for having been preserved, together with
his religious brethren, from the plague which made
such ravages in the city of Lyons. This favour
he attributed to the powerful intercession of St.
Joseph.

Pere Binet, also a Jesuit, penetrated with the
most tender devotion towards the saint, whose
glorious privileges he undertook to eulogize, asked
pardon for himself and all mankind, for having

so long neglected to do honour to his virtues, and to implore his protection. "May all future ages," says he, "join their hearts and voices to ours, in multiplying tributes of love and veneration by which to indemnify thee, our good Father and Patron, for the neglect of past ages" (1650).

F. Peter Moralès wrote before these two fathers. His work was published at Lyons some years after his death, in 1614. This learned theologian informs us himself, in the preface to his work, that he undertook it out of gratitude to the Blessed Virgin and St. Joseph, who had procured admittance for him into the Company of Jesus. The thousand pages of his work testify with what gratitude and piety he had studied the life of the holy patriarch. It ranks among the best works in honour of St. Joseph and the Holy Family.

We may also consult the Venerable Peter Canisius, Francis Suarez, Stephen Menochius, Bollandus, all members of the Society of Jesus, and, finally, the commentators of the New Testament, and those authors who have written the life of Jesus Christ and of His Blessed Mother. There is not one among the above-named, who has not spoken of St. Joseph in strains of the highest eulogy ; and all dwell, with particular emphasis, on the pre-eminence in rank which he holds among all the other saints. If, in anticipation only, the pious Isidore de L'Isle experienced so much consolation, when he foresaw the future manifestation of St. Joseph's glory, through the medium of the eloquent tongues and pens of certain highly-gifted individuals, whom Almighty God was to raise up for that glorious work, what would be his sentiments were he now to revisit this place of exile, when he would experience the satisfaction of being enabled to enumerate (at the moment in which I now write, 1709) upwards of three hundred authors, whose pens have furnished us with biographies, or panegyrics, of St. Joseph, in less than three hundred years, commencing with Gerson !

CHAPTER XI.

Eleventh Motive—Example of Persons Eminent for Holiness.

THOSE eleven stars which bowed down in adoration before the ancient patriarch Joseph, would appear as if intended, in the designs of God, to prefigure certain personages of the New Law, who, in our latter times, were to signalize themselves by the extraordinary homage which they were to render to the Joseph of our days. We shall not here repeat what we have already alluded to, concerning the Sun of Justice, and the mysterious Moon, which represent Jesus and Mary, paying St. Joseph the most profound homage it is possible to conceive, that of the most unqualified obedience to all his wishes and desires. What we have now particularly to observe concern‑ing those eleven stars is, that they encircle our saint, not in order to eclipse him, but rather to increase his lustre, by adorning him with a brilliant halo of glory.

The first of these stars which appeared above the

horizon was, as we have before mentioned, the illustrious Chancellor Gerson. From the moment that he was capable of speaking or writing, he consecrated his pen and his voice, his zeal and his learning, which was superior to that of any doctor of his age, to the glory of St. Joseph. He thus led the way for those who came after him, and began to explore that mine of precious gems, that wondrous treasure of heavenly graces and prerogatives, which this privileged being had so studiously concealed from the eyes of men, beneath the sacred veils of humility and simplicity. He also has the honour of being the first who used all his eloquence to induce ecclesiastics to celebrate the feast of St. Joseph in a solemn manner, and to recite his Office: with this intent, he composed a Mass in his honour, also various hymns and panegyrics. His zeal was not confined to these efforts; not content with the endeavours which he made by means of letters, as solid as they were fervent, to implant his cherished devotion in the hearts of princes, prelates, and doctors; he also devoted the greater part of a sermon, which he preached upon the feast of the Nativity of the Blessed Virgin, before the Council of Constance, to the praises of her august spouse, and in terms so eloquent and energetic, as to have left that mighty assembly penetrated with admiration of the orator and devotion to the saint. In short, Gerson, during the whole course of his long life, laboured indefatigably to promote the glory of his hero. It is true, however, that these labours were not productive until nearly a century afterwards; but this delay will not deprive him, in the eyes either of men or angels, of the merit of having discovered the long-hidden source of that ocean of graces

which now-a-days inundates and fertilizes the field
of the Catholic Church.

The second star which irradiates St. Joseph's
crown, is that master, so meek, so enlightened, of the
spiritual life, that perfect model of prelates, St.
Francis de Sales. He always speaks of him with the
greatest affection, and dedicated to St. Joseph his
treatise on the " Love of God," styling him his protector and his beloved father. He would keep no other
picture in his Breviary except one of St. Joseph.
He once said to a holy Jesuit : " Oh, Father! know
you not that I am devotedly attached to St. Joseph ?"
Being asked by the rector of the professed house at
Lyons to preach twice on St. Joseph's feast, " Father," he replied, with his usual sweetness and
urbanity, " it is indeed a rare occurrence with me to
have to felicitate myself upon preaching two sermons
in one day : however, as a proof of my love for St.
Joseph, I consent to preach this day a second time."
He desired that this devotion, which he had himself
so strongly imbibed, might also serve his first daughters of the Visitation as a spiritual food, well calculated to strengthen and improve them in the interior
life. He made St. Joseph the special patron of this
new order, which he had recently founded, and
placed the first church which he built at Annecy,
under the patronage of this saint. Finally, being
eager to bequeath to posterity a lasting pledge of the
tender affection he bore him, among other rules
which he wrote for the novices, was a special injunc-
tion ever to look up to St. Joseph as their master and
guide in the paths of the interior and contemplative
life, in which all the spouses of Jesus Christ are
called to walk.

The third of these mysterious eleven stars is the blessed Gaspar Bon, of the order of Minims. It may be said that he deserves to be ranked amongst those who have been most zealous in paying court to St. Joseph, for he was always conversing in spirit with the Holy Family in the House of Nazareth. The sacred names of Jesus, Mary, and Joseph, were ever in his heart and on his lips; and these three sweet names may be compared to three honeycombs; whence it is not surprising, that from his mouth should proceed words and sentiments of the tenderest devotion. It was an admirable practice with him never to ask a question, or reply to one, without having invoked these three names, both before and after. In his last moments, he begged of the religious who attended him to repeat these holy names frequently for him, in order to alleviate the pangs of his agony, and mitigate the horrors of death, by their celestial melody; and he expired while actually repeating the names of Jesus, Mary, and Joseph.

We shall now direct our attention to the fourth star which did homage to St. Joseph, namely, the Ven. Father Peter Cotton, of the Society of Jesus, who is not less eminent for his talents as an orator, than for his virtues as a religious. His zeal in promoting the glory of St. Joseph was almost miraculous. In each of his sermons and exhortations he never failed to say something in praise of his beloved patron. It was by his advice and exertions that the Church of the Novitiate-house at Lyons was dedicated to St. Joseph; it being the first church which was erected to his honour in France. This devout client of St. Joseph was so happy as to die on his dear patron's feast-day, as had previously been revealed to him.

It is stated that the Blessed Virgin appeared to him during his last illness, and said that she had come to assist him to die happily, as she was grateful for the tender devotion he ever evinced towards her dear spouse. All these circumstances prove, that such an enviable death was a reward for all the services which he had rendered to St. Joseph, who, in acknowledgment of them, introduced him into the regions of the blessed, on the very day when the Church militant was celebrating his own merits.

The fifth star which shed its lustre around St. Joseph shall be, and deservedly, the Ven. Father Louis Lallemont, S.J., who, for regularity and exactness to religious discipline, deserves to be universally looked up to as a living copy of the spirit of St. Ignatius, of whom he was a faithful disciple and imitator. He had a remarkable *attrait* for the interior life ; and in order that he might always have a finished model before his eyes, he applied himself to the meditation of St. Joseph's virtues. This was his method : In the morning he considered, first, the fidelity of our saint to grace, exciting himself to acts of humility on account of his own faithlessness ; secondly, his habitual recollection, which he preserved so well in the midst of exterior occupations, he examined how far distant he was from his example. In the evening, he placed himself in spirit with St. Joseph, and studied his conduct with regard to the Blessed Virgin and her Divine Son, asking for himself grace to imitate him. He had a peculiar secret of inspiring others with a devotion to this great saint; and such was his confidence in him, so efficacious his intercession with him, that he never failed to obtain through him all his requests. Therefore, when

trying to induce the faithful to honour him, he always
inspired them with this great confidence, and asked
favours for them himself, assuring them, at the same
time, that they would infallibly obtain all they desired from the goodness of St. Joseph. The following
is a proof of this : Whilst Rector to the College of
Bourges, he had an opportunity of becoming acquainted with two young men, teachers of the lower
schools, whose piety and virtue he greatly admired.
On the approach of St. Joseph's feast, he called them
both to him, and promised to obtain for each any grace
they wished for, provided that they would exhort
their pupils to choose St. Joseph as a patron, and to
perform some particular devotion in his honour upon
his feast-day. The two masters most joyfully acceded
to the proposal, and so efficacious did their exhortations prove, that every individual in both classes
approached the most holy Sacrament, in honour of
the saint, on the day of his feast. On the same day
the two teachers went to the Father-rector, and each
revealed to him, in confidence, the favour he was
anxious to obtain through St. Joseph's intercession.
The first (who was the celebrated Pere Nonet) asked
for grace to be enabled to speak and write worthily
concerning our Lord: we are not aware as to what
the request of the other was, because, when relating
the fact, his humility did not permit him to mention
it ; we can only say that he obtained it.

As to Pere Nonet: the day after the feast, having
changed his mind, he returned to the Father-rector,
saying, that upon more serious reflection, he thought
it would be better to ask for some other grace which
might tend more immediately to his own advancement in perfection, The father replied that it was

now too late, for St. Joseph had already obtained for him the favour he had first asked. Of the plenitude of this gift some idea may be formed by his glowing sermons, and the innumerable spiritual works which he wrote, but especially that which he composed on the excellencies of Jesus Christ, which is all radiant with celestial light, and the flowers of divine love, capable of softening and converting even the hardest hearts. The inference to be drawn from all this is, that Pere Lallemont was one of St. Joseph's most cherished favourites, and that he had all his treasures at his disposal. As a last testimony of the extraordinary devotion which he felt towards this powerful protector, he begged that his image might be placed in the coffin with him.

We shall now contemplate the sixth, and, may I be permitted to add, the most brilliant star in St. Joseph's diadem, Theresa of Jesus, that illustrious virgin, whose sanctity and doctrine have so gloriously illumined the Church of Christ. If it redounds to the glory of St. Theresa that she should have been the individual chosen by Heaven to reform the order of Mount Carmel, she has no less reason to exult in having also been chosen to diffuse the devotion to St. Joseph throughout the entire Christian world, and to have established it upon that grand scale upon which it has ever since been perpetuated. In order to enhance the glory of His Church, Jesus Christ did not deem it expedient to found it upon the mighty ones of this world, on its pomp and power; in like manner, and for similar reasons, He did not consider it necessary to make use of princes or potentates, of men remarkable for learning, or otherwise eminent, in order to diffuse, far and wide, the glory of His adopted father, and to procure universal homage for him. He reserved the success of this great scheme for a virgin until then unknown, that to Himself alone might be attributed the glorious work.

Let us now see what an admirable model of devotion to St. Joseph was this virgin reformer of Mount Carmel. From her earliest childhood she conceived the most tender affection, and a truly filial confidence, in the spouse of the Mother of God; when speaking to him, she affectionately called him her father and her lord. Of the sixteen reformed houses which she founded, she placed thirteen under the protection of St. Joseph, and gave them his name. Great as were the circumspection and reserve with which she studied to conceal from human observation the graces and privileges with which God had favoured her, whenever the glory of our saint was in question, the case was quite the reverse; her tongue, as well as her pen, betrayed the secret of her affections; she could not refrain from manifesting the extraordinary graces which she owed to his intercession.* It is only necessary to read her life, in order to comprehend her zeal for this saint's honour, and his goodness

* The tender and filial devotion of this saint to St. Joseph appears in all her writings, and by the touching eloquence and simple tenderness of her words, she communicates it to her readers. In her admirable advice to her religious, she says: "Although you may have many saints for patrons, nevertheless, have also a peculiar devotion for St. Joseph, who has such great power with God" (*Avis*, lxv.).

St. Theresa has bequeathed to her order her holy zeal for the glory of St. Joseph. The Carmelites have never ceased their efforts to spread this devotion; they may be said even to equal the ancient Carmelites, of whom Benedict XIV. gave this testimony: "It is to them," says this great Pope, "according to the

in her regard. " I never remember," says she, " to
have asked anything of him which I did not obtain;
the recital of all the graces, of every description, with
which God has endowed me, and of the many dangers,
both of soul and body, from which He has delivered
me through the prayers and merits of my beloved
saint, appears to me altogether miraculous. Other
saints are invoked for certain particular favours, to
obtain which their intercession has often been successfully employed ; whereas our saint has universal
power, as experience proves; and our Lord would
have us understand thereby, that as He was subject
to St. Joseph in all things during His earthly pilgrimage, so also now in Heaven He is pleased to
condescend to all his wishes. This is well known
by experience to many persons whom I counselled
to recommend themselves to this saint; and the
graces which they have received have penetrated
them with gratitude and affection for him. My own
experience of the many signal favours which he has
obtained for me from God, makes me doubly anxious

opinion of many learned writers, that we ought to ascribe the
rapid spread from East and West of the laudable custom of honouring St. Joseph with peculiar devotion" (*De Beatif et Canoniz.*
lib. iv. part ii. chap. xx. No. 17). There were more than 150
churches belonging to the Carmelites dedicated to St. Joseph,
at the end of the eighteenth century.

From the time that St. Theresa began publicly to honour St.
Joseph, numerous religious orders vied with each other in propagating this devotion. Crowds gathered round the altars of this
glorious saint in all parts of the world, and his name was everywhere invoked. It is to St. Theresa that the glory is due of
having brought this devotion, so dear to all Catholics, to the
degree of splendour and universality in which we now find it
(*Life of St. Theresa,* by Rev. F. Marcel Bonix).

to draw all hearts to him. Among all those who are
sincerely devoted to him, and who make an open profession of honouring him, I know not a single individual who does not daily advance in virtue; so
powerfully does he assist all those who place themselves under his protection. For several years past,
I have always asked some particular favour from him
on his feast-day, and he has invariably obtained it
for me. I have even remarked, that when I failed
to make the very best selection, this amiable saint
would, nevertheless, always make the favour he
obtained for me eventually turn to my greater
spiritual advantage. If I had the permission, I
should find the greatest pleasure in making a detailed recital of the many favours bestowed on others,
as well as on myself. I shall now implore of those
who may, perhaps, find it difficult to believe what I
have asserted, to make a trial of it themselves, for
the love of God; and their own experience will convince them how advantageous it is to claim the
patronage of this glorious patriarch, and to be ranked
amongst his devoted servants. What I have just
said, I particularly address to those who are anxious
to acquire a spirit of prayer; for such are the persons
who should especially endeavour to ingratiate themselves with this great master of the interior life. It
is to me incomprehensible how any one can contemplate the Queen of Angels bestowing her maternal
care upon the Divine Infant Jesus, without, at the
same time, gratefully acknowledging the kind and
valuable assistance afforded by her holy spouse on
those occasions, to the mother as well as to her
Divine Son."

From these passages, and several others that we

could quote, it is easy to infer how incomparable is the dignity of St. Joseph, how vast the extent of his power in Heaven, and how zealously he makes use of his credit for the benefit of those who invoke him with confidence, and are truly devoted to him. The zeal with which St. Theresa had endeavoured to promote the glory of her beloved patron during life, continued unabated even after death: of this the following fact will convince us. Several Carmelite houses of which she was foundress, in the first transports of their joy on hearing of their dear mother's canonization, were desirous of placing the churches which were attached to them under the invocation of St. Theresa, and to substitute her name for those of the saints to whom they were originally dedicated. They submitted their judgment on this matter, as on others, to the Father-provincial of the Carmelites, who, having himself a great devotion to the new saint, highly approved of the design of his spiritual daughters. All this, however, seemed contrary to the wishes of her whom they were so solicitous to honour. She openly condemned it; for, appearing to a religious in the monastery of Avila, she expressed her disapprobation in the following words: "Thou shalt tell the Father-provincial to deprive the monasteries of my name, and to restore to them that of St. Joseph." The order was immediately executed. Therefore, whoever is desirous of giving pleasure to this great saint, must learn to love St. Joseph as she did, and if devoted to her, let their devotion to him be infinitely greater. This was perfectly well understood by that rich and pious benefactor, who, wishing to erect a chapel in the Church of the Barefooted Carmelites at Rome, in

honour of their holy patron, placed it opposite to
that which was dedicated to their holy mother,
knowing how agreeable to the saint was the constant
view of an object so dear to her heart; he desired
also to remind the faithful, that they should jointly
invoke these great servants of God, who were both
so closely united in Him, with a full and firm confidence that Joseph will grant all their requests for
the sake of his faithful servant Theresa, and that
Theresa will surely be favourable to them for the
sake of her beloved patron St. Joseph.

The seventh star whose brilliancy imparts additional lustre to the glory of our saint, is a daughter of
St. Theresa—the Ven. Clare Mary, of the illustrious
house of Colonna. She exerted all the influence
which her high rank commanded, in order to extend
the devotion to him, and with this view used every
means she was mistress of to obtain various privileges from the Holy See, by which to add new
splendour and dignity to the due solemnization of his
feast.

But she was no less solicitous to establish a fervent
devotion to St. Joseph among the religious of the
monastery which she had founded at Rome, under
the title of the "Regina Cœli." Here is a private
chapel dedicated to St. Joseph: on the day of his
feast, Clare Mary always adorned it magnificently; she
then opened the case containing his relics, which she
requested might be carried in procession by the nuns,
whilst they sang the canticles which she had composed
in his honour. A faithful imitator of her holy mother
St. Theresa, Mary Clare had recourse to him in all
her wants, with the most unbounded confidence.
She wrote thus to a religious who possessed her

confidence:—"The feast of St. Joseph passed off
very well: I felt a great increase of devotion to him;
I look upon him as a father to whom I can fearlessly
have recourse; I present myself thus before him,
with all my miseries, and implore of him to obtain
for me a great love of God." She so often experienced the effects of St. Joseph's benign patronage,
that she attests, like St. Theresa, never to have had
recourse to him in vain. He was her secure asylum
in all the necessities of the monastery. One day,
Mary Clare happened to find a pious picture repre-
senting our Lord crowned with thorns, and clothed
in derision with a purple garment; she placed near
it an image of St. Joseph, saying to him with her
usual pious simplicity: "You are the person whom
I expect will draw from the treasury of the merits
and sufferings of Jesus Christ, all that may be necessary and advantageous to our house." Never did
her devotion appear more admirable than when
she became superior of the monastery; she then
had it in her power to make him some small
return for his many favours, by giving alms in his
honour; on his feast-day she always gave a full suit
of clothes to a poor old man, and alms to the indi-
gent, as far as her vow and profession of poverty
would permit. Among the poor persons whom she
assisted in honour of St. Joseph, it happened one day
that an unfortunate carpenter, who was a debtor to
the convent, came in for the greater part of the alms.
Hearing that his name was Joseph, and the trade
which he professed giving him an additional trait of
resemblance to our saint, her holy protector, she in
consequence remitted his entire debt; and even this
did not satisfy her piety; for, upon being informed

that he had several children, she procured by her
charitable exertions a marriage portion for one of his
daughters.

The eight luminary which shed its brilliant rays
around St. Joseph was another daughter of the
reformer of Carmel, the Venerable Margaret of the
Most Holy Sacrament. Her's was a soul so dear to
the Divine Infant Jesus, that this amiable Saviour
deigned Himself to bestow on her the title of the
"Spouse of His sacred Infancy." Jesus, Mary, and
Joseph were the usual objects of her contemplation,
as well as of her warmest affection; and to St. Joseph,
as chief of the Holy Family, she paid a special tribute
of respect, and considered him, after Jesus and Mary,
as the most perfect model for imitation. When
venerating the different mysteries of the Divine
Infancy, she always united her heart to that of St.
Joseph, desiring that she herself might be enabled to
comprehend them as he did; and that she might
worthily participate in the overflowing graces and
immense advantages to be derived from them, by the
proper use and application of them to our souls.
Such were the pious practices of her early life, that
interesting age of candour and artless simplicity, in
which God loves to communicate Himself, for "He
ever seeks a pure heart, and there is the place of His
rest." On one occasion her mistress, who suspected
that something extraordinary was passing in her soul,
asked her several questions regarding St. Joseph.
The youthful Margaret's answers were profoundly
sublime, and so much the more admirable as being
perfectly in accordance with all the most enlightened theologians have written concerning the great
saint. One of the sweetest practices of devotion

adopted by Margaret in the midst of those stated daily occupations in which she happened to be engaged in the monastery, was that which she mentioned in a letter to a confidential friend and sister in religion. She says:—" I am delighted to find you installed in your present post. I conjure you to unite yourself to our dear and amiable Child Jesus, who, in St. Joseph's workshop, did not consider Himself the master, but merely as an assistant. Unite your labours to those of that Blessed Child : accustom yourself to look upon the sister whom you have been appointed to assist, in the same light as that in which He considered St. Joseph. I am also an assistant to one of our sisters, and I will endeavour to be faithful to the practices which I now recommend to you." We could mention many traits of Margaret's solid devotion towards this saint, but we have already said enough to give the reader an idea of the high veneration and filial confidence evinced by this holy religious towards the worthy spouse of Mary, and the guardian of the " Immaculate Word."

The ninth star, and not the least brilliant in St. Joseph's crown, was another Margaret, a Dominicaness of Civita Castellana. The usual subjects of her meditation were the sacred maternity of Mary, the birth of the Word Incarnate, and the services which St. Joseph had the privilege of rendering to both, whether in the cave at Bethlehem, in Egypt, or in their own humble dwelling at Nazareth. These sacred mysteries inspired Margaret from her infancy with so tender an affection for our holy patriarch, that the divine love impressed his image on her heart, together with those of Jesus and Mary.

The tenth of these mysterious stars was Ven. Jane

of the Angels, an Ursuline religious, at Lyons. She
lived in the constant practice of the most heroic
virtue, because she ever had the life of St. Joseph
before her, making it the subject of her serious consideration, and taking it for the model of her own
life, as far as the measure of grace bestowed upon
her would permit. On the eve of his feast she practised fasting and other austerities; and after her holy
communion on the following day, she chose him anew
as her annual patron, and at the same time renewed
the offering of her filial love. The venerable religious had personal reasons for being so devoted to
him: she had been delivered by his intercession from
evil spirits that tormented her, and cured of a dangerous illness, which nearly brought her to the grave.
It would even appear that it was the saint himself
who inspired her with the extraordinary affection
which she bore him; for, appearing to her once encompassed with resplendent rays of glory, he exhorted
her in the most amiable manner to bear patiently the
pain she was enduring, and to place all her confidence
in God, who, while He mortified her flesh, gave an
increase of health and vigour to her soul. The saint
also intimated to his pious servant, that it would
gratify him that she should make nine communions
in his honour, on the days of the week corresponding
with that on which his festival would fall.

The eleventh and last star which adorns the diadem
of our glorious saint, is that true servant of God,
Mary-Catherine of St. Augustine. God called her
out of France, where she was a mother to the poor,
in order to send her as a sister-hospitaller to the
Hospital of Mercy at Quebec, the capital of Canada,
or, as it was then called, New France. Her tender

devotion to the chaste spouse of Mary, who was also the particular patron of the newly-made Christians of those foreign countries, inspired her with a desire of adding the name of Joseph to her own. This she did immediately, and was thenceforth called Mary-Josephina. As it may contribute to the honour of our saint, we shall now relate a vision which this religious had on the feast of the Ascension of our Lord. She beheld a solemn procession, composed of all the blessed inhabitants of Heaven, in the midst of which appeared the King of Glory. Whilst the august cortege ascended high in air, and advanced triumphantly towards Heaven, Mary-Josephina distinguished St. Joseph, who preceded all the others, directed their movements, and was stationed nearer to the eternal gates than any other of the saints. When all had entered into Heaven, and the adorable humanity of Christ our Lord had been seated on the throne prepared for Him on the right hand of God, Mary-Josephina heard her holy patron speak : "Behold," said he to the Eternal Father, "behold the talent which you gave me when I was an inhabitant of the Earth : I restore it to you this day, not merely doubled, but increased as many hundredfold as there are souls in this vast multitude which have been ransomed by Him." "Just and faithful servant," replied the Eternal Father, "as you have been the head of My family on Earth, it is our will that you retain the same power now in Heaven ; and you shall not be styled servant any longer, but lord." Jesus Christ then declared that He would continue as usual to obey all the wishes of His adopted father. Mary-Josephina, turning towards her glorious patron, exclaimed: "Great saint! ask the King of Glory that I may have the happiness never to be deprived of His love, but to experience a continual inci ase of it; He cannot refuse *you* this grace." Her prayers were heard; but on condition that she never would forget the promise she made to God of resigning herself unreservedly into His hands, having no other ambition than that of conforming herself in all things to His ever just and amiable will. She was also shown the place which she was to occupy in Heaven with Jesus, Mary, and Joseph.

I am sure the clients of St. Joseph must rejoice to see how great is his power in Heaven. Can anything appear more wonderful than that the King of Glory should now in Heaven still condescend to submit to the will of His adopted father? Our amazement, however, will cease if we give our attention to what St. Bernardine of Sienna has written on this subject. These are his words: Who can doubt that Jesus Christ, who during His mortal life lived on terms of the strictest intimacy with St. Joseph, and rendering him the respect and obedience of a son, has confirmed his title to all his prerogatives in Heaven? To these, doubtless, He has added other gifts of a higher order. If, observes the same saint, filial piety caused our blessed Saviour to glorify not only the soul, but also the body of His Blessed Mother, on the day of her assumption, may we not also piously believe that St. Joseph, who was greater than all the saints, had been equally privileged on the glorious day of our Lord's ascension, when so many holy souls, who had been long sighing for the adorable presence of their Redeemer, were delivered by Him from their long captivity? We give the precise words made use of by the saint: " We may piously believe that the most

affectionate Jesus, Son of God, as He assumed His
Mother into Heaven glorified in body and soul, thus,
too, assumed the most holy Joseph on the day of his
ascension."—" Pie credendum est quod piissimus
Filius Dei Jesus, sicut matrem assumpsit in cœlum
corpore et animam gloriosam, sic etiam, in die resurrectionis suæ, sanctissimum Josephum." These
words he made use of in a sermon which he preached
at Padua to a crowded audience; and what is most
singular, just as he was in the act of delivering them,
a golden cross appeared shining over his head, as if
to ratify by this miraculous apparition what he happened at the moment to utter regarding St. Joseph's
resurrection (*Bern. de Bustis*, p. 4, Mar. serm. 13,
p. 4).

CHAPTER XII.

Twelfth Motive—St. Joseph is the Special Patron of the Agonizing, and of a Happy Death.

SHOULD it happen that, after the foregoing examples,
the reader may not as yet have determined to choose
St. Joseph as his patron, we trust that the motive
which we are now about to offer for his consideration
will not fail to produce that desirable result. As the
sentence of death has been pronounced on all, without
exception, it follows that all and each, without exception, should endeavour to secure the interest and

friendship of him who is all-powerful in procuring every assistance for his clients at that awful and decisive hour, to enable them to die happily. If a person engage in a law-suit, on the event of which depends an immense gain or utter ruin, does he not call in the aid of some eminent lawyer, of one on whose zeal for his interest he may safely depend? Now every Christian at the article of death, is about to hear an irrevocable sentence pronounced upon him, upon which will depend his eternal life or death. The rage and temptations of the Devil at that critical moment—the remembrance of past sins—the uncertainty as to the real state of one's soul at that awful moment—the terror of the future—all combine in disputing as it were his claim to the kingdom of Heaven, and in torturing his spirit with the dread apprehension of being condemned to the eternal loss of that God, who loved him even so well as to die for him, who alone can make him happy—to that Hell of fire where the worm dieth not, and the fire is never extinguished! Why not at that critical moment call on some saint to plead his cause, and to obtain a favourable sentence for him at that awful tribunal, whence there is no appeal should he once have the misfortune to be condemned? Who is there better qualified to perform this charitable office than St. Joseph? He is acknowledged by all Christendom to be the special advocate of dying Christians; whence it is that congregations have been everywhere established and altars raised in his name, and that the feast of his blessed death is celebrated in many places.

Among the many motives for which St. Joseph has been constituted the particular patron of dying persons in preference to other saints, there are three which more especially engage us to consider him as such : 1st, St. Joseph is the adopted father of our Judge, whereas the other saints are only His friends; 2dly, his power is more formidable to the devils; 3dly, his death was the most singularly privileged, and the happiest ever recorded in the annals of mankind.

In the first place, St. Joseph is the father of Him who is to pronounce our eternal doom. Moses was constituted only chief or leader of the Jewish people, and, nevertheless, so great does his authority seem to have been, even where God Himself is in question, that when he asks Him to grant favours to that ungrateful and almost incorrigible race, his prayer seems to become a command, which paralyzes as it were the hands of the Divine Majesty, and deprives them of the power of chastising the guilty, until Moses gives them liberty (*Exodus*, xiii.). But how immeasurably greater is your power with the Sovereign Judge, O great patriarch! You, whose sublime vocation it was to be a guide, guardian, and father to Him who will one day judge both the living and the dead. Let us now for a moment suppose that a devout client of our saint has received his last awful summons, and is warned to prepare for death. His holy patron immediately presents himself before the tribunal of Jesus Christ, to whom he addresses this prayer: "Ah! do not refuse, for my sake, to take compassion on this poor creature, and strengthen him now with an all-powerful grace; enable him to make an act of the most perfect contrition, and to die in Thy holy love. I implore of you to grant me this favour, O

Sovereign Judge! by the sweet name of 'Father,' with which you have so often honoured me; by the joy and rapture with which I received your infant form into my arms in the stable at Bethlehem, when I sheltered you in my bosom from the piercing cold. Remember it was these arms that transported you into Egypt beyond the reach of Herod's fury. I implore this favour by those divine eyes, whose tears I so often wiped away; by that blood which I received as a priceless treasure at your circumcision; by the labours and fatigues to which I devoted my life, in order to provide sustenance for you." With Jesus Christ such an appeal must be irresistible: the many affecting instances here brought forward by St. Joseph of his tender love for his Divine Redeemer, must serve as so many chains to bind the hands of Jesus, who will only be permitted to say as formerly to Moses: "Suffer me at least, father, to do justice to the sinner." But Joseph will not yield; he only unshackles the hands of the Judge, on condition that He pardons the criminal. But, in truth, Joseph has no need to enforce his authority, for, as Gerson says, a prayer of his has all the force of a command. How great a happiness, then, is it not for a dying person to possess so eloquent an advocate in the father of his Judge, one who can so powerfully plead his cause—a cause, on the issue of which an eternity of happiness or misery depends!

It is, moreover, a great advantage to a dying person, to have a saint interested for him, whose very name is terrible to the damned. Amongst many other honourable titles bestowed on him by the Church, may be found that of " Conqueror of hell." This glorious title he merited, when, in order to save the Divine Infant from the death which impious Herod had decreed Him, he transported Him into Egypt : for as Herod was a figure of the infernal monster, as well as the instrument made use of by him, who is the arch-persecutor of Jesus and of all the souls who were purchased by His most precious blood ; so Joseph, in conquering this prince and defeating his designs, conquered the devil also ; and this first victory enabled him to gain another far more glorious. Origen remarks, that the order given by the angel to St. Joseph to go into Egypt, comprised also the power to drive away all the devils who had fixed the centre of their empire in that infidel land. Scripture informs us, that no sooner did the holy patriarch, with the Child Jesus and His mother, enter Egypt, than the idols were overturned, the oracles destroyed themselves, the father of lies was chained down, the infernal spectres and the spirits of darkness took flight at the aspect of the "Sun of Justice," though then hardly risen, and enveloped in the mourning garb of humanity ; all, as had been foretold by the prophet Isaiah (chap. xix.). The glory of these victories, doubtless, belongs to the Infant God ; but He was pleased to achieve them by the arm of St. Joseph, as being the head of His family, the guide and saviour of the "Saviour of the world." Seeing himself once overcome, the devil thence began to tremble at the name of Joseph ; but has he not greater reason at present to fear him, when he sees the brilliant lustre with which his merits, his sanctity, his dignity, and his power shine forth ? Joseph is one of the first potentates of heaven ; he there occupies the rank which

is due to the king's father and the queen's spouse.
Lucifer is aware of this, and hence it is that with
fear and trembling he approaches the bed of a dying
person who, during life, had been a true servant of
St. Joseph. He knows that our Divine Saviour,
in order to reward this great saint for having saved
Him from the sword of Herod and a temporal death,
has given the special privilege of preserving those
dying persons who, during life, looked up to him
as their protector, from the power of the devil and
eternal death. Is it likely that St. Joseph will fail
to make use of so great a privilege? Ah! surely
not; and we shall presently give the reader some
interesting details which will prove what a sincere
friend and benefactor he has been to his clients. It
is the experience of so many signal marks of his protection, that induces a multitude of Christians (and
whose numbers are daily increasing) to recur to him,
sure to find beneath his wings their best security
against the arts of Satan at that tremendous crisis,
when his fury is raised to its highest pitch, at the
aspect of his prey about to escape from him for ever.

A Christian not only requires a powerful protector,
who will shield and fortify him against the danger
of that last and violent combat; he also looks for a
friend, whose love will suggest to him a thousand
ways of administering comfort, and of alleviating, in
some measure, the grievous anguish of that last
hour. Who more qualified to undertake so necessary, so consoling a ministry, than he who received
himself such powerful assistance, such exquisite
consolation, at that bitter hour? For you alone, O
Joseph! was reserved the happiness of beholding
Jesus and Mary bending over your bed of death.

These two noble hearts strove to leave nothing undone within the limits of their humble state, to repay all the services rendered to them by you during so many years, with so much zeal and affection. During your last illness, they both served you with their own hands, and in a manner worthy of the charity of God made man, and his blessed mother; for those comforts which their poverty could not procure, they endeavoured to compensate by redoubled tenderness and solicitude, which was a subject of admiration to the whole court of heaven. It is said that, on the day previous to St. Joseph's death, bands of the angelic choirs descended from heaven, to console and cheer him with their sweet concerts. And if God has deigned to grant consolations of a similar nature to many of His servants, as we learn from authentic statements, how could He refuse them to the greatest of all His saints, to the guardian and the adopted father of the Incarnate Word? We are told that at the death of the Ven. Isabella, a Carmelite nun, four consoling angels stood at each corner of her bed, singing on their harps these words from Isaiah (cap. iii.): "Say to the just man that it is well."—"Dicite justo quoniam bene est." But to whom can these words of consolation better be applied than to St. Joseph? Does not the Holy Ghost Himself bestow on him the epithet of the just man? The angels may therefore, with justice, have thus addressed him : "Speed you to a better world, O happy Joseph! your death is truly that of the just, because of you alone can it be said, that you breathe forth your spirit in the embraces of Him who is justice and sanctity itself, of Him who is the source and giver of life! Go, then, noble chief of the patriarchs, go, and bear to them the good tidings of their approaching redemption. Behold, we are now about to form a crown of lilies for the Virgin spouse, a crown of roses for the first persecuted member of Christ's infant Church, and a crown of brilliant stars for the adopted father of the Redeemer, for him who is so much our superior in all virtue and prerogatives; we go to prepare for him a throne near that which shall be occupied by his blessed spouse, the Virgin Mother! Thrice happy Joseph! greater in heaven than was the patriarch Joseph of old at Pharaoh's court, you will there be the first officer in the court of the Most High, the dispenser of His treasures, the protector of the Church, and the advocate and patron of all Christians."

But if the angelic concert proved such a source of joy and comfort to St. Joseph in his last moments, who shall be able to conceive the sweet transports of his soul when the divine words of Jesus fell upon his ear? St. Bernardin of Sienna, contemplating St. Joseph's happy death, attended as it was by all that was great in heaven, cannot find language to describe the consolations, the supernatural illuminations, the languors, and ecstasies of love with which this blessed soul was favoured. In return for all the affectionate caresses which Jesus received in His childhood from this holy, this tender father, He now lavishes upon him a thousand testimonies of affection and sympathy in his suffering state, with all the devoted tenderness of filial love, on so trying an occasion. For his past labours, Jesus infuses into the soul of His adopted parent torrents of interior joy; for all the tears shed on His account, He repays him by so many heavenly consolations; for all the anguish and solicitude he endured, He gives him so many secure pledges of confidence and peace. While with one hand He supports his drooping head, He places the other on that bosom which had been the resting-place of His sacred infancy, and pierces it with the darts of His divine love. Mary then humbly returns thanks to her cherished spouse for his holy companionship, his indefatigable care and tenderness in her regard; and her words acted on the dying saint as so many darts of love which terminated his existence : whence some have said that St. Joseph's death was caused only by the violence and ardour of his love! However the case may be, the Church at one time compares his death to a peaceful slumber, such as a child enjoys on its mother's bosom; at another time, to an aromatic flambeau, which is gradually being consumed while it burns, and diffuses all around an odour of exquisite sweetness. The death of all the saints is a subject of holy envy, because they all die in the embraces of our Lord; but this can be said of them only in a spiritual manner, and signifies the close union of love which binds them to our Lord. But St. Joseph actually expired in the embraces of our Lord, for he breathed his last in the arms of Jesus, and in the act of receiving His last blessing and embrace. If, as seems probable, he retained the use of his speech and of his senses to the last, could he have more worthily terminated so holy a life than by repeating often the sweet names of Jesus and Mary? O thrice blessed death! If I cannot have the happiness of breathing forth my soul in the arms of Jesus and Mary, may I at least with my dying lips join your name, O great and privileged Joseph! to those of Jesus and Mary!

The bonds of affection which united this blessed
mother and her Divine Son to holy Joseph, were not
severed by his death. Both in anguish closed his
eyes, and both paid him the tribute of their tears;
for let not any one deem it unworthy of Jesus that
He should weep on such an occasion. Surely His
affection for Joseph was much more tender and lively
than that which He afterwards felt for His friend
Lazarus? If His groans and tears at the tomb of
Lazarus astonished the spectators, and elicited from
them the remark: "Behold, how He loved him!" is
it not very reasonable to suppose that such mournful
demonstrations were far more justly due to the
deceased person, who was not only a friend, but also
His guardian and His adopted father? So that those
persons who visited the mortal remains of St. Joseph,
might also have said of Jesus: "Behold, how He
loved him" (*St. John*, xi.). Thus reasons John Eckius,
a pious contemplative. Gerson adds, that Jesus
Himself washed this virginal body, that He crossed
the hands over the breast, that He afterwards blessed
it, in order to preserve it from the corruption of the
tomb, and charged the angels to guard it until it
should have been laid in Joseph's ancestral sepulchre,
between the Mount of Sion and that of Olives. The
general opinion is, that he died about the age of
sixty, and before our Divine Lord quitted Nazareth
in order to receive baptism from St. John the Baptist.

From all that we have been saying it may be inferred,
how just and reasonable it is that all Christians should
choose St. Joseph as their patron at the critical and
inevitable moment of death. Father of their Judge,
whose anger his authority will soften and pacify—
Conqueror of devils, his presence will chase them

away from the bed of death—favoured himself by
the most happy and tranquil death ever known, will
he not come with his holy spouse to assist those
Christians at the hour of death who shall have invoked and professed themselves his devoted servants
during life? Therefore, as we must all die, we should
all hasten, while it is yet time, to secure St. Joseph's
protection as our patron at the hour of our death.
The Church exhorts us to do so in the hymn in which
she celebrates his happy passage to a better world.
As a docile child of this holy mother, I joyfully conform to her wishes. In anticipation of that dread
hour, I will now call upon my august protector in
the words of the following prayer :

" Blessed Joseph! it is not without important
reasons that you have been preferred to so many
other saints, and honoured as the special patron of
dying persons, of those who are desirous of securing
for themselves the greatest of all graces, that of a
happy death. Your death was so consoling, so precious, that it is a subject of envy to all the just on
earth. You had Jesus and Mary at your side, both
anxious to make you some return for all the services
you rendered to them during your life ; both admi-
nistered to you in turn all the little comforts which
their extreme poverty would allow them to procure ;
Jesus comforted you by the words of eternal life ;
Mary consoled you by bestowing on you a degree of
care and attention which the utmost tenderness alone
could suggest. How often did the arms of Jesus
support your languishing head !—how often did
Mary wipe off the perspiration of death from your
wan and ghastly countenance ! Ah ! how could you
not have died of love when you beheld Jesus and

Mary—a God and the Mother of a God—supporting and consoling you in your agony? The holy old man Simeon died in peace, and full of joy, for having beheld Jesus for a few moments; and you, O blessed Joseph! who for so many years had Him constantly before your eyes, who a thousand times bestowed upon Him the caresses of a good father, and received from Him those of a fond son; you whom He considered a duty to obey to the last moment of your life; you who were to breathe out your last sigh whilst receiving a last embrace from Jesus; you, in a word, who knew that Mary herself was to close your eyes, oh! with what far greater justice may you not sing with Simeon, before you expire, that canticle of love and joy: 'Now, O my Jesus, my Son, and my God! Thou dost dismiss Thy servant, Thy father, Thy guardian, in peace!' Most holy and blessed patriarch, since your death has been so sweet, so honourable, so precious in the sight of the Lord, I now at this moment earnestly implore your protection for my last hour; obtain for me, I conjure you, at that moment so terrible for the sinner, grace to detest most sincerely all the sins of my life; to hope with unshaken confidence in the infinite mercy of my Redeemer and my God, who for my salvation commenced His life in the crib, and consummated it upon a cross! And finally, may I cherish also the most unbounded confidence in Mary and in you. What I would wish to say when in the act of expiring, I now repeat with all the ardour of my soul:

"Jesus, Mary, and Joseph, I conjure you to assist me in my agony!"

END OF THE FIRST BOOK.

SECOND BOOK.

GRACES AND FAVOURS
DUE TO THE PATRONAGE OF
SAINT JOSEPH.

CHAPTER I.

Protection of St. Joseph, as experienced by St. Theresa and the Order of Mount Carmel.

THE reader, doubtless, has not forgotten all that we have said concerning St. Theresa's tender devotion to St. Joseph, and the exertions she made to diffuse it throughout the entire universe; we shall now lay before him a few facts, which will show that the love of St. Joseph for his servant Theresa, was that of a father towards a favourite child, and that of this he has given miraculous proofs, both to the saint herself, as well as to the entire family of Carmel. These statements are taken from Bollandus, who procured them from the most authentic sources.

St. Theresa began from her very childhood to experience the good effects of St. Joseph's benign patronage. She mentions in the autobiography, which was written in compliance with the wishes of her superiors, that, after struggling for three years with the most violent and irremediable maladies, which deprived her of rest, and of all hope of recovery, she at length had recourse to St. Joseph, who restored her miraculously to health.

About the commencement of the Carmel reformation, our Lord ordered her not to defer any longer the foundation of her first monastery, at Avila, promising to give her every requisite assistance towards the accomplishment of that good work, because He foresaw that He would be served by the inmates of that house with the utmost perfection. He also desired her to give the name of St. Joseph to this, which was the first of the reformed houses, and informed her that, at either side of the entrance to it, He would Himself place the most faithful and vigilant guards, namely, Mary, his own mother, and Joseph, her chaste spouse.

The holy foundress was one day in great anxiety, because she actually had not money enough to pay the workmen's wages, and could not devise any possible means of procuring it. St. Joseph, on this occasion, appeared to her, and offered, not only to become answerable for the debt, but also to be her treasurer; he assured her, that she should not want for money, and induced her to make an agreement with the men, and to go on with the work. The saint had not a fraction, but, nevertheless, she complied with St. Joseph's request. He was not wanting on his part, and supplied her with money in so many extraordinary ways, that those who witnessed them deemed them altogether miraculous.

Elsewhere she also relates, that, being at prayer on the feast of the Assumption, in the church of the Dominicans, she felt as if some person had thrown around her a mantle of dazzling whiteness. She

could not at first discover to whom she was indebted
for this honour; but, shortly after, she beheld the
Blessed Virgin on her right hand, and St. Joseph on
her left; both covered her with this rich vesture,
giving her to understand, at the same moment, that
she was purified from all her sins! Thus clothed,
while her heart was overflowing with inexpressible
joy, it seemed to her that she took both hands of the
Blessed Virgin in hers, who, smiling graciously upon
Theresa, condescended to express her great satisfaction at the saint's tender devotion to her holy spouse,
and recommended her to apply to St. Joseph for
whatever she stood in need of for the monastery,
with a firm confidence of obtaining her request: as
a pledge of this promise, she presented her with a
precious gem. The saint likewise thought she saw
round her neck a magnificent necklace, from which
was suspended a golden cross: after which, these
two glorious personages took their flight towards
heaven, accompanied by myriads of angels, leaving
the soul of Theresa in an ecstacy of joy, and burning
with a desire, as she says herself, of consuming her
strength and her life in the service of God, of becoming a complete holocaust to His greater honour and
glory.

On another occasion, St. Joseph saved her life
miraculously, and also the lives of several of her
spiritual daughters, who were travelling with her on
a foundation : the new monastery was to be under
his special protection, and to bear his name. At a
critical part of the road, the coachman lost his way,
and the horses were galloping full speed towards a
precipice. St. Theresa, seeing the terror of her companions, when on the very brink of the abyss which

yawned before them, thus addressed them : "My dear sisters, the only means by which we have a chance of escape, is to have recourse to our good father, and to implore his assistance." They did so, and immediately a voice was heard to proceed from the abyss, saying: "Stop! stop! if you advance another step, you will all perish;" at which the horses stopped, and the religious, having asked what direction they were to take, the voice pointed out to them a safer road than that which they were pursuing. They obeyed, and found themselves at once out of all danger. The coachman and guides went in search of the person who had spoken to them from the abyss, in order to express their gratitude, but they could not find the slightest vestige of a human being. St. Theresa, who well knew who their real benefactor was, could no longer keep the secret. "My dear daughters," she said, much affected, "in vain do the guides seek for him to whom we owe our preservation—our liberator is no other than our great and good father, St. Joseph." On another occasion, St. Theresa got a violent fall, from which, however, she received no injury; and this she attributed to St. Joseph's protection.

We shall now mention some special favours granted by St. Joseph to the order of Carmel: we quote them from the historian of St. Theresa's reformation. Two Barefooted Carmelites of Grenada were in the act of coming out of their monastery in that town, when they met a man who seemed to be far advanced in years; he had a pleasing countenance, and his aspect was venerable. He joined them, and asked them whence they came. The elder replied, that they came from the convent of the Barefooted Carmelites.

"Father," returned the stranger, "can you tell me why your order is so devoted to St. Joseph?" The same religious replied, that it was because their holy mother, Theresa of Jesus, so greatly honoured that glorious saint, who powerfully assisted her in the foundation of her different monasteries, and obtained from heaven innumerable graces for her, that in gratitude to him, she gave his name to the greater number of the houses founded by her. "I am aware of that," said the stranger; "look at me, and be as devoted to St. Joseph as your holy mother was: whatsoever you shall ask through his intercession, you shall obtain." Having spoken thus, he suddenly disappeared, and the religious, on looking round, could see no person. On reaching their convent, they related their strange adventure to the superior. "The stranger was St. Joseph himself," said the superior to them; "and it was rather for me, than for you, that this apparition was permitted; for I have not been as fervent a client of this great saint as I ought to have been; but henceforth I shall consider it a duty to become so." This event happened in 1584, two years after St. Theresa's death.

The saint did not long defer the fulfilment of his promises. The Carmelites had founded a convent at Consuegra, in Spain, but the premature death of the pious founder deprived them of all pecuniary resources, just as they had commenced the building of their future residence. They knew no person who was either able or willing to assist them, and were actually reduced to a state of extreme destitution. A father of the reform, who then happened to be at Consuegra, suggested to them a means of obtaining relief. He wrote to the prior, and said to him :

"Your monastery is under the protection of our holy father, St. Joseph; it therefore belongs to him. Experience has often proved to you how great is his power with God; if you desire his assistance now, order a general Communion in his honour: I feel confident that this will be sufficient to induce him to deliver you from your present distress." This advice being complied with, on the following day, the same father was walking through the public square, when he was accosted by a notary, who informed him, that having heard that the nuns were anxious to borrow funds, and even at interest, if necessary, he was most willing to accommodate them, but could not obtain the consent of his wife, who seemed to have a great objection to his doing so. Upon hearing this, the religious went himself to the lady to induce her to enter into her husband's charitable views. To his surprise, he found her so kind and so generous, that, far from offering any objection, she appeared to consider it quite an honour and a favour to be permitted to employ her fortune in the construction of the monastery. Other circumstances with which this unexpected change was accompanied, were so singular, and yet seemed to be brought about in so simple and agreeable a manner, that it would be impossible not to recognize the intervention of a saint jealous of his promises, and anxious to reward the faith of his devout servants.

A no less wonderful instance of his power occurred in Zumaya, in Biscay. Some of the most respectable ladies of the place had assembled together with a view of consecrating themselves to God in the religious state, and the institute which they seemed inspired to embrace was that of the Barefooted

Carmelites, or daughters of St. Theresa. They wrote
to inform their pastor, the Bishop of Pampeluna, of
their intention. The latter only partially approved
of their design. He repaired to Zumaya to propose
to them another rule less austere. These pious ladies
renewed their entreaties, and even seemed to question whether the prelate could conscientiously refuse
them the means and permission to pursue their vocation. The bishop, however, was determined not to
yield, and desired them to choose among those orders
which do not oblige their members to go barefoot;
he gave them only the time during which he cele-
brased Mass to decide, adding, that if, during that
interval they had not come to a decision, he would
oblige them to embrace any order he thought fit to
to choose for them; saying which, he went to the
church and began Mass. The holy women, instead
of deliberating, spent the time in supplicating our
Lord, that it would please Him to admit them to
take the rule and habit of the Theresians. Their
prayer was heard, through the intercession of St.
Joseph : the saint appeared to the bishop during
Mass, reprimanded him warmly for having
afflicted these good souls by refusing his assent to
their pious wishes, and commanded him to authorise
them to embrace St. Theresa's rule. After Mass, the
bishop, not without some embarrassment, informed
them of the apparition, and the order he had received. He completed their joy, by giving them his
full consent to embrace the order of their predilection, placing the new house under the invocation of
the saint, who, in so extraordinary a manner, had
professed himself its firmest upholder and warmest
advocate.

CHAPTER II.

Protection of St. Joseph over Religious Houses.

ST. JOSEPH, as father and guardian of the Holy Family, is entitled to be the patron of all Christian families, but especially of those who, by the profession which they make of the Gospel counsels, are the most perfect copies of that blessed family, which is called by excellence, the " Holy Family." We alluded to this matter before (in the seventh chapter, first book), and shall now illustrate the doctrine therein explained by a few examples.

In the early part of the seventeenth century, the order of the Chartreuse experienced a great affliction; no subjects were offering themselves—the novitiate houses were empty—its members gradually fell off, and the complete dissolution of the establishment was apprehended; just like an army, which for want of recruits must dwindle away to nothing. At this painful crisis, a general chapter of the order was held at the Grand Chartreuse; the most ancient of the fathers proposed having recourse to St. Joseph, whereupon it was unanimously decreed to choose St. Joseph as the patron of the order, and to observe his festival in the most solemn manner. The effects of this arrangement were soon felt: shortly after vocations manifested themselves, and the novitiate-houses were soon so well filled, as to remove all further apprehensions of the failure of this venerable order.

The branch of the Chartreuse at Lyons, which was that most destitute of subjects, made a vow to have

Mass celebrated every week in honour of St. Joseph, by all the priests who were residing in the house. This practice, together with the great confidence with which the religious were animated towards him, proved so agreeable to the saint, that he ever after took care to supply the novitiate with subjects full of fervour, and determined to embrace all the austerities of the institute.

A convent of nuns experienced a similar mark of St. Joseph's protection. The elders began to be seriously alarmed, seeing that, for a considerable time past, no one offered herself to receive the habit. The superioress felt an inspiration to have recourse to St. Joseph, and ordered the prayer composed by the Church in honour of the saint, to be recited daily after the Community Mass. Hardly had they commenced this practice, when a young person offered herself, who most earnestly desired to consecrate herself to God in that house. She was admitted, and persevered : the sisters ever after looked upon her as St. Joseph's special daughter.

St. Joseph has often proved a friend to poor convents, when, in their temporal necessities, they had recourse to him : St. Theresa and the order of Carmel can furnish many proofs of this, as may be seen in the preceding chapter. I shall here only mention what a superior of one of the professed houses of the Jesuits told me : these houses live upon alms. He said that he had been recommended by two fathers, respectable both for their years and virtues, to apply to St. Joseph whenever their houses were in want, and that he had never yet done so, without experiencing the happy effects of the saint's benign patronage.

CHAPTER III.

St. Joseph is the particular Patron of those who aspire to Great Interior Sanctity.

THE Almighty seems, in a special manner, to have entrusted to St. Joseph's care those souls who practise habitual recollection, and probably as a reward for the hidden and interior life which He led at Nazareth. If one of the greatest advantages for a person really anxious to make continual progress in perfection, is an enlightened and prudent director, all Christians who aspire to the interior life, are, for that reason, invited to abandon themselves to the direction of our saint, with perfect confidence of being happily conducted by him to the consummation of their pious wishes. In favour of this truth, we shall here give the reader the testimony of a young man, who, in the midst of the world, preserved the innocence and simplicity of the dove. This young man happened one day to meet a father Jesuit, who, after some moments' conversation, recognised him to be a singularly gifted soul, enriched with such sublime graces and favours, that he had never until then met with any person so highly favoured, or so far advanced in perfection. The father's admiration and astonishment increased on hearing the young man say that he had been eighteen years in service, and had never received a lesson in the spiritual life from any one; and yet he spoke like a saint and a theologian on the most sublime and abstruse matters. Upon being asked whether he had a devotion to St. Joseph, he replied

in the affirmative, and that it was then six years
since the Almighty had inspired him with a devotion
to the saint, whom he then made choice of for his
patron.   His language actually seemed like inspiration, when speaking of the sanctity of St. Joseph ;
and he concluded by saying, that St. Joseph was the
particular patron of those who are so happy as to
possess a particular *attrait* for the hidden life.

The following is another exemplification of this
truth.   A religious of St. Clare, who was preparing
to perform the spiritual exercises, intended to choose
her holy father, St. Francis, as her patron during
the retreat, when suddenly St. Joseph became present
to her imagination, and she felt painfully undecided
as to which of the two she ought to choose for her
patron.   In this state of uncertainty, she determined
to decide the matter by lots, and having written the
name of each saint on a slip of paper, she drew St.
Joseph's, and therefore considered him the patron
destined by God for her.   Some time after, in compliance with a strong inspiration, she was about to
choose a patron for life among three or four saints,
to whom she had a great devotion from her childhood; to this patron she was especially to entrust all
her spiritual interests.   The name of Joseph being
much in her thoughts, she wrote his name also with
the others ; and so fortunate was she, that she drew
his name the very first, and afterwards three times
successively.   This religious no longer entertained
the least doubt but that St. Joseph was selected by
God Himself to be the father and guardian of her
soul during the remainder of her life.

But surely it is not necessary to have recourse to
lots, in order to ascertain if such be the will of God,

when the mother of Him who regulates every human event, declares to us that Joseph her spouse ought to be our spiritual guide. A perfect religious was much troubled by violent temptations, especially during her spiritual exercises : what gave her most concern during these conflicts was, that she feared she had abandoned herself to pusillanimity and discouragement, thinking she would never attain that precious liberty of spirit which is the peculiar privilege and inheritance of the children of God. In her anguish she had recourse to her good mother, the Blessed Virgin, and begged that through her intercession peace and tranquillity might succeed to the tempest of her soul, saying, that her only motive in asking this favour was, that she might be united to God in prayer with a heart more pure, more fervent, and more perfectly disengaged from all transitory things. O Holy Virgin! she added, if you will not grant me this favour yourself, deign at least to show me one amongst your favourites in heaven to whom I may have recourse with confidence as to the father of my soul, to obtain the favour I now ask. Scarcely had she concluded this simple supplication to the Mother of Mercy, when she felt her heart overflowing with spiritual joy and peace ; at the same moment she beheld with the eyes of her soul St. Joseph himself, who was represented to her as being beloved by Mary above all the other saints, in the first place, because he was her spouse, and secondly, on account of his transcendent virtues, which have entitled him to be preferred to all the other saints, as the worthy master of the interior life and the spiritual father of souls. The religious from that moment placed herself entirely under the direction of St. Joseph, whom she ever after regarded as a tender parent, who not only possessed the will, but also the means of serving her. The effects of his protection were soon experienced by his devoted daughter, for she was delivered by him from all her interior pains; and when afterwards assailed by any temptation, she had only to cast herself like a child into the arms of her good parent, and was immediately restored to peace of mind and interior recollection.

But to descend more to particulars, let us see how great an advantage is St. Joseph's assistance to those souls who are desirous of advancing in the science of prayer. Here it will suffice to quote the testimony of St. Theresa, that great mistress of prayer and contemplation. It was by his aid that she was enabled to soar so high on the wings of the dove, or to speak more properly, of the eagle: and those souls who were anxious to make a progress in prayer, she always recommended to call on St. Joseph for his assistance. "Whoever," says she, "cannot find a director capable of guiding him through the paths of prayer, need only have recourse to St. Joseph in order to arrive happily at the possession of his heart's treasure." In the mean time, until you know this yourself by happy experience, I will give you an example which will prove most consoling and encouraging to St. Joseph's clients, and to all who thirst for the unspeakable happiness of being closely united to God by prayer. Père Barri, one of our saint's historians, relates it as follows: "I am myself acquainted with two individuals who could not endure the holy exercise of prayer, on account of the difficulties which they experienced in it. Both, hoping to surmount them, chose St. Joseph as their guide and special patron;

and very soon did they feel the effects of his patronage : the mountains were laid low before them ; the field of prayer, which had appeared so sterile and rugged, was now covered with flowers and verdure, so that meditation or mental prayer became the most consoling and agreeable of all their spiritual exercises."

Another religious, says the same father, told me herself, that she was most anxious to be delivered from distractions at prayer; and in order to obtain this grace, she was irresistibly impelled to have recourse to St. Joseph. She prayed most fervently to him, and the fruit of her confidence was a very eminent spirit of prayer, and also a total exemption from anything in her dreams capable of giving the least uneasiness to her conscience.

St. Joseph is also remarkable for imparting a great love of the cross to those who are devoted to him. He and his blessed spouse appeared one day to the Ven. Anne Rodriguez, a Franciscan nun. Whilst Mary recommended her to her divine Son, Joseph presented her with a vase, containing two sorts of meat, one of which was most agreeable to the palate, and the other equally bitter and distasteful. " My child," said he, " take whichever of these you prefer." The religious, who was a fervent client of the saint, took the bitter meat. St. Joseph then showed her a beautiful, but very weighty cross, saying to her : "Daughter, you have made an excellent choice; henceforth you shall indeed always share the cross for your portion, with all bitterness ; but rejoice ! for therein you will possess ample means of rendering yourself exceedingly pleasing in the sight of God, and He will turn all your mourning into joy."

CHAPTER IV.

St. Joseph's Paternal Vigilance over those amongst his Clients
whose Salvation is in Danger.

ST. JOSEPH may be compared to the good father in
the Gospel, who loves those among his children
who obey, and are an honour to him, but whose
tender and compassionate heart also yearns for the
return of that ungrateful child who had abandoned
and dishonoured the best of parents. The meaning
of this is, that if he grants favours to the just to
enable them to advance in perfection, neither does
he withhold his paternal care and solicitude from
poor sinners. Of this, we here give a very ancient
but authentic example : it is a quotation from that
famous work on St. Joseph, written by Père Isidore
de L'Isle, and which the author dedicated to Pope
Adrian VI., about the year 1522. A Venetian gen-
tleman, who had acquired the pious custom of praying every day before an image of St. Joseph, but
who seemed otherwise extremely careless with regard
to the most indispensable duties of religion, happened
to be attacked with a serious illness, and seemed in
imminent danger, not only of death, but also, what
was infinitely more deplorable, of eternal death ! Happily for him, at those periods of the sickness when
his case appeared most desperate, a heavenly physician, even St. Joseph himself, came to his relief.
The sick man distinctly saw a personage enter his
chamber, whose countenance bore a striking resemblance to that of the image which he was in the habit
of saluting daily. Such an unexpected apparition

was cheering to him as a sunbeam, which suddenly
dispels the gloom of some darksome prison into which
it penetrates. He then saw clearly and distinctly all
the sins, in the habit of which he had so long almost
unconsciously lived; he conceived the deepest horror
of them, as well as the most lively contrition : but
this did not satisfy his fervour; he made a general
confession of his whole life, with abundance of tears.
But a most singular grace that his generous protector bestowed on him was, that, just at that precious
moment when the priest had pronounced the last
word of the form of the absolution, the fortunate
penitent gave up his soul into the hands of its
Creator. It may well be supposed that St. Joseph
failed not to accompany that soul, so highly favoured
by him, to the feet of the Sovereign Judge, to be its
defender, if necessary, at that dread tribunal.

The following example we hope will serve
to impart courage to those weak and timid souls
who, after having had the misfortune of falling
into some grievous sin, yield to the dangerous
temptations of absenting themselves from the tribunal of penance, rather than undergo the confusion of confessing it : it will, moreover, show
them that in St. Joseph's intercession they will be
sure to find a powerful means of overcoming this
base, this pernicious shame. The person to whom
this occurred told it herself to Père Barri, when he
was writing a life of St. Joseph. This person had
the misfortune to commit a great sin contrary to a
vow which she had made, and found it impossible
to conquer the false shame which sealed her lips at
the sacred tribunal of penance. For a long time she
lived at enmity with God, and a prey to that most

grievous of all torments, remorse of conscience, the inevitable consequence of sin. This unhappy creature knew well that her sufferings would endure until the thorn which lacerated her should have been extracted, and that her wound would never heal until she had discovered it to the spiritual physician. She at length thought of calling on St. Joseph to assist her weakness, and invoked him to enable her to overcome the repugnance which seemed indomitable. For this intention she recited during nine days the hymn and prayer of the saint, after which she felt so strong and courageous, that rising superior to herself, she hastened to cast herself at the feet of her confessor, and made her accusation without the least difficulty. From that happy moment, she always regarded St. Joseph as her liberator, entrusted him with the care of her soul, and always wore his image about her, and even at night, as a preventative against bad dreams. She moreover acknowledged that St. Joseph was pleased to recompense her fidelity and devotion to him by extraordinary graces.

The same writer mentions two singular conversions, both of which are attributed to St. Joseph's intercession. The first was that of a young man at Lyons, who had led a very edifying life, and had even resolved to quit the world, in order the better to secure his eternal salvation : but afterwards, his parents having opposed his vocation, he was so weak as to renounce it. The world soon cooled his youthful fervour and piety, and he gradually abandoned all his former holy practices ; the absence of all restraint, the allurements of pleasure, and the force of bad example, made him forget his duties, and he abandoned himself to all the excesses of the most licentious life. But all that was not yet sufficient to gratify the violence of his passions; like another prodigal, he quitted his father's house, buckled on the sword, and enlisted as a soldier. In his new profession, he cared not to acquire any other glory than that of being cited as the most shameless libertine of the entire regiment. All this was permitted by Divine Justice, to punish both the parents and the child: the latter for having, through mistaken compliance, closed his ears against the voice of God; the former, for having, in their blind affection, dared to oppose the designs of heaven. However, the parents were now inconsolable on seeing their son, whom they refused to give to God, in the hands of the devil; they wrote him innumerable letters, bathed in their tears, exhorting him to a change of life, and to return to his parental home, where he would be received with open arms. At last, seeing that all their invitations, all their entreaties, were not capable of softening the obdurate heart of their son, they had now recourse to a more noble, a more efficacious means, which was that of invoking St. Joseph; and they implored him to take their unfortunate child under his protection, and to save him from perdition. The saint had compassion on them; he inspired the young soldier with such lively feelings of regret and piety, that becoming an altered man, he quitted the army and returned to his parents, of whom he humbly asked forgiveness for the anguish he had cost them. He thenceforth entered on a life worthy of his former fervour, and so seriously and perseveringly, that we may apply to him the words addressed in the Gospel to the prodigal son : " He was dead, and is come to life ; he was lost, and is found."

The second conversion which was effected by St. Joseph's intercession, took place at Paris. A religious of the Society of Jesus had a near relative, who for many years was a disgrace, no less to the name of Christian, than to the priesthood, with which dignity he was invested. This zealous religious having employed, though in vain, the most kind and paternal remonstrances, together with the most awful and serious warnings, at length begged of God, that if all other means failed, it would please Him to send this wretched man a grievous illness, which might serve to reclaim him from his wanderings; for in truth there is not a more effectual means than tribulation for restoring reason to those whom vice has deprived of it, according to this passage of Holy Writ: "Tribulation giveth understanding." In order to neglect nothing on his part to secure the efficacy of this remedy, he had recourse to St. Joseph, and asked his friends to say two novenas together, one of Masses, the other of Communions, in his honour. The favour so vigorously demanded was not refused; the unworthy minister fell sick, and appeared not to have many moments to live. It was only then he became sensible of all the disorders of his life; he sincerely detested them, and hastened to be purified in the sacrament of penance. In order to render this miracle more striking, St. Joseph added another extraordinary favour to it, for the priest was quite suddenly restored to perfect health, and rose from his bed with a perfect determination to live thenceforth in a manner conformable to his saintly character. He devoted himself with zeal and perseverance to works of piety, and seemed to have but one object in life, namely, to promote, by word and example, the glory of his Divine Master in all things.

CHAPTER V.

St. Joseph is not unmindful of the Temporal Wants of his Clients.

ALL parents and heads of families are particularly bound to honour St. Joseph, and to recommend those under them to the care and guardianship of him whom God Himself chose to be the chief and governor of the "Holy Family." Children are undoubtedly the most precious ornaments and the greatest blessing a Christian family can possess, and parents cannot be too solicitous to procure for them a good and virtuous education. In order to secure the success of so important an object, let them have recourse to St. Joseph, and with so much the greater confidence, that in taking upon him the duty of watching over the sacred infancy of our Saviour, he, at the same time, assumed that of presiding over the interests of the children of the Church, who were ransomed by that Saviour's blood.

In the year 1631, an immense crater of Mount Vesuvius burst forth, vomiting such a deluge of fire and ashes, that, like a vast inundation, the burning lava threatened to overrun all the neighbouring countries, but particularly a place called Torre del Greco. In this place there lived a woman of the name of Camilla, much devoted to St. Joseph; she had a boy of five years old, her nephew, staying with her, and whose name happened to be Joseph. In order to escape from the fury of the flood, she took

the child in her arms and fled; but being closely
followed by the lava, and finding the passage closed
up by a large rock which jutted out into the sea, she
was now exposed to the twofold danger of either
being consumed by the fire if she stopped, or else
drowned if she advanced another step.   At this
critical moment she remembered her holy patron,
St. Joseph, and said: "I recommend to your care
your little Joseph; it is on your intercession I depend for his safety."   Saying this, and having not
a moment to lose, she placed the child upon the rock,
and then boldly leaped down from it as it were into
the sea which rolled beneath.   The leap was a most
fortunate one, for instead of falling directly into the
waves, as appeared inevitable, she alighted on the
beach without having sustained the least injury.
She was safe; but her anxiety was most painful as
to the fate of the poor child whom she had left to the
mercy of the flames.   She began to run here and
there, bewildered and almost frantic with grief, when
suddenly she heard herself called by name, and beheld her dear little nephew running towards her full
of life and joy.   "May God be praised!" exclaimed
Camilla, as she clasped him in her arms, " who has
rescued you from being stifled by the ashes, or consumed by the terrific flames?"   "It was St. Joseph,
dear aunt," said the child, joyously: "you recommended me to St. Joseph's care; he took me by the
hand and brought me here to you."   On hearing
this the pious Camilla shed tears of joy, and fell on
her knees to thank her amiable protector for the two
miracles which he had at the same moment performed
in her favour.

Amongst the various pious exercises which are

practised in honour of St. Joseph, there is one very
well known, and which consists in meditating on the
principal events of his life, reduced chiefly to seven,
and usually styled the Seven Joys and Dolours of St.
Joseph. The practice of this exercise owes its origin
to a celebrated event, which has not been forgotten
by any of the saint's historians. It is related as follows : Two Franciscan fathers were in a vessel on
the coast of Flanders, when suddenly a violent storm
arose which sunk the ship, together with three hundred passengers. The two religious had sufficient
presence of mind to grasp at a plank belonging to the
wreck, and thus endeavoured to sustain themselves
upon the angry billows : but their agony may be
imagined, seeing death before their eyes, and the
vast tomb which threatened each moment to swallow
them up. In this perilous situation, with all their
endeavours to retain their hold on the plank, they
began to fear that it would be washed away from
them, and then death would be inevitable. They
always had a particular devotion to St. Joseph ; they
now most earnestly called on him as their true hope
and the star of their salvation ; and at length he
came to their assistance : he appeared to them standing on the plank that had supported them, in the
form of a fine majestic youth. The kind and friendly
manner of his salutation was in itself sufficient to
impart consolation to their hearts, and even a miraculous vigour to their limbs ; he acted as a pilot,
and conducted them safely to shore. Once more on
land, the religious, prostrate on the earth, poured
forth their gratitude to God ; they afterwards thanked
the young stranger, and begged to know his name.
" I am Joseph," said he, and then spoke of the seven

joys and dolours of his mortal life, told them how acceptable to him it was that Christians should meditate on them, and that such persons should receive special marks of his protection. He then disappeared, while their hearts overflowed with such pure and lively joy as they had never until then experienced.

The city of Lyons has been singularly favoured by St. Joseph, and it would occupy an entire volume were we to recount the many extraordinary favours granted by him to the pious prayers of its inhabitants. Père Barri has mentioned a certain number of them in his work, and we here give only the most remarkable of these. Sister Jane of the Angels, Prioress of the Ursulines, was attacked with pleurisy, which was accompanied with fever and the most agonizing pains. All the remedies proved ineffectual, and the invalid was prepared for death. One day on which the violence of the disorder had deprived her of the use of her senses, without however affecting her mind in the least, she seemed to behold St. Joseph coming down from heaven; his benign and gracious aspect seemed to indicate that he was about to grant some extraordinary favour; her cell appeared to have been transformed into a little Paradise. Issuing from a bright cloud, the invalid perceived a young man of most prepossessing appearance, richly attired, holding in his hand a burning wax taper—she knew him to be her angel-guardian; near him stood the glorious patriarch St. Joseph, brilliant as the sun, and whose aspect altogether was one of incomparable beauty and majesty : his features were not those of an old person, but of one in the maturity of manhood. He first saluted Jane with an expression of great sweetness; he then spoke to her, and exhorted her to persevere constantly in those pious practices which she was in the habit of performing in his honour, after which he restored her completely to health. The vision then instantly vanished, and the invalid arose from her bed perfectly cured. In the meantime the physician called in; she went to meet him, and it may be conceived how great was his astonishment to see a person whom he expected to find no more, full of life and vigour. In gratitude to her benefactor, and in order to merit a continuance of his powerful patronage, she thenceforth devoted herself with redoubled ardour to his service.

During the plague which afflicted the city of Lyons in 1638, a vast number of the inhabitants were preserved or recovered from it by the intercession of St. Joseph. For brevity sake we shall cite only two instanses of this:—An advocate attached to the parliament of Dauphiné, who happened to be at Lyons, found that one of his children, a boy of seven years old, was attacked by the plague, and had all the symptoms that usually denote the near approach of death in such cases. The father, who was a good Christian, did not lose confidence; he invoked St. Joseph, and made him a promise that if his child recovered, he would hear Mass during nine days in his church, and burn wax-lights in his honour, and that he would place there an *ex voto*, the inscription on which would record the benefit due to his intercession. In the meantime the physicians continued their visits to the sick child, whom they found in so deplorable a state, that they ordered him to be at once taken off to the Lazaretto, saying, he had not

two hours to live. Their directions were attended to,
but no sooner had the child arrived at the Pest-
house, than he was perfectly cured, and the happy
father, overwhelmed with gratitude to his glorious
benefactor, immediately accomplished his vow. Another child in the same town, called Martin, was
seized with the plague. The distracted mother,
almost in despair of his recovery, was recommended
to call on St. Joseph to protect her child, who was
only four years old. "O yes," she said; " I will indeed recommend him to St. Joseph, for my child was
born on his glorious festival." She then began immediately to pray to the saint. The child's father came in
two hours after, and found him apparently near his
end; he mentioned this to his wife, who was of the same
opinion; however, she still had hope in prayer, and
persevered in calling on St. Joseph as she knelt at
the foot of the child's bed. While his mother was
still in prayer, the dying boy suddenly asked for
something to eat, and in a few moments after he rose
up from his bed perfectly recovered. As a token of
gratitude, the happy mother presented a handsome
painting to St. Joseph's altar, which represented the
illness and cure of her son. This miracle was one
of those which contributed wonderfully to increase
the confidence and devotion of the public towards St.
Joseph, and thus became the source of a multitude
of graces no less extraordinary, which the saint was
pleased afterwards to pour down upon that city.

We have made previous mention of a beautiful
little chapel dedicated to St. Joseph in the interior of
the Augustinian monastery at Antwerp; it is, however, no less celebrated for the many favours which
have been granted in it to the fervent clients of the

saint, than for its perfection as a work of art.
Amongst the inmates of that monastery was a religious, by name Elizabeth, who for three years
was a martyr to a most painful malady, the stone.
The excess of her pains brought on a burning
fever, and the physicians actually despaired of
her recovery. Finding that she no longer had
anything to hope from human aid, she now
looked only to heaven for relief; and having always
been devoted to St. Joseph, it was to him she now
partially had recourse. She solicited and obtained
permission from the superioress to offer up as many
prayers, vows, and mortifications, as she should
judge expedient, in order to render herself more
worthy of the care of the heavenly physician whom
she had chosen. She ceased not day and night to
invoke him, and engaged as many as she could to do
so for her. The longer she persevered in these holy
exercises, the more did her confidence increase, so
much so, that one day she told the superioress that
she felt almost certain of her recovery. It was on
the 10th of June, 1659, when her agony became
intolerable, that, with the assistance of her atten-
dants, she placed herself on her knees before an
image of St. Joseph, and calling loudly upon him for
relief, she instantly not only obtained a cessation of
all pain, but also the complete removal of her complaint. From the peculiar nature of her case, all
allow, and among others an heretical physician, that
her cure was miraculous.* The fame of this prodigy

---

* According to the Bollandists, this happened on the 10th of
June, 1649; a verbal process was made on the 9th of January
following. Among other signatures are seen those of Marie

inspired with confidence a poor mother whose sonl was afflicted with a malady not less dangerous and painful, and her fervent prayers to our saint obtained his miraculous recovery.

In the monastery of St. Elizabeth at Lyons, one of the religious, Margaret Rigaud, met with a dangerous fall, which, for the moment, deprived her of the use of her senses, and caused the blood to issue from her mouth, nose, and ears; however, with the aid of strong remedies and great care, her life was preserved, but the organs of her head were so weakened, that for several months she could not recline it on the pillow, and her intellectual faculties were so impaired that she found it impossible to apply them to anything. The physicians and surgeons, after holding a consultation together, agreed that the only chance she had of recovery was to go through the operation of trepanning. So great a shock did this decision cause the poor patient, that they thought it better to run the risk of waiting a few days. In the interim, the superioress determined to try a more easy and effectual course, and ordered all the sisters to make a novena of communions in honour of St. Joseph. The pain continued as violent as ever; and at length, towards the end of the novena, some of the sisters, giving up all hopes of obtaining their request through St. Joseph, thought it would be well to substitute St. Anselm, to whose protection they usually had recourse on meeting with these kind of accidents. But one of

Martens, prioress of the convent, of Catharine Martens, infirmarian, and of Elizabeth Sillevorti, the name of the invalid in question.

the sisters, who had a remarkable love and veneration for the spouse of the ever-blessed and immaculate mother of the Saviour, redoubled her entreaties, and begged of him to effect the cure himself; she represented to him that it would be quite derogatory to his honour, which they were so desirous to promote, to yield the glory of such a miracle to any other; and she promised him that the invalid herself, if restored to health, would not fail to offer up a second novena of mortifications and acts of devotion and thanksgiving. Whilst the pious sister persevered night and day in prayer, without intermission, the invalid was perfectly cured, and precisely at the moment when such an event was least expected. She happened to be quite alone, and in the excess of her joy she dressed quickly, and ran through every quarter of the monastery, exclaiming: "A miracle! a miracle! St. Joseph has cured me!" The sequel proves that her cure was complete, for on the same day she assisted in choir, and recited the Office with the other religious, though a little before she could not bear even the distant sound of their voices; she resumed all her usual occupations with an energy that would lead one to suppose that she had never lost her strength. In a word, St. Joseph not only obtained the restoration of her health, but also favours of another kind, which greatly contributed to her spiritual advancement.

We conclude this chapter with the relation of a circumstance which we read in the life of the Ven. Mother Mary of the Incarnation:—Madame de la Peltrie was a Frenchwoman of eminent virtue. One day she accidentally met with an account of a mission which the fathers of the Society of Jesus had

undertaken in Canada : whilst reading it, she felt
strongly moved with a desire to co-operate in the
salvation of the poor Canadians. As she was meditating on the best means of effecting her holy designs,
she was visited by an alarming and unusual illness,
which baffled the skill of the physicians, who completely despaired of her recovery. In this sad condition the good lady did not forget her pious desires,
and God Himself, in the midst of her pains, fortified
her in her holy resolves, and inspired her to make a
vow to St. Joseph. She was aware that it was to
the special protection of this great saint that the
missionaries had recommended the conversion of the
idolatrous nations of the new world; she, therefore,
promised the saint, should it please him to obtain
her recovery, that she would found and endow at
her own expense a convent for the education of
young girls in that country. No sooner had the
invalid pronounced her vow than her prayer was
heard; all her pains, which had been extremely
violent, departed instantaneously, and nothing
remained of that cruel malady but a little lassitude. The physician, on finding her so very
different from what she had been on the previous
day, was equally rejoiced and astonished.
"Madam," says he, "what has become of those
excruciating pains—where are they gone?" "Why,
my dear sir," she replied, smiling, "I believe my
pains are gone to Canada!" She soon after fulfilled
her vow, and built the monastery which was destined
to receive and educate the young Canadians; and it
was Mother Mary of the Incarnation whom Providence designed to become its first superior. It was
revealed to the latter afterwards in a vision, that St.

Joseph was the patron of the New World, and that it was owing to his intercession that she had been called to labour there in the salvation of souls. This it was that induced her to give the new monastery St. Joseph's name, and to adopt as its seal the image of that glorious patriarch, holding the child Jesus in his arms.

CHAPTER VI.

St. Joseph, the Protector and Guide of Travellers.

As our glorious saint received orders from heaven to transport the infant Jesus into Egypt, in order to protect Him from the malice of Herod, he thus acquired another peculiar privilege, viz., that of being the guide and protector of travellers. It was doubtless of him that the prophet Isaiah spoke when he said: " Behold the Lord will ascend upon a swift cloud, and will enter into Egypt" (xix. 1), if, as we have reason to believe, Joseph carried the Divine Infant in his arms into Egypt, and brought Him back from Egypt to Nazareth. Was he not then that beauteous cloud beneath which the Orient from on high concealed its early beams? Yes; while in the heavens above, the sun was regulating the courses of the stars, and eclipsing them by his splendour, on earth, enveloped in swaddling clothes, and reposing on the arm of His adopted father, lay the glorious, the mighty Sun of Justice, a helpless, persecuted babe, altogether dependant upon the will

of two of the poorest of His creatures! Thus speak
Albert the Great and the Abbe Rupert. Joseph,
now-a-days, renders the same kind offices to his
devout clients when any danger threatens them on
their travels. Of this fact we give the following
instances :

A religious in the monastery of Montserrat, in
Spain, was remarkable for a great devotion to our
saint, and, amongst the inexhaustible subjects of
meditation which he gathered from the life of the
holy patriarch, there was not one that served to
animate his fervour more, or afforded him greater
consolation, than his flight into Egypt with Mary
and the Divine Infant. One day, when this good
religious was returning to his convent, he lost his
way, and wandered into the mountains; night was
stealing on, and he became seriously alarmed at the
danger to which he was exposed of being devoured
by wild beasts, or else of falling into the hands of
the brigands who dwelt in those wild and unfre-
quented districts. In this painful situation, he had
just recommended himself into the hands of Providence, when he suddenly perceived a stranger leading
an ass, upon which rode a lady with a child in her
arms. The religious, having inquired of the stranger
the direction of the road which he had missed, the
latter kindly invited him to follow them, saying,
that though the way was perilous, and the darkness
momentarily increasing, yet he was intimately acquainted with the place, and would safely conduct
him to his destination. They continued their journey together, and so saintly was the conversation of
the lady and her guide, that the religious felt his
heart inflamed with a great love of heavenly things,

and experienced an inward peace and consolation somewhat similar to that formerly felt by the disciples of Emmaus, when Jesus, in the disguise of a traveller, joined them on their journey. At length the little party reached the direct road to the monastery, upon which the stranger took leave of the monk, and instantly disappeared: the latter felt convinced that these mysterious fellow-travellers were no other than the Holy Family, to which he had such a devotion ; and their heavenly words made so deep an impression upon his heart, that ever after he found them a source of the greatest comfort and joy.

The Venerable Mother Mary of the Visitation, a Barefooted Carmelite, was also honoured by St. Joseph's special protection on one of her journeys. While yet very young, she led a most holy life in her father's house; but it being the design of God that she should serve Him in a cloister, He was pleased to make use of a very singular means to procure her entrance into it. He impressed her with so lively a sense of her own miseries, that she firmly believed herself to be the scandal of the country. Her confessor and other ecclesiastics urged her to endeavour to subdue the vivacity of this feeling, by the excessive indulgence of which, she might fall into a state of pusillanimity, which is always so injurious to pious souls, and a great obstacle to their progress in virtue. All their efforts were unavailing ; she resolved to set out secretly by night, with the intention, as she afterwards said, of flying from herself if possible. Accordingly, she left the house with no other companion than a crucifix, which she bathed with her tears. After having wandered

about in this state of excitement for the greater part
of the night, she met a venerable old man, who asked
her whither she was going. "I am going," she
replied, "into solitude, in order to flee from myself
and from my sins." The old man then described a
circle around her with his staff, after which pointing
out to her the road that led to Palencia, "Take it,"
said he, "or you are lost." He then suddenly disappeared. The young fugitive soon discovered that
the person who had been speaking to her was St.
Joseph, whom she regarded as her particular patron
from her very childhood; that the circle which had
been traced around her, and the road which she was
warned to pursue, was nothing less than an order to
go to Palencia, and there enter a cloister. She
directed her steps towards that town, but had not
as yet reached it when she was overtaken by some
of her relatives, who, on hearing of her flight, had
set out for the purpose of bringing her back to her
family, and were determined to compel her to return.
They overwhelmed her with reproaches, to which the
young girl listened without making a reply; and
finding herself interiorly strengthened by the order
she had received from heaven, she remained immove-
able in her resolution. The mild yet firm manner
which she adopted on this occasion, quite overcame
her friends, who at length consented to accompany
her as far as Palencia; and as if directed by some
secret impulse, they conducted her to a convent of
Barefooted Carmelites, which was under the invocation of St. Joseph. She was at once admitted and
received as a choir-religious; but this rank appeared
to her far above her deserts; and it occurred more
than once that, whilst chanting the Divine Office,

feeling deeply humbled and ashamed of herself, she would close her breviary, and raising her hands and eyes towards heaven, exclaim : " And my soul, O God ! and my soul !" She feared the loss of her soul if she were to remain as a choir-nun; she most earnestly implored to be permitted to join the lay-sisters, and was actually allowed to do so in order to give an example to the entire community of consummate virtue, even at her early age.

Among the probationary exercises practised by the novices of the Society of Jesus, is that of going on pilgrimages in order to make an essay of the apostolic life. On these occasions they have neither money nor provisions of any kind, and are thus exposed to all the probable inconveniences which naturally result from such a life of fatigue, hunger, thirst, and other similar privations. Three novices on one of these pilgrimages found themselves one day in the midst of a vast plain, far from any human habitation, and exhausted with lassitude, hunger, and thirst, without even so much as a morsel of bread or a drop of water to refresh them ; but being all full of fervour, and eager for sufferings, they mutually consoled and encouraged one another, hoping that as it was vain to expect any relief from earth, heaven would soon provide for their wants ; and in truth it so happened that the extreme necessity to which our three young pilgrims were reduced, was the means of procuring a signal favour for them. They suddenly beheld in the plain a man accompanied by a female, who carried an infant in her arms. Those three strangers approached the novices, and, with a gracious salutation, placed before them the most exquisite meats. The delicious repast, so miraculously provided for them,

did not excite their pleasure and astonishment more
than the angelic sweetness and amiable courtesy of
these mysterious strangers, whose name and quality
they were most anxious to learn, in order to be enabled
to testify their gratitude for a favour which seemed
like something supernatural. However, they were
too humble, and perhaps too timid also, to ask any
questions. Their pious curiosity, however, was fully
satisfied when they heard the following words distinctly pronounced : " We are the founders of the
Society of Jesus," after which their kind hosts instantly disappeared! It is not difficult to imagine
what joy our pilgrims must have felt when they discovered they had the happiness of being served by
Jesus, Mary, and Joseph. They immediately fell
prostrate on the earth to thank and venerate them,
after which they pursued their journey, blessing God
and animating each other to make new efforts thenceforth to prove themselves the worthy children of their
celestial benefactors, who during their mortal lives
had been the most perfect models of the holy state
which they had embraced. In Joseph they could
admire the vigilance of the superior; in Mary, the
virtue of the perfect religious ; and in Jesus, the simplicity and docility of the novice.

The Venerable Sister Cecilia Portaro, of the third
order of St. Francis at Milan, was singularly devoted to St. Joseph. One of her practices was that
of fasting on bread and water every Wednesday in
his honour; in all her wants, spiritual and temporal,
she had recourse to her dear patron, and became
worthy of receiving a very remarkable favour from
him. It occurred as we shall now relate :—Cecilia
had gone on a pilgrimage to Notre Dame de Drepane,

in Sicily, accompanied by some other pious ladies.
As they were returning homewards, the vessel that
was to take them to their destination weighed anchor
without them, leaving them quite alone at night on the
seashore, some distance from Palermo. Whilst her
terrified companions bitterly bewailed the luckless accident, Cecilia lost no time in useless regrets, but
immediately had recourse to her ordinary refuge, and
as the event proves it was not in vain. Quite suddenly
there appeared before them a venerable old man in the
dress of a traveller, with a staff in his hand, who promised to guide them safely through the darkness. "My
dear children," said he, "you must not be encum-
bered with your luggage, here is a little boy who will
carry it for you." "Kind friend," said the travellers,
"we most joyfully accept your charitable offer; but
you will be obliged to make a very long journey, for
the place in which we would wish to pass the night
is at a great distance, namely, St. Joseph's-street."
"Ah! that is the very street in which I live," replied
the old man; "come, let us proceed, my children;
be not afraid." He then accompanied them to the
very door of the house, and placed their luggage on
the threshold. When the travellers turned round to
take leave of the good old man, he and the boy had
disappeared. Astonished at such a prodigy, they
began to ponder all the circumstances of the case, and
at length came to the conclusion that in their charitable guide they beheld St. Joseph, Cecilia's patron,
and that the boy must have been either his adopted
Son, or else the guardian angel of one amongst
them.

The Ven. Sister Jane Rodriguez, of the third order
of St. Francis, was also rewarded by this saint's
visible assistance for her great devotion to him. She

happened once to be travelling on foot with a companion, when the horizon was suddenly obscured by dark clouds, which portended a violent tempest. Jane's companion looked around in alarm for some place of shelter, but without success. At the same moment a stranger made his appearance, and graciously offered to accompany them, assuring them that on this occasion they should not suffer the slightest inconvenience from the rain. Soon after the rain began to fall in torrents, and the heavens seemed bursting over their heads, and nevertheless not the least moisture reached even the feet of the travellers. On witnessing so great a miracle, Jane approached nearer the stranger, and on examination recognised St. Joseph, her blessed protector. He completed their happiness by conversing with them on the vanity of the world and its false advantages, on the inestimable value of divine grace, and on the love of God above all things, until Jane and her companion had reached their journey's end, when the saint quickly vanished from their sight.

Father Jerome de Pistoia, a Capuchin friar and apostolic missionary, repaired to Venice by order of the Sovereign Pontiff, whence he was to embark with one companion for the Isle of Candia. After leaving Venice at some distance behind them, the holy fathers, who were travelling on foot and by night, lost their way, and wandered they knew not where. Feeling exhausted and fatigued, and being destitute of all human resources, they knelt down to invoke Jesus, Mary, and Joseph, whom they asked to befriend them in their present extreme necessity. It is not likely that such a prayer would prove fruitless, Father Jerome being one of our saint's most fervent clients. The religious perceived something like the light of a lamp at some distance; towards it they directed their steps, and discovered a small house which was occupied by a man advanced in years, also a woman and her infant boy, all three remarkably beautiful! They invited our travellers in, and treated them with an admirable charity. On awaking next morning, the two religious found themselves in the midst of a meadow, and could not, in any direction, discover the house where they had received hospitality; upon which they concluded that their kind hosts were no less noble personages than Jesus, Mary, and Joseph, who condescended to hear their simple and heartfelt petition, and to whom they now poured forth their most grateful thanks for so singular a favour (*Chron. of St. Francis*). The words of the learned Eckius, which we shall quote, teach us the fruit to be derived from the extraordinary facts related in this chapter. What he says is as follows:— "Let those who are obliged to undertake perilous journeys, and to traverse wild and inhospitable countries, place themselves under the protection of St. Joseph, and confidently ask of him all the assistance they may stand in need of on such occasions."

CHAPTER VII.

St. Joseph, the Protector of his Servants at the awful hour of Death.

IT is true that St. Joseph is the special patron of all Christians in their last agony; but he reserves the tenderest pledges of his love for those who throughout their lives give him the most signal proofs of their

love and veneration. The patriarch Joseph of old
relieved the Egyptians during the raging famine, by
distributing amongst them the corn which his prudence had amassed; but for his own brethren he did
something more; not content with having filled their
sacks with wheat, he also made them a present of
the money which they gave him as the price of it.
Our glorious St. Joseph will treat with similar, if not
far greater generosity, his devout clients; he will
repay them with usury, at the hour of death, for all
the honour they shall have rendered to him. But as
facts will prove the truth of what we have been saying
better than anything else, we here offer the following
details to the reader:—

The Ven. Sister Pudentia Zaguoni, celebrated in
the Franciscan order for her eminent virtue, had a
particular devotion to St. Joseph, and received some
singularly precious favours from him at the hour of
her death. On that trying occasion the saint appeared to her, and for her greater consolation held in
his arms Him who is the joy of the angels, the beauty
and the bliss of paradise, the life of pure souls, the
most blessed Infant Jesus! We shall not attempt to
describe the transports of holy joy into which this
vision threw the soul of the invalid; let it suffice to
say that the religious present were in some degree
participators in her happiness when they heard her
conversing with St. Joseph and the Divine Infant;
thanking the former for having turned all the bitterness of that dread hour into heavenly sweetness, and
pouring forth her gratitude to the Divine Child for
having come in so amiable a form to invite her to the
marriage-feast which He had prepared in heaven for
holy virgins, whom He has been pleased to dignify

by the title of His spouses. It appeared also to the by-standers, that St. Joseph placed the Divine Infant in the arms of their dying sister, thus giving her death a closer resemblance with his own at Nazareth, for he had the happy privilege of expiring in the sacred arms of Jesus his Divine Saviour.

The venerable servant of God, Alexis de Vige-Vano, a Capuchin, crowned a life full of merits by a singularly happy death. A few moments before he expired, he begged of one of the brothers who assisted him to light several wax tapers. The latter, who was surprised at his making such a request, asked to be informed of the reason of it, to which he replied, that as he expected a visit from our Lady, with her holy spouse, St. Joseph, he desired to receive them with all possible respect. It became quite evident a a moment afterwards that this glorious visit did actually take place, for the dying man cried out in an ecstacy of joy : "Behold the Queen of heaven ! behold St. Joseph ! Pray, father; kneel down and receive them with all possible respect." But the sick man was the first to reap advantage from the presence of Mary and Joseph, for just at the same moment he gave up his soul to God. This occurred on the 19th of March, a day consecrated by the Church to honour St. Joseph's triumph in heaven, who called this good religious on that festive day to participate with him in that eternal jubilee which rewards the virtues and merits of all the saints, and especially of the devout servants of St. Joseph.

St. Vincent Ferrer relates the following fact, wherein we find that Joseph came to the relief of a dying person in company with Jesus and Mary. A pious merchant of Valencia, in Spain, was in the habit of inviting three poor persons, consisting of an old man, a woman, and a child, to dine on Christmas Day in honour of the Holy Family. He remembered those words of our Lord: "That whatever is done to the least of His brethren, is done unto Himself," and thenceforth He regarded these poor persons with the eye of faith, and served them with the utmost care and affection. The charitable merchant appeared after his death to some pious persons who were praying for him; he told them just as he was about to breathe his last he beheld these three blessed personages, who addressed him in the following words of consolation: "We are now come to invite you to dwell for ever with us in our eternal tabernacles, in return for the affectionate reception you so often gave us while in your earthly habitation." The merchant then added that they immediately transported his soul to the eternal banquet in Paradise. O truly fortunate merchant! to have engaged in so advantageous a traffic, to have placed your capital in the hands of Jesus, Mary, and Joseph.

One of the most illustrious members of the reformed Carmelites, the Ven. Sister Anne of Saint-Augustin, enjoyed the happy privilege of being visited at the hour of her death by St. Joseph, who, on this occasion, was accompanied by a multitude of the blessed. Some of the religious present actually beheld this heavenly band sent by our Lord to conduct His faithful spouse in triumph to the eternal tabernacles; they particularly distinguished St. Joseph and St. Theresa. The dying nun, on perceiving that her cell was transformed into a Paradise, appeared overwhelmed with joy; and also, judging from her countenance and movements, she seemed to be occupied with the reception of the celestial guests who were coming in crowds to meet her. Not being able any longer to contain the excess of her joy, she cried out three times : " My fathers ! my fathers ! my fathers !" inviting by these, the last words she uttered, all the religious who were present to behold this great and wonderful spectacle, and to venerate St. Joseph, who came with his beloved daughter, St. Theresa, to transport her happy soul to the mansions of the blessed. In corroboration of this fact, a Carmelite of great virtue, who lived in another monastery, was in the act of praying for the recovery of the sick nun, when she was favoured with the privilege of seeing her ascending gloriously towards heaven, having St. Joseph on one side and St. Theresa on the other, and followed by legions of angels and saints (*Hist. of Reformation of Mount Carmel*).

An Augustinian monk appeared several months after his death to another religious of the same order. He informed the latter that he was suffering the most excruciating torments in purgatory, and that he had very narrowly escaped the flames of hell ; but that our Lord had been pleased to rescue him from eternal damnation for the sake of St. Joseph, His adopted father, to whom this religious was greatly devoted during life ; and that the guardian and nursery-father of the " Incarnate Word " is all-powerful at the tribunal of the Judge of the living and the dead.

We now beg permission to add to our pious author's details the account of a favour granted by St. Joseph a few years since to a person with whom we happened to be intimately acquainted.

John Grange, lay-brother in the Society of Jesus, had a truly filial love for St. Joseph. One of his constant practices was to recite daily his litanies and other prayers in his honour. Under the guidance of this great saint, he made the interior life his principal care and study; and in order that he might be less liable to have his recollection disturbed in his employment of cook, he preferred working alone, rather than allow others to assist him, as thus he would be obliged to break silence. His health, at all times delicate, was considerably impaired in the winter of 1834, and the superiors sent him to Saint Acheul, in order to enjoy a little rest. However, instead of being served by the change, he grew much weaker, and a rapid consumption was hurrying its victim to the grave. Although aware of his danger he, persevered as usual in the faithful discharge of all his religious exercises, and never did he cease to invoke, both with heart and voice, as far as he was able, him whom he had so long honoured as the patron of the agonizing. Those who assisted him during his illness remarked, that whenever they suggested to him the invocation of Jesus and Mary, he never failed when repeating these names to add that of St. Joseph. He soon received the reward of his lively and constant devotion to our saint. A few moments previous to his death, the infirmarian having remarked that he kept his eyes fixed with great complacency on a certain corner of the chamber, asked him what it was he was looking at with such attention and pleasure. "St. Joseph," he replied. "St. Joseph," exclaimed the infirmarian; "doubtless he is come to take you home." "Soon," answered the sick person. He expired shortly after, leaving his brethren persuaded of the happiness which is experienced by a devout soul at this last passage, when it only departs from the body in order to fall into the hands of so powerful and generous a friend. This happy death occurred on the 20th September, 1834.

————————

CHAPTER VIII.

St. Joseph's Protection in Various Necessities, both Spiritual and Temporal.

I SHALL conclude the second part, pious reader, by presenting you with a variety of instances wherein the benign influence of St. Joseph's patronage may be easily recognized. These will form, as it were, a kind of bouquet, the flowers of which, though carelessly arranged, will, notwithstanding, prove very agreeable, both on account of the richness and variety of their colours, as well as the delicious fragrance resulting from a combination of their odours. This spiritual bouquet will, I trust, be most acceptable to our great saint, as it will serve to impress us more forcibly with the truth of the testimony which has been given of him by one of his most devoted friends, who says, " that St. Joseph is a saint who may justly be styled ' The Help of Christians' in all their necessities, both temporal and spiritual."

Don Quiroga, a celebrated Spanish captain, was greatly devoted to St. Joseph. During the frequent wars which he was obliged to sustain against the inhabitants of the Ladrone Isles, he had continual recourse to his protection, and this protection proved an impenetrable shield against every danger to which he was then so much exposed. This he particularly experienced in one of the islands where he frequently had to encounter these barbarians, whose forces were far superior to his own; and yet the victory was always on his side without the loss of even a single man—not one of his soldiers was even wounded. Don Quiroga attributed his good fortune entirely to St. Joseph's intercession; and, indeed, it would have been impossible for him not to see with what solicitude his heavenly protector watched over the preservation of his little army. One day it was furiously attacked by a large body of natives from the interior of the islands, who discharged upon them a volley of poisoned arrows. The inevitable destruction of the Spaniards would have been the consequence, if St. Joseph, whom Don Quiroga invoked, had not come miraculously to the rescue. The saint appeared in the air, and was seen by the Christian army to shiver in pieces the deadly weapons, which fell harmless at the feet of those whom they were designed to destroy (*History of the Ladrone Isles*).

Father Anthony Natale, of the Society of Jesus, a celebrated missionary, had a great *attrait* for the interior life, and consequently a great devotion to St. Joseph. He neglected no opportunity by means of which he might promote the honour of the saint. He published, among other tracts, one in which he exhorted all Christians to venerate him specially; and he proposed issuing another on his virtues and prerogatives, but death prevented the execution of his pious project. His apostolical labours extended to one-third of Sicily, and to insure their success, he placed his missions under the protection of St. Joseph. Among other homages rendered to that saint by him, was the daily recital of a rosary of prayers which he had composed specially in his honour. The beads which he used for this purpose he esteemed highly, though of the most common description, because, as he used to say, "they are the beads of St. Joseph." Happening to miss them one day, he really felt as if he had lost a treasure; he prayed to the saint that he might find them, and his prayer was heard; for one morning, when making his act of thanksgiving after Mass, a beautiful child approached, and with an air of familiarity handed him the beads.

In the eleventh chapter of the first book we have mentioned the Ven. Sister Clare-Mary of the Passion as being one of those persons whose devotion to St. Joseph was most remarkable : we shall now speak of a few of the many favours which this worthy daughter of St. Theresa received from him. The following passage, which we quote from a letter to her director, wherein she gives an account of conscience, will enable the reader to form some idea of her confidence in the saint. She says : "My dear St. Joseph's feast was indeed a most happy day for me; I never before felt such fervour; I presented myself at his feet, with all my miseries, and begged of him to obtain for me a great love of God." Her confidence was amply rewarded by such a multiplicity of graces and favours of every kind, that she might truly say with her mother, St. Theresa, that she never asked anything of St. Joseph which she did not obtain. St. Joseph was her refuge in all the wants of the monastery, of which we give the following instance :—

A sister who had accompanied her to Rome on her foundation of the monastery called Regina Cœli, was about to return again to her own convent. Sister Clare was however afraid that the reputation of the house would suffer, and that seculars would be scandalized, seeing a religious leave the monastery. In this perplexity she made this simple appeal to the saint.: "Beloved patron, behold the evil now impending over this poor little convent of the Queen of heaven, your spouse." At that very moment she heard a voice within her, saying: "It will rise again the third day." The event proved the truth of this promise, or rather of the prediction. "It inspired me with hope and joy," continues Clare, "for I hoped that as our divine Lord's passion began by opprobrium, and ended in the glory of the resurrection, so also this house, after some days of humiliation, should also have its hour of triumph. This hope has been since realized beyond all human probability." It was also at the request of his devout servant that St. Joseph delivered Sister Anne-Theresa of the Incarnation from a most dangerous polypus in the nose, whose branches, as the physicians said, extended even to the eyes, and would most assuredly cause her death. The Ven. Clare, visiting her one day, said to her: "Take courage, my dear sister, St. Joseph will protect you;" then turning towards a picture of the saint, she thus addressed him: "Glorious saint! by that joy with which your soul was enraptured when holding the blessed Infant Jesus in your arms, and by all the love you bore His virgin mother, your august spouse, I entreat of you to grant me this favour." She then left the room, promising the invalid that she would offer up her communion for her on the morrow. After receiving the holy communion on the following day, she returned to the sufferer, and found her with a violent headache, her nose much swollen, and having all the appearance of gangrene. St. Joseph's fervent client was not the least disheartened or troubled; but, on the contrary, with an unusual air of confidence and gaiety, she said to Sister Anne: "Have confidence, my dear sister, you shall be cured; St. Joseph will obtain this favour for you; and I promised him that I would get three Masses said, and would clothe a poor person in his honour." She then desired her to use her pocket-handkerchief; the invalid had a great horror of doing so, on account of the great pain it caused her. "Obey, my dear sister," said Clare; "obey, and you will soon see the benefit of it." She obeyed, but was seized with such violent, such excruciating pain, that she thought her head was splitting asunder. Shortly after she sneezed, and the brain was at the same time relieved from the first seeds of that painful malady. The root of the polypus once extracted, the patient was soon quite well, to the great astonishment of the physicians and surgeons, who on that very day called to visit her, in order to assure themselves personally of the truth of such a prodigy.

We have elsewhere spoken of Sister Jane of the Angels, an Ursuline religious at Lyons, who received the most signal favours through St. Joseph, and, among others, that of which we are about to speak. By the permission of God, she had been for a long time cruelly tormented by an evil spirit. Hoping to be delivered from her unhappy state, she made a vow .to recite daily, for the space of a year, the

Office of St. Joseph, to practise some weekly corporal
austerities, and also to make a novena of communions.   On the ninth day, whilst the priest was
exorcising her, the malignant spirit was himself
heard to say, that St. Joseph had commanded him
to quit this body; and, as a token of his having done
so, that the name of Joseph would be found engraven
on the hand of his holy servant, which actually happened as he said; and from that moment she never
was molested by him.

St. Catherine of Bologna, so called from the city
where her body has been preserved, entire and un-
decayed, for many ages, lived for some time in a
monastery at Ferrara, where she performed the office
of portress.   It happened that an old man, in the
garb of a pilgrim, often came to ask alms of her.
Catherine always served him cheerfully, and received
his visits with pleasure, because he used to converse
with her about his pilgrimages to Jerusalem, and of
the happiness he experienced on beholding the various
localities of that holy city, which had been sanctified
and honoured by the mortal presence of our Divine
Lord.   One day, after receiving his alms as usual,
the pilgrim presented Catherine with a vase made of
some unknown composition, saying that this vase
was used as a drinking-cup by our Divine Lord when
a child, and had belonged to His blessed mother.
Catherine received the sacred relic with joy and
reverence, and returned thanks to the generous
stranger, who, on taking his leave of her, begged she
would keep the vase until he should return to claim
it.   The blessed portress felt perfectly convinced
that it was a present from the glorious spouse of
Mary, and preserved it carefully as a most precious

treasure. Being elected superioress of a monastery
at Bologna, she confided the vase to the care of the
superioress of the convent she was about to leave,
with a charge to return it to the old man, should he
ever come to claim it; but that in case he did not
come, she intended to bestow it on the monastery of
Ferrara, on condition that it should be annually
exposed on the feast of St. Joseph for public veneration. This was done accordingly, and the holy
relic verified its authenticity by the multiplicity of
miraculous cures which it wrought.

It is a remark of St. Augustin, that the beneficent
influence of the power and glory of the patriarch
Joseph was limited merely to the kingdom of Egypt,
whereas the patronage of the second Joseph is
enjoyed by the whole world. What amazing progress has not the Catholic faith made since the missions of various parts of the East and West Indies,
and of the vast empire of China, have been placed
under St. Joseph's special protection! In a thousand
different occasions the missionaries and the people of
these barbarous countries have experienced his
paternal assistance, and have found this glorious
saint to be one of the firmest supports of the cause
of Jesus Christ.

The following will serve to remove a very erroneous
idea, which has sometimes been entertained by St.
Joseph's clients. If they do not happen always to
obtain what they ask through the intercession of this
great and good saint, why should they be discouraged? Let faith come to their assistance, and assure
them that the saint hears their prayers on those
occasions, in a manner more conducive to their real
advantage, although perhaps in a way less conform-

able to their narrow views; and that the objects of their
ambition may, if obtained, prove so many real evils.
Deplorable, indeed, would be the case of a sick person
whose wishes were always gratified by the physician.

A nobleman, who loved and venerated St. Joseph,
was in the habit of celebrating his feast-day annually
as devoutly as he could. He had three children;
one of them died on St. Joseph's feast, and, strange
to say, a second died the following year on the same
day! This double affliction was so keenly felt by
this fond father, that he resolved not to celebrate
the saint's festival the following year, fearing that
he might also lose his third and last child. Accordingly, being unwilling to encounter that memorable
day at home again, and also in order to dissipate his
grief and anxiety, he determined to travel. As he
was walking one day in a pensive mood, he happened
to raise his eyes, and saw two young men hanging
from a tree; at the same moment an angel appeared
to him, and spoke as follows: "See you those two
young men? Know, then, that if your sons had
lived, they would have met with a similar fate; but
owing to your devotion to St. Joseph, that saint has
obtained from God the favour of an early death for
them, that your house may not be dishonoured, but
more especially to secure for them, by a premature
death, the blessing of a happy eternity. Go, celebrate St. Joseph's feast, and fear not for the child
that remains to you; he will be a holy bishop, and
enjoy a long life." All this happened exactly as the
angel had predicted.

Although the following fact relates rather to Mary
than to Joseph, I will mention it here, as being calculated to increase the devotion of St. Joseph's

clients, when they learn what delight it affords the
mother of Jesus to see her holy spouse worthily
honoured. In 1648, there was a Moorish slave
living at Naples, who was obstinately attached to his
false religion, and could not endure to hear the
dogmas of Christianity spoken of. What contributed to render his conversion much more difficult, were
the counsels and example of another slave, by whom
he was even surpassed in the pertinacity with which
he adhered to error, and who strove without ceasing
to fortify his companion's prejudices against the
Catholic religion. The unfortunate Moor, completely under the influence of his monitor, resisted
every effort that was made to enlighten him on the
impiety and absurdity of Mahometanism. Deluded
as he was, he however continued faithful to a practice he had adopted during the last two years, of
placing a lamp every evening before an image of our
Lady, which was painted on the wall of his master's
garden; and to meet the expenses of this, he laid
aside a part of his wages. His master, a Neapolitan
nobleman, having taken notice of his pious practice,
inquired the motive of it. "My motive," said he,
"is to place myself under the protection of the Virgin Mary; and I am sure she is a most amiable and
beautiful lady, though the darkness conceals her
features from me." The pious nobleman, thinking
this a favourable opportunity for trying to effect his
conversion, immediately sent off to the Jesuits' College for one of the fathers, who was specially devoted
to the service of the poor slaves. The father having
accordingly repaired to the palace, sent for the Moor
and his companion; but all his exhortations only
elicited mockery and insult, and produced no other

fruit than that of affording the father an occasion of
practising patience. Whenever he returned to fulfil
the same kind office, his labours were requited in the
same way. He then saw that prayer was the only
chance of success within his reach; he therefore
redoubled his fervour in that holy exercise, and
solicited the prayers of others, that God would
vouchsafe to enlighten and soften the hearts of those
two unfortunate creatures. The prayers proved efficacious. It happened that on the night of the
Assumption, the Moor was sleeping soundly in a
coach-house, when he was awakened by a voice,
which called him by name, saying, "Abel, Abel,
arouse thee, and listen." He awoke, and on opening
his eyes beheld the coach-house brilliantly illumi-
nated, and in the midst of the light a majestic lady
robed in white, and accompanied by a venerable old
man, who held a silver vase filled with water. Abel,
quite overcome with mingled feelings of awe and
terror at the sight of so extraordinary a spectacle,
exclaimed: "Who are you, and how did you make
your way hither, the doors being all locked?" The
lady replied: "I am Mary, whose image you venerate in the garden, and the personage near me is
my dear spouse, St. Joseph. I have come down
from heaven for the special purpose of engaging you
to become a Christian, and also to request you will
take the name of Joseph in baptism." "Madam,"
answered the Moor, "command me aught else, and
I will obey you, but to become a Christian is more
than I can undertake for you." The Blessed Virgin,
instead of being discouraged or annoyed by so un-
gracious a reply, approached the slave in the most
kind and affectionate manner, and placing her hand

upon his shoulder, said to him with great tenderness : "Come, come, Abel, you will not surely refuse to gratify me : do become a Christian." Hard as was the heart of Abel, it was incapable of resisting such an appeal; it was indeed quite changed, and melted away, as it were, like ice beneath the influence of a burning sun. "Madam," he cried, "your sacred hand has moved and inflamed my heart; I will obey you, I will become a Christian, I will take the name of Joseph. But how will a poor ignorant man like me be able to say all the prayers of the Christians ?" "I myself will teach you," replied the Mother of Mercy; and taking the Moor's right hand, as a mother would her child's, she taught him how to make the sign of the cross, and made him promise never to forget it. She then bade him go and learn the other prayers of the good father who had so often exhorted him to become a Christian. The Moor finding his confidence increase in one who had given him so many proofs of the tenderest regard, asked our holy Lady what was necessary to be done in order to become a Christian. Upon which the Mother of God took the vase from St. Joseph, and pouring the water on his head, said to him : "This is what the priest will do in order to confer the sacrament of baptism upon you, and at the same moment your soul will become as white and as pure as the robe I wear." After thus speaking, the Blessed Virgin seemed as if about to depart; the Moor, full of simple confidence, endeavoured to detain her, but in vain. "Madam," he said, "promise me at least that when I am in affliction, you will return in order to impart consolation to me." She promised to do so, and disappeared.

When Abel found himself once more alone, he immediately hastened to inform his master of all that had happened. In the morning, the father who had charge of the slaves was informed of it. On his arrival the Moor earnestly asked for baptism. His companion in slavery, who had so long retained him in infidelity, was also converted on hearing of the miraculous vision; and after some days' instruction, both were sufficiently prepared for baptism, together with ten other slaves, whom their example had induced to enter seriously into themselves, and who, on conviction, abjured all their errors.

The ceremony was performed with great magnificence and devotion. Abel, who was the principal object of interest, received the name of Joseph, conformably to the orders of the Blessed Virgin; and he proved not unworthy such august patronage. The Mother of Mercy soon after showered down new favours on him whom she might so truly consider her adopted son. On one occasion, the latter being oppressed with a most grievous sadness, had recourse to her protection. "Holy Virgin," he cried, "now is the moment to fulfil your promise." That moment she actually did appear to him, and said: "Joseph, have patience." These three little words, falling like a sweet and healing balm into his heart, gave him, as he said himself, a foretaste of the bliss of Paradise.

[N.B.—We are not indebted to the author of this work for the following facts: they are taken from other writers, who have been eye-witnesses of certain miraculous graces due to St. Joseph's intercession.]

Sister Mary Theresa Nicholi was a professed

religious in the monastery of Sainte-Marie-de-la-Prière, at Malamoco, in the diocese of Chiozza, in Italy. This religious suffered from a complication of various maladies, which, for the space of ten years, seemed incurable. She was first attacked by a violent fit of apoplexy, from which certain remedies restored her. This was soon followed by epilepsy, accompanied by a dreadful shock of nerves, so that her limbs became quite crippled, and she continued motionless, and apparently lifeless, for several hours together. To this succeeded an universal paralysis; then acute pains in different parts of her body, palpitations of the heart, malignant fevers, which twice brought her to her agony, and finally a contusion of the muscles, which shortened her right leg by half a foot. To this complication of disorders, which, considering their intensity and duration, would alone be sufficient to exhaust an ordinary stock of patience, we may add the incalculable number of violent and bitter remedies with which the physicians wearied the poor invalid during a protracted illness of so many years. At length Almighty God judged that the time was come to put a term to the trials of His faithful servant, and to raise her up from her bed of suffering. It pleased Him that she should be informed of a famous miraculous cure, which had been lately wrought at Venice through the intercession of St. Joseph. This news inspired her with the hope that she might obtain, through the mediation of that glorious saint, what all the art of physic could not effect. She therefore resolved to perform the pious exercise of the seven Wednesdays in his honour, and she was joined in prayer by a great number of her companions.

On the first Wednesday, which fell on the 26th of May, 1710, after holy Communion, she got one of those frightful attacks which we have described, and for a quarter of an hour was apparently lifeless. On returning to herself, her sisters encouraged her to call on the saint with a lively faith. She did so; and having asked for three threads of the mantle worn by his statue at Venice, she swallowed them, and at the same moment felt some invisible hand, which at the same time restored her right leg to its proper and natural length. Finding then that she had acquired at unusual degree of strength, she arose from the chair on which she had been reclining, and walked about the room without the least difficulty, thanking and blessing God and St. Joseph. All her infirmities had vanished. But as her leg still continued a little painful, she was advised to use a walking-cane, and to feel great confidence that through the intercession of the holy patriarch it would, ere long, be perfectly cured. In these dispositions, she made a vow to continue every year of her life the devotion of the seven Wednesdays. Her vow was favourably received, for she obtained the favour she solicited. The following year, 1711, the last of the seven Wednesdays fell upon the 17th of June: on that day, while making her act of thanksgiving after holy Communion, she was seized with an attack such as she had the preceding year, only with this difference, that on the present occasion she did not lose her senses, and was able to invoke the assistance of St. Joseph, and also to call for a bit of the thread of which the famous mantle was composed, which she swallowed with a lively faith. Now, as on the former occasion, she found her leg so fortified, that she rose up without requiring assistance, and from that moment walked with as much facility as if she had never experienced the loss of the use of her limbs. She resumed all her former duties and avocations, renovated in mind and body, and consecrated the remainder of her life to the greater glory of God, to the honour of St. Joseph, and the great consolation of his devout clients.

The fact which is now about to engage our attention, is of a more recent date than the foregoing. It occurred in the year 1834, in one of those seminaries which were attached to St. Acheul, well known by the appellation of St. Joseph du Blamont. A chapel had been just erected there, to be dedicated to the holy patron of the house. The ceremony was about to take place on the third Sunday after Easter, the day on which the Church celebrates the feast of the Patronage of St. Joseph, and a novena was offered up preparatory to it, in which all the students joined with the most edifying fervour. On the first day of the novena, the superior of the house happened to meet with a gardener who lived in the neighbourhood, and perceiving that the man appeared very sad, he inquired the cause. He replied, that he had two children a long time ill, and that the doctors said they never would recover unless he changed his present situation; and that even though he were to make such a sacrifice, they could not answer for the lives of his children, so rapid was the progress of the disease. "But," continued the gardener, "where can I go? Here we have bread to eat, and if we go elsewhere, how can I afford to support so many? There are my wife, my mother, and six children; all my earthly hopes are dependant upon the labour of my

hands." The superior spoke words of consolation to
him, advising him to have recourse to the Sovereign
Physician, through the intercession of St. Joseph.
It may be observed, that several members of the
poor man's family were called after St. Joseph. He
returned home, determined to offer up a novena, in
union with his wife and children, and begged that
the superior would recommend him specially to his
great patron. Accordingly, laying aside all the
remedies, he began to pray with his family, and on
that very day the fever and inflammation began to
abate ; a few days after, all the bad humours, together with the fever itself, had entirely disappeared.
On the ninth day, being the feast of the Patronage
of St. Joseph, the good man went to Blamont, taking with him his two children in perfect health; and
asked permission for them to assist at all the offices of
the day, in which he himself joined most heartily in
thanksgiving to his dear benefactor. " I hope,"
said the superior, when offering his congratulations,
" that you will give to each the name of Joseph in
confirmation." " They already bear that name,"
replied the gardener, " and their mother also." At
his request, the superior wrote a detailed account of
the two cures; the gardener got it framed, in order
to preserve it always in his family, and thus, as he
said himself, transmit to his children's children that
token of his gratitude to St. Joseph. To these
favours, however, we must add another and a very
important one, granted to one of the children at the
same time. He was remarkable for an extremely
odd and unmanageable disposition ; and, dating from
the novena, there never was a more gentle or trac-
table creature, or one more devoted to duty; and

this moral cure, as experience afterwards proved, was not less complete or permanent than the physical.

The college "du Passage," near Saint-Sebastian, in Spain, made choice of St. Joseph as its patron; and, as a consequence of its great devotion to him, was favoured with many blessings through his hands. Indeed, it would be impossible to render him greater homage and respect than that which he received from this house in 1831. The month of March is particularly consecrated to him, and is hence called the "Month of Joseph," as May is styled the "Month of Mary." During the entire "Month of Joseph," six wax lights, which were kept in order by the pupils, burned without intermission, from morning until night, before the statue of the holy patriarch—emblematic of a pure and fervent spirit, loving God, and His saints, the noblest of His works, in Him. Every day during the Holy Sacrifice, the altar was covered with letters and billets, containing the spiritual necessities and wishes of each client. A fervour so lively, so general, could not fail to produce great fruit, and in effect was rewarded by the most abundant graces and favours. Some of the students who stood in need of conversion, returned fervently to God before the end of the month; almost all the others acquired renewed energy in the pursuit of their studies, and made the most remarkable progress in all the virtues of their age and state of life, and, with few exceptions, continued to give entire satisfaction to their masters. In the month of April, a public proclamation was made, as was usual in that college, of the marks which each pupil merited for the three following points: "Application, Progress, Conduct." The result on this occasion was a brilliant testimony of what devotion to St. Joseph and his protection are capable of effecting in the formation of even childhood itself, to the practice of those sacrifices which virtue demands. Among the fifty pupils of which the last, or youngest, division was composed, only one bad mark was found; and even fifteen of the very youngest children merited to receive each the best mark in every department.

Dating from the same period, that is, from the "Month of Joseph," several of them adopted the habit of making the examen of conscience regularly every evening, and of comparing one day with another; they also began to prepare the subject of their meditation on the preceding evening, and to rise earlier than the prescribed hour in order to have time to make it. Many of them also were so full of fervour, as to adopt the practice of private austerities, of which their tender age seemed quite incapable. When St. Joseph's feast was over, each, in the impulse of his gratitude, spoke freely of the particular favours for which he was indebted to the intercession of the saint. One found that his memory had become wonderfully retentive, though naturally quite the reverse; another could perform his class duties with more facility and success; a third found not the least difficulty or repugnance in the observance of the rule, which until then had appeared to him so painful and fatiguing. There was no one, in short, who had not some substantial proof that his prayers were heard.

CHAPTER IX.

Pilgrimages in Honour of St. Joseph.

FROM the earliest ages of the Church, numerous sanctuaries have been dedicated to the Blessed Virgin; many of these sanctuaries, favoured by heaven, have become celebrated pilgrimages. It was the same, though in a lesser degree, with the tombs in which repose the ashes of saints, especially of martyrs, so great graces were granted through their intercession, which kept up the confidence of the faithful.

St. Joseph, considering his virtues, and the high dignity to which he was exalted, had doubtless the greatest claims to the homage of the people; but, as some theologians say, his body having left the tomb, in perfect life, at the moment of our Lord's resurrection, no trace remained of him here below to be a remembrance of him, or an object of veneration. Divine Providence, no doubt, had its own designs in permiting this momentary forgetfulness.

The glory of St. Joseph, of late years especially, is always increasing, far from suffering, from the brilliancy of that of the Sacred Heart and Immaculate Conception. The devotion to him appears to derive fresh lustre from it. To judge even by the rapid progress which the devotion to this great saint is making, and by the favours granted to those who invoke him, it seems to be the will of heaven that we should unite in our love and veneration the three august personages who were united by it on earth, to be the most perfect instruments of its glory and our sanctification.

ST. JOSEPH-OF-THE-FIELDS.

Such is the name of the first pilgrimage which, to our knowledge at least, has been established in honour of St. Joseph. It owes its existence to a religious of the Society of Jesus, Father Debrosse, a zealous servant of St. Joseph. One day that this fervent religious was thinking by what means he could infuse into the hearts of the faithful the tender devotion with which he was penetrated to St. Joseph, the thought occurred to him of forming a pilgrimage; and his project was so well received, that it was soon put into execution. On the 19th of March, 1840, the beautiful chapel was blessed which stands at a league and a half from Laval. Above the altar, which, as well as the chapel, is Gothic, is a statue of St. Joseph, bearing the Infant God in his arms. Two reliquaries have been deposited in this holy place by the Marquis and Marquise d'Ambray, on their return from Rome. They contain relics of the mantle of St. Joseph and of the veil of the Blessed Virgin.

A still greater favour entitles this sanctuary to the veneration of the faithful. His Holiness Gregory XVI., by briefs, in 1840 and 1842, granted both plenary and partial indulgences to the pilgrims who visit it. Therefore, on Wednesdays especially, the chapel can often not contain the numbers who visit it, and pious persons have founded Masses for all the Wednesdays in the year.

The heart of St. Joseph is touched by this devotion,

and he has obtained signal graces, of which we will mention a few.

A confidential person, employed in the community of Mercy, at Laval, was attacked by a serious illness, which was not understood. After three months of useless remedies, the physician abandoned all hopes of a cure. The invalid, having nothing more to expect on earth, had recourse to heaven, had herself taken to the chapel of St. Joseph-of-the-Fields, to ask there either her cure or, at all events, the grace of a happy death. She heard Mass and received the holy Communion there, and found herself cured. The next day her strength had so completely returned, that she resumed her ordinary occupations.

The superioress of the hospital of Laval was at the extremity of a dangerous illness ; with one exception, the physicians in consultation declared she could not recover. The community, greatly alarmed, began a novena to St. Joseph, and made a vow to receive a postulant gratuitously if the invalid recovered. From that moment the superioress became better, and in a few days her cure was complete. In thanksgiving, about forty persons, almost all from the house, went to St. Joseph-of-the-Fields. The chaplain said Mass, and spoke on the immense credit St. Joseph enjoys in heaven, and the use he makes of it in favour of his devoted servants. The postulant who was received in accordance with the vow, has now finished her noviciate, and happily promised the religious vows.

A workwoman of Laval was attacked with a nervous affection, which brought on violent convulsions ; for more than a year these had occurred seven or eight times in the day. After a novena to St. Joseph, she was entirely cured, and for the two years

since she obtained so signal a favour, she loses no
opportunity of testifying her gratitude to her powerful
protector.

The Rev. Father the Abbot of La Trappe, had
asked several important favours of St. Joseph, both
of himself and his monastery, and had promised, if he
were heard, to contribute, as far as his poverty would
permit him, to the decoration of his chapel. All the
graces were granted, and the reverend father, in fulfilment of his vows, gilded, with his own hands, the
altar of St. Joseph-of-the-Fields.

We might add many other facts, but we will confine ourselves to these. The numerous *ex-votos* which
the gratitude of the faithful have placed in his chapel,
prove how many graces have been obtained by our
illustrious saint for his faithful servants.

PILGRIMAGE OF ST. JOSEPH-OF-THE-OAK.

A religious of the Society of Jesus came to Vire, in
the beginning of the Lent of 1854, to preach a mission
there; but owing to unexpected occurrences, the
three fathers who were to have assisted him in this
important work, were prevented from attending.
Vire contains about 10,000 inhabitants, and there
was every prospect of the mission being productive
of great fruit: but how was this possible? A single
evangelical labourer could not suffice to such a harvest.
The father wrote to his superiors, and implored help;
all his efforts were in vain, none could be given.
The feast of St. Joseph arrived. On the eve, preparing his meditation, the Father met with those
words of St. Theresa—"I never remember to have
solicited St. Joseph without having obtained what I

asked; and for many years I have asked some particular grace on his feast, and have never failed to be heard." The next day he had no sooner finished his meditation than he wrote three letters, and giving them to the priest of the parish, said: "Our mission will be given; here are three letters which I place under the protection of St. Joseph; I have asked him for missioners, and he will come to our assistance. St. Theresa says she never failed to obtained of this great saint what she asked on his feast."

The clergy and people of Vire had greatly desired a mission; but they had now given up all hopes of it; they only laughed, and said: "You have moved heaven and earth already in vain: do you still hope? All the saints in heaven have failed: do you think St. Joseph has missioners ready to set out at his pleasure?" The obstacles were certainly great, but Divine Providence would glorify St. Joseph, and show the power of his intercession. Some days passed on, when, at the moment he was least expected, a Father arrived: he had come all the way from Belgium. Two others come the next day, sent from the Jesuit's house at Angers. Each letter had brought a missioner; and what is still more remarkable, one of them was obliged to leave a work of importance to go to Vire, and only determined to do so after having prayed to St. Joseph to direct him as to what was best to do. This favour, obtained so unexpectedly, being known to the whole town, prepared the way for the most happy results which followed the labours of the evangelical workmen.

The four religious themselves had felt too strongly the effects of the protection of St. Joseph, ever to forget it; from that time they laboured to promote the devotion to him. He who had first arrived at Vire, to show his gratitude, caused a picture of St. Joseph to be engraved, with motives for honouring him; and this homage, dictated by his heart, was accepted by the holy patriarch, and recompensed by another favour. A new pilgrimage was to be established, so this Father was chosen to found it.

The Abbé Pettier, priest of the parish of Ville-dieu, in the diocese of Angers, had been very intimate with 'the missioner, both having been brought up at the college of Combrée. They had, however, been separated for many years; but the Father, now at Poitiers, in publishing his little work on St. Joseph, sent a copy of it to his old friend. Pleased with his attention, the Abbé pressed him to pay his parish a visit. The Father consented, but it was only as a missioner that he would come. Ville-dieu is a small town of La Vendée. We cannot here enter into any details upon its inhabitants. We can only say, that notwithstanding the wars and horrors of the revolution, the traditions of faith are as alive as ever : the Vendean of to-day, like the Vendean of former years, is strongly attached to his duty and his religion. Shall we be surprised, then, that Providence should have selected this country, and these good people, to second its designs for the glory of St. Joseph?

On his arrival at Ville-dieu, the Father commenced the exercises of the forty hours' prayer ; then, by a retreat, he prepared the children for their first communion. Before his departure, M. Pettier took him to see an immense oak-tree, renowned through all the country for its wonderful size. Whilst admiring its amazing circumference, no less than eighteen mètres, observing the hollow which time has formed in its trunk, the idea occurred to him of consecrating it to St. Joseph. "Your parish," he said to the good priest, " is composed of working people ; let us place their holy patron here, they will come to honour him ; and strangers who visit the oak will find, with an object of curiosity, food for devotion." All Ville-dieu was delighted with the project, which the good priest readily seconded. On Pentecost Sunday, 11th May, 1856, the two families of Massé and Pohn yielded their right to the tree, and on thè 24th of August following, St. Joseph took possession of his sanctuary.

Such is the origin of the pilgrimage of St. Joseph-of-the-Oak. From all parts of the country, the clergy and inhabitants came to salute St. Joseph on its erection, and to do him honour.

A granite altar is placed in the inside of the oak, and on a pedestal which surmounts it is placed the statue of St. Joseph. It is of stone, and the size of life. The Infant God, sweetly sleeping, rests on the heart of St. Joseph ; and the holy patriarch, with an indescribable expression of respect and affection, con-templates the august Child confided to him. Doubt-less a great master might have produced a more per-fect work of art ; but it would have been difficult to have said to the people with greater simplicity : " Go to Joseph ; for see how good he is, and how the Infant God depended on him."

– Three years have hardly elapsed since our country possessed this sanctuary, and already it has become a celebrated pilgrimage. Mgr. Angebault, the Bishop of Angers, granted forty days' indulgence to those who should visit and pray there ; and his Holiness Pius IX. was pleased to open the treasures of the

Church in its favour; and on the 21st of June, 1857, addressed from Rome a most favourable brief to the parish priest of Ville-dieu. From this time the concourse of pilgrims has greatly increased, not only from the country round, but from considerable distances.

St. Joseph is not unmindful of these testimonies of devotion; his favours are proportioned to the faith of his servant. We will mention one or two here.

A very pious lady had long been soliciting the conversion of her husband, an excellent man in many respects, but who unhappily had for more than forty years neglected his religion. The day of grace at length arrived · the missioner who had erected the sanctuary of St. Joseph-of-the-Oak, came to the town where this family lived; the pious lady, with re-animated confidence, began a novena, with her children and others, to obtain the so much desired conversion. The novena finished, between hope and fear, she told her husband what she had done and what she wished. He who had so many times refused, now made not the slightest difficulty; he chose his confessor, and appointed the hour for his confession. This was at noon; and it was through the midst of all the children of the town, collected for catechism, that the missionary, for whom he had asked, met him at the confessional. Observing that a more favourable time and place might have been taken: "Father," he answered, "this is done on purpose; I wish that in another hour the whole town should know of the steps I have taken: I act freely and without being ashamed of it." Some days afterwards the happy lady and her children accompanied the newly-reconciled to the holy Table. Convinced that it was to St. Joseph she owed this immense grace, the lady sent to the sanctuary of Ville-dieu a golden heart, on which was engraven these words : " Testimony of gratitude to St. Joseph-of-the-Oak, for a conversion obtained by his intercession."

A child of eight years old accompanied a servant whom his master had sent to cut down an oak. Whilst the man was in the tree, the child took up the hatchet, and with one blow cut his thumb through, so as only to leave a strip of the skin, and the forefinger was almost as much injured. Carried home covered with blood, his poor mother cried out : " Great St. Joseph-of-the-Oak ! if you do not take pity on my boy, he is maimed for life." The surgeon was called ; he expressed great fears that at all events the child could never use them again. However, he dressed the wounds ; but what was not his surprise, on returning in a few days, to find them in a fair way of being cured. Now they are perfectly sound, and the child uses them as if they had never been injured : only they are marked by large scars, as undoubted witnesses of the seriousness of the wounds and of the protection of St. Joseph. The missioner, of whom God had made use to found this pilgrimage, being there on the anniversary of the erection, in 1858, a woman accosted him after the procession, saying : " Rev. Father, I have been long looking for you ; I want to show you what St. Joseph has done for my son :" and at the same time she put into his the hand of the little boy.

A priest came to pray at the sanctuary of Ville-dieu ; he had travelled fifty leagues. He returned a few months later, and asked to be allowed to place a lamp before the altar of St. Joseph, and to keep it up during his lifetime : his prayers had been heard.

A young person in vain entreated the consent of her family to enter a community : she always met with the most decided opposition. In her grief she confided her cause to St. Joseph-of-the-Oak; she promised to send a heart of gold to his altar, if her parents would yield on another attempt. She spoke, and received this answer : " My child, we leave you free ; you shall enter when you please." Two other similar facts occurred in the same town within three months, in which it was impossible not to see the intervention of heaven.

These details will seem very incomplete to those who know the generous benevolence of St. Joseph towards the pilgrims to this sanctuary. But we do not undertake to write a history of this sanctuary ; we only wish to make it known to our readers.

To these two sanctuaries, to which the people of Maine and Anjou flock, another will soon be added— St. Joseph of Segré. This sanctuary, in testimony of the lively faith of the people, will surpass the two first, to judge, at least, by the generous efforts, the noble devotedness of which it is the object. May it also be to the good inhabitants of Segré a source of grace and blessings !

[NOTE OF THE AUTHOR.—We should like to add here an account of several marvels which have been sent to us for insertion by the persons concerned ; but as they have not yet been examined, we deem it more prudent not to do so. We beg, therefore, those who write, not to neglect to send the proofs they may have of the wonders they relate.]

END OF THE SECOND BOOK.

THIRD BOOK.

DEVOUT PRACTICES

IN HONOUR OF

SAINT JOSEPH.

CHAPTER I.

Practices for each Day.

THE holy patriarch Jacob, wishing to give his favourite son, Joseph, then a boy, a mark of his tenderness and predilection, ordered a tunic of various beautiful colours to be made for him (*Gen.* chap. xxxii.). I am of opinion that this variegated garment was a figure of the various privileges, virtues, and marks of respectful homage by which St. Joseph is so eminently distinguished among all the other saints. Bearing a striking resemblance to the Queen of heaven, by the lustre of his virtues and prerogatives, does it not follow, that the devotion which is testified to him, should resemble in some degree that which is rendered to Mary? and the homages which he receives, should they not "abound in variety"? (*Psal.* xliv.) It is my intention now, pious reader, to present this mysterious tunic to your view, by suggesting various practices of devotion, which will enable you to testify your love and respect for this glorious saint.

I.—IMAGE OF ST. JOSEPH.

Venerate his image; and with this view, let it occupy a distinguished place in your oratory; for in every family, the portraits of the most illustrious benefactors, patrons, or relatives, constitute the most valuable part of the furniture. Imitate in this respect the devout St. Francis de Sales, who would have no other picture in his Breviary but St. Joseph's; also F. Louis Lallemant, who would have St. Joseph's likeness always about his person, and even in the grave.

II.—PRAYER AT MASS.

If you are a priest, you can, by virtue of a general authorisation, given by the Congregation of Rites, when you recite the prayer *Et cunctis,* insert the name of Joseph, placing it before that of the Apostles Peter and Paul.

III.—PATRONAGE OF ST. JOSEPH.

If Providence has placed you at the head of a family, or of a religious community, entrust it to the care of a saint to whom the Eternal Father confided all that was most dear to Him, namely, Jesus and Mary. In this you will follow St. Theresa's example, who placed each new monastery that she founded under the tutelage of her dear master and patron, St. Joseph. When the King of Egypt was about to raise Joseph of old to the dignified position which he afterwards held, he said to him: "You shall be the head of my house." Apply the same language in your own case to the "ruler of the family of Jesus."

IV.—REMEMBRANCE OF ST. JOSEPH.

Frequently think of St. Joseph in the course of the day, especially when the striking of the clock warns you to venerate the great mystery of the "Incarnation," which took place in the chaste womb of the Blessed Virgin Mary, his spouse. Also, when you hear the bell tolling to announce the agony of a dying person, as is usual in many places, think then of him who is the special patron of the agonizing, and repeat the following, or a similar aspiration: "O holy Joseph! worthy spouse of the Mother of Life, remember me when I am in my last agony!"

V.—INVOCATION OF ST. JOSEPH.

St. Mary Magdalen de Pazzi, beholding the glory of St. Joseph in one of her ecstasies, exclaims: "Oh! how great a share had not the glorious St. Joseph in the chalice of Jesus' passion, by the services which he rendered to His ' Sacred Humanity'! In Paradise, St. Joseph's purity increases the lustre of Mary's: he always favours with especial protection those souls who are enrolled beneath the standard of Mary! How resplendent does the sanctity of Joseph appear, when united to that of Jesus and Mary!" Thus it is that the saint speaks. You see, then, that to make your devotion to St. Joseph complete, it ought to comprise devotion to all three, viz., to Jesus, Mary, and Joseph, who have been so closely allied to one another by family ties, affection, and holiness. Be you also united to them, by cherishing, with all the fervour of your soul, a true devotion to the adorable infancy of our Divine Lord, to which Mary and Joseph vowed all their love and energies. Frequently invoke these three sweet names, in imitation of the blessed Gaspar Bon, who lived and died with these sacred names in his heart and on his lips.

VI.—IMITATION OF ST. JOSEPH.

Since the most solid devotion to our holy patrons consists in striving to imitate their example, you should endeavour to practise each day some particular virtue for which St. Joseph was remarkable; for instance, vigilance over your inferiors, if you be the father of a family, or a superior. A particular practice of the Ven. Louis Lallemant, of whom we have already spoken, was this : he made choice of St. Joseph for his master and model in the interior life. With this view he daily practised the four following exercises, two in the morning and two in the evening. The first was, to enter in spirit into the heart of St. Joseph, and to reflect how docile it had been to the inspirations of the Holy Ghost; then, looking down into his own heart, he humbled himself for his negligence or resistance, and animated himself to follow the impressions of grace more faithfully in future. The second exercise was, to consider with what perfection St. Joseph united the interior life to the laborious avocations of his state of life ; then, reflecting upon his own occupations, he examined whether he had any faults to correct as to his usual manner of performing them. By this self-discipline, Père Lallemant arrived at a very high degree of union with God—a union which he knew the secret of preserving uninterrupted, even amidst the most distracting duties. The third exercise consisted in uniting himself to St. Joseph, whom he considered in his character of "spouse of the Mother of God," and as such, favoured beyond all other creatures with the most extraordinary lights regarding the ineffable virginity and maternity of Mary; he endeavoured then to excite in his soul an increase of love towards this great saint, for the sake of Mary, his blessed spouse. The fourth exercise was, the consideration of the profound adoration, the loving and paternal services which St. Joseph rendered to the blessed Child Jesus; and he asked his permission to unite with him in adoring, loving, and rendering service to that amiable and Divine Child. This he earnestly desired to do, with sentiments of the tenderest affection and veneration the most profound. We now invite those happy souls, whose sole aim is to please God, and to advance perseveringly in perfection, to adopt henceforth the practice of these holy exercises, than which we deem nothing more conducive to the perfect accomplishment of their pious desires. Should it happen, however, that they appear too sublime for some timid souls, we here give them an exercise more in accordance with their weakness.

VII.—HONOUR THE SEVEN PRIVILEGES OF ST. JOSEPH.

Assign each day of the week to honour one of the glorious privileges of St. Joseph. On the first day, honour him as the spouse of Mary; on the second, as the adopted father of Jesus; on the third, as a most pure virgin; on the fourth, as vicar and lieutenant of the Eternal Father; on the fifth, as the chief and protector of the Holy Family; on the sixth, as the happiest of men in his life and death; and on

the seventh, honour him as being the most exalted of
all the saints in heaven.

VIII.—TO CULTIVATE A SPECIAL DEVOTION TO THE SEVEN DOLOURS AND SEVEN JOYS OF ST. JOSEPH.

He himself taught this practice to the three Franciscan friars, of whom we have spoken in the fifth
chapter. This devotion, then, cannot fail of being
pleasing to him.

The Church, besides, by numerous indulgences,
has testified her approbation of this devotion. His
Holiness Pius VII., in a rescript of the 9th Decem-
ber, 1819, has granted the following indulgences in
perpetuity to any of the faithful, who, with a con-
trite heart, should recite the following devotion in
honour of the Seven Dolours and Seven Joys of St.
Joseph :—

1. One hundred days, once a day.
2. Three hundred days, every Wednesday, and on
the nine days preceding his principal feast, and that
of his Patronage.
3. Plenary indulgence on each of these feasts, confession, communion, and prayers for the intentions of
his Holiness being understood. For reciting these
prayers the whole month, plenary indulgence any day
of the month at choice, with the usual conditions.

Gregory XVI., by a rescript of January 22nd,
1836, granted to the faithful who should recite these
prayers for seven consecutive Sundays, the following
privileges :—Three hundred days indulgence every
Sunday, plenary indulgence on the seventh, on the
three usual conditions.

Pius IX., by two decrees of the Congregation of

Rites, one on the 1st of February, the other on the 22nd of March, 1847, has granted a plenary indulgence on each of these Sundays; adding, however, to the usual conditions, that of visiting some church or public oratory, to pray for his intentions.

By the decree of the 22nd of March, Pius IX. grants these plenary indulgences to those who, being unable to read, recite instead of the devotions of the Seven Dolours and Joys, seven Paters, Aves, and Glorias. (*See the Italian work, entitled Raccolta di Indulgenze*).

PRAYERS IN HONOUR OF THE SEVEN DOLOURS AND JOYS OF ST. JOSEPH.

1. Chaste spouse of the Immaculate Mother of Jesus! glorious St. Joseph! permit me to commemorate the mental agony which you endured with regard to your sacred spouse; deeming yourself under the painful necessity of leaving her, until the angel banished your doubts, and filled you with unspeakable joy, by revealing the mystery of the Incarnation : by your anguish and holy joy on this occasion, obtain for me, I implore, both now and in my agony, the joy of a good conscience, sincere charity towards all men, and the consolation of dying with you in the embraces of Jesus and Mary.

Pater, Ave, Gloria, &c.

2. O thrice happy Joseph! deeply impressed with a sense of the sweet and sacred duties which, as a father, you were called on to render to the "Word Incarnate," permit me to commemorate the sorrow which filled your breast on beholding that Divine Infant lying on straw, in a manger, weeping, shivering with cold, and enduring all the privations of the most

abject poverty. But how great was your consolation shortly after, to hear the canticle of peace intoned by the blessed spirits, and to witness the kings of the earth humbly prostrate at the Infant's feet, while their countenances beamed with love, joy, and admiration, and offering their most precious gifts to Him whom they acknowledged as heaven's King! By your anguish and holy joy on this occasion, obtain that my heart may be always a pure and holy sanctuary, where Jesus will love to dwell by His grace and His real presence in the adorable Eucharist; and that, when the trials of life and the shades of death shall have passed away, my ears may be enchanted with the harmonies of the heavenly choirs, and that I may enter into the possession of those joys that neither eye hath seen, ear heard, nor the human heart conceived. Amen.

Pater, Ave, Gloria, &c.

3. Thou wert, O great St. Joseph! a man according to God's own heart, for His law was thy meditation. Permit me to commemorate the acute sensibility of thy tender heart, when, by the law of circumcision, it became thy painful duty to cause the first effusion of the precious blood of the innocent "Lamb." The sword which pierced His infant flesh wounded thy heart; but the sweet name of "Jesus," which, in accordance with the revelation of the angel, thou didst bestow on Him, imparted a holy and soothing unction to thy soul. By thy anguish and holy joy on this occasion, pray thy blessed Son, that, being purified in the laver of His precious blood, and all inordinate inclinations being circumcised, I may have the sweet and saving name of "Jesus" always engraven on my heart, and be so happy as to invoke it

with great love and efficacy at the hour of death. Amen.

Pater, Ave, Gloria, &c.

4. O faithful St. Joseph! to whom the mysterious secrets of our redemption were confided, permit me to commemorate the sorrow which filled thy afflicted heart on hearing Simeon's prophecy concerning the sufferings of Jesus and Mary. But how much wert thou comforted on hearing immediately after that the Child Jesus was destined for the resurrection and salvation of many! By thy anguish and holy joy on this occasion, obtain for me grace to participate in the dolours of Mary, and the bitter passion of her beloved Son, that by patient suffering, and heartfelt compunction, I may one day rise to a glorious resurrection, through the merits of Jesus Christ, and the intercession of His most blessed mother. Amen.

Pater, Ave, Gloria, &c.

5. O zealous guardian of the Son of God, and pious comforter of His dear mother! permit me to commemorate the trials and anxiety thou didst undergo in their service, but especially in thy flight into Egypt, and the hardships of thy exile, for which, however, thou wert in some degree consoled, by seeing the idols fall prostrate in the presence of the only true God. By thy sufferings and holy joy on this occasion, obtain for me, I beseech thee, grace to destroy all the idols of self-love, to which I may have erected an altar in my heart, and that, henceforth, devoting all the energies of my soul to the service of you and Mary, I may live and die as thou didst in union with them. Amen.

Pater, Ave, Gloria, &c.

6. Angel of the earth! vigilant guardian of the

Virgin of virgins and her Blessed Babe! permit me to commemorate your painful anxiety for their safety, when, on returning home, you found the throne occupied by a tyrant no less cruel than Herod; but soon, reassured by an angel, you joyfully re-established your family in the holy house of Naza-reth. By your anguish and holy joy on this occasion, obtain for me, I most earnestly implore, the great blessings of interior peace, and a pure conscience during life, and that I may die invoking the sweet names of Jesus and Mary. Amen.

Pater, Ave, Gloria, &c.

7. Mirror of sanctity! glorious St. Joseph! permit me to commemorate the affliction which you experienced on losing the Child Jesus, and the agony of your grief upon finding your search useless after the space of three days. But how inexpressible was your joy upon finding your precious treasure in the house of prayer! By your poignant anguish and ineffable joy on this occasion, obtain for me grace never to be separated from Jesus by grievous sin. And should I have the misfortune to forfeit His friendship, even partially, by venial sin, may I never suffer the day to close until I shall have made my peace with God; but especially at the hour of death, may I be closely united to Him by love, confidence, and perfect com-punction. Amen.

Pater, Ave, Gloria, &c.

℣. Ora pro nobis, sancte Joseph.

℟. Ut digni efficiamur promissionibus Christi.

℣. Pray for us, O holy St. Joseph!

℟. That we may be made worthy of the pro-mises of Christ.

OREMUS

Sanctissimæ Genitricis tuæ Sponsi, quæsumus, Domine, meritis adjuvemur, ut quod possibilitas nostra non obtinet, ejus nobis intercessione donetur : qui vivis et regnas in sæcula sæculorum. Amen.

LET US PRAY.

Vouchsafe, O Lord! that we may be helped by the merits of thy most holy mother's spouse; and that what of ourselves we cannot obtain, may be given us through his intercession : wholivest and reignest, world without end. Amen.

DEVOUT PRAYERS TO JESUS, MARY, AND JOSEPH.

Jesus, adorable Saviour, whom it pleased, for our sake, to be born of a virgin mother; grant that we may honour, by a perpetual homage, the consoling mysteries of Thy sacred infancy; grant that we may become in spirit like little children, and thereby worthy to imitate the humility, simple confidence, purity, innocence, and all the other virtues of which Thou, Divine Infant, hast given us an example in that state of weakness and humiliation. Amen.

Jesu, tibi sit gloria, qui natus es de Virgine, cum Patre, oumque_ Spiritu, in sempiterna sæcula. Amen.

To Jesus, from a virgin sprung,
Be glory given and praises sung ;
The like to God the Father be,
And Holy Ghost, eternally. Amen.

O singularly-privileged being! thrice happy Mary! thou art truly worthy of the united homages of men and angels, because from thee arose the Sun of

righteousness, Christ our God. Ah! by the services
thou hast rendered to His sacred humanity in its
state of helpless infancy, do not refuse to teach us
how we may worthily honour Him as thou didst
here on earth, so as to merit one day to be made
participators of His glory in heaven. Amen.

Monstra te esse matrem,	Show thyself a mother,
Sumat per te preces,	Offer Him our sighs,
Qui pro nobis natus	Who, for us incarnate,
Tulit esse tuus.	Did not thee despise.

Hail, immaculate spouse of Mary! Hail, faithful
guardian of her virginal integrity! Hail, happy
father of the Holy Family! You endured toil and
fatigue in order to provide sustenance for the " Incarnate Word;" you rescued Him from the power
of impious Herod; you were His instructor, guide,
and father at Bethlehem, in Egypt, and at Nazareth.
By your paternal love and solicitude in His regard,
obtain for us grace to serve Him worthily in this
life, and help us at the hour of death, that when our
last trial is over, we may have the happiness of
enjoying Him with you in heaven, where He liveth
and reigneth one God, with the Father and the Holy
Ghost. Amen.

Salve, Sponse Matris Dei; salve, Pater Jesu mei, Joseph admirabilis, Joseph ter amabilis! Amen.	Hail, spouse of the Mother of God, Hail, father of my Jesus: Joseph most admirable, Thrice amiable Joseph.

Adopt the pious practice of reciting every day, in
honour of St. Joseph, some of the prayers found
below, in the fifth chapter.

CHAPTER II.

Practices for Different Periods of the Year.

THESE practices are threefold. Some answer as a preparation for his feasts; others are suitable to the feasts or solemnities themselves; and a third class may be profitably made use of at any time, as being calculated to re-animate the devotion of his clients. It may not be useless to add here a few remarks on this subject.

1st.—Pious persons are, and always have been, accustomed to prepare for the worthy celebration of all great solemnities, by some particular practices of devotion, because they are aware, that on those solemn festivals the divine favours are more abundantly infused into hearts well disposed for their reception, than at other times; like the dew of heaven, which, though it fall indiscriminately upon every spot of the earth, yet serves really to nourish only such portions of it as, by previous cultivation, give a promise of bearing fruit, plants, or flowers. You cannot be ignorant that one of the most usual and approved devotions on the occasions of which we speak, is that of the novena. If you generally prepare for the due celebration of the feasts of the Blessed Virgin by a novena, surely a devout client of St. Joseph will not be less anxious to honour worthily the glorious spouse of Mary on his festivals. This devotion will prove peculiarly agreeable to him, and will oblige him to grant you some one of those great favours which he has in reserve for his most faithful servants, as experience has so often proved. Many examples may be seen in the Second Part of this little work. I will, however, mention here the case of a poor man who resided at a village near Lyons. Being attacked with the plague, which desolated the city in 1638, he asked the vicar of the place if, independently of all human resources, there were any other means of saving his life. The vicar replied that he felt confident the sick man would obtain his recovery through the powerful intercession of St. Joseph, if, in order to secure that favour, he would make a vow to celebrate St. Joseph's feast every year of his life, by approaching devoutly the sacraments of penance and the Eucharist, together with a preparatory novena, in which he would recite seven Paters and Aves, invoking each time the names of Jesus, Mary, and Joseph. The good old man actually made a vow, and all symptoms of the plague immediately vanished.

We have given below some spiritual exercises suitable for a novena.

FIRST DAY—MARCH 10.

"She was espoused to a man called Joseph."—*St. Luke*, i.

Consider his glorious titles.—1. He was the true and worthy spouse of Mary, specially predestined, from all eternity, for so noble an alliance, supplying, in a visible manner, the place of Mary's invisible spouse, the Holy Ghost. 2. He was a virgin, and his virginity was the faithful mirror of Mary's; for, like her, he also made a vow ever to remain a virgin. 3. He was the cherub placed to guard the new terrestrial paradise, the real propitiatory which contained the price of reconciliation between God and man, between heaven and earth.

Virtues to imitate in St. Joseph.—1. His love of purity. 2. His guard over all the senses. 3. His mortification, by undertaking all that was painful and laborious for mind or body in the spirit of penance.

Graces to ask of St. Joseph.—Most blessed St. Joseph! you who were chosen by the adorable Trinity to be the spouse of the Mother of God, are indeed worthy to receive the united and most fervent homages of men and angels, who can never sufficiently testify their respect and joy, seeing you are raised to a dignity which no other creature, either man or angel, was deemed worthy to share. I am the most worthless of all creatures, yet I cannot refrain from laying at your feet this day the affectionate sentiments of my heart, and in union with all the angels and saints, thus reverentially salute you, saying with them : " Hail, most worthy spouse of Mary ! Hail, fairest lily of virginity ! inseparably united to the Mystical Rose. Hail, beauteous cherub ! faithful guardian of that paradise of grace and perfection in which the 'Incarnate Word' so delighted' to dwell ! Ah ! refuse not, thrice happy and chaste spouse, to ask for me grace to imitate your great love of purity ; obtain for me strength to overcome all those temptations from which you have been preserved by reason of your privileged and most sublime vocation, as well as by the exalted degree of virtue to which your co-operation with divine grace raised you even in this world. Amen."

Practices of devotion and mortification.—1. Perform

some corporal austerity, if your health will permit.
2. Mortify your curiosity as to sight and hearing,
unless, of course, duty be in question. 3. Speak
little, to honour the silence and recollection of St.
Joseph, not one of whose words is recorded in the
Gospel. 4. Address an aspiration occasionally in the
course of the day to St. Joseph.

Spiritual Lecture.—Read the second chapter of the
first part of this work, and learn of the Blessed Virgin
how to honour St. Joseph. Read some examples to
be found in the second part. Terminate all your
lectures by the following prayer :—

Ant. Missus est Ange-
lus Gabriel ad virginem
desponsatam viro cui no-
men erat Joseph, de domo
David ; et nomen virgi-
nis, Maria.

Ant. The angel Gabriel
was sent to a virgin es-
poused to a man whose
name was Joseph, of the
house of David, and the
name of the virgin was
Mary.

℣. Ora pro nobis, sancte
Joseph.

℣. Pray for us, St.
Joseph.

℟. Ut digni efficiamur
promissionibus Christi.

℟. That we may be
made worthy of the pro-
mises of Christ.

OREMUS.

LET US PRAY.

Sanctissimæ Genetricis
tuæ Sponsi, quæsumus,
Domine, meritis adjuve-
mur, ut quod possibilitas
nostra non obtinet, ejus
nobis intercessione done-

We beseech thee, O
Lord! that we may be
assisted by the merits of
the spouse of thy most
holy Mother, and that
what we cannot obtain

tur : qui vivis et regnas in sæcula sæculorum. Amen.

may be granted to us through His intercession, who livest and reignest with God the Father, in the unity of the Holy Ghost, world without end. Amen.

Sentences relating to the prerogatives and virtues of St. Joseph.

Honoravit eum Spiritus Sanctus patris vocabulo. (*Ger. Serm. de Nat.*)

"He is honoured by the Holy Ghost with the name of Father of Jesus." (*Gerson.*)

Joseph fuit, super omnes homines purus, similis Virgini gloriosæ. (*Idem.*)

"Of all the children of men, not one so nearly resembled the Blessed Virgin as St. Joseph." (*Gerson.*)

Ecclesiæ fides in eo est ut non modo Deipara, sed etiam putativus pater atque nutritius virgo habeatur. (*St. Pet. Damianus.*)

"It is perfectly in accordance with the faith and spirit of the Church, to honour as a virgin not only the Mother of God, but likewise Joseph, His reputed father, and the guardian of His infancy." (*St. Peter Damian.*)

In hoc justo et æque casto viro peccati originalis fomitem vel exstinctum vel depressum fuisse. (*Gers. et alii opud Canisium,* tom. ii. ch. 13.)

"In this man, equally just and chaste, the fire of concupiscence, proceeding from original sin, was extinct, or at least rendered incapable of action". (*Gerson.*)

SECOND DAY—MARCH 11.

" We have found Him of whom Moses in the law and the prophets did write, Jesus the son of Joseph of Nazareth."—*John*, i. 45.

Titles to consider in St. Joseph.—1. He deserved the title of father of the Son of God, because he was the representative of God the Father on earth. He alone, amongst all creatures, had that honour, and could exercise all a parent's authority, with regard to Jesus Christ. 2. He was the father of Jesus by the choice which Jesus made of him, and by the affinity which his alliance with Mary established between them. 3. He was the father of Jesus by the choice which Mary made of him to be her spouse; by the right with which he was invested of giving our Saviour the glorious name of Jesus; and by all the labours which he undertook in order to provide for His wants, to shield Him from danger, &c.

Virtues to imitate in St. Joseph.—1. His humility and mean opinion of himself, combined with so much real greatness. 2. His entire dependence on the will of the Eternal Father. 3. His paternal love for Jesus.

Graces to ask of St. Joseph.—I ardently desire to honour and glorify you, O blessed St. Joseph! and where find a title more glorious or more dear to your heart, than that which the Gospel bestows upon you : "We have found Jesus the son of Joseph of Nazareth." Thus spoke the first disciples of Jesus; and were they deceived? No; but were it even so, surely Mary was under no delusion when she said : " Thy father and I have sought thee," &c. Yes, great saint! in all justice and truth this honourable title

belongs to you, for you alone have been chosen by
the Eternal Father, from amidst the countless multitude of the children of Adam, to hold His place on
earth to His only and well-beloved Son. He has
communicated to you what appears incommunicable,
namely, a degree of His paternity! I rejoice to contemplate you in this exalted character, O blessed
saint! but greater still is my joy to behold you endowed with a plenitude of grace fully proportioned
to your admirable dignity! Oh! the depth of the
tenderness infused into your heart by the Eternal
Father for His only Son, who was yours also! Oh!
surely the most intense love of the fondest parent is
but as a feeble spark when compared with yours for
the mysterious being whose infant form encompassed
the Divinity itself! By this your inconceivable love
obtain for me a strong and tender love to Jesus.
Especially in His exile of love in the holy Eucharist,
may I become one with Him, as He and the Father
are one. For the sake of the Divine Jesus in His
infant years, be thou, O exalted saint! a father to
me also; and may divine love transform me, through
your intercession, into a little child in docility and
meekness, though a giant in forbearance, endurance,
and courage, under all the crosses with which it may
please Divine Providence to visit me. Amen.

Practices of devotion and mortification.—1. To renew yourself, in the love of Jesus Christ, by a serious
and determined renunciation of all voluntary faults
or imperfect habits, which serve to alienate us effectually from Him. 2. Impose some penance upon
yourself, to repair the misfortune of having loved Him
so little hitherto. 3. Make a visit to our Lord in
the most blessed Eucharist, to ask for an increase of

love to Him, and to offer Him that love with which Joseph was inflamed.

Spiritual Lecture.—Read the first chapter of the First Book, and some examples in the Second. Conclude as the preceding.

Ant. Fili, quid fecisti nobis sic? Ecce pater tuus et ego dolentes quærebamus te.

Ant. "Son, why hast thou done so to us? behold thy father and I have sought thee sorrowing." (*Luke,* ii. 48.)

Prayer as usual, &c.

Sentences relating to the titles and virtues of St. Joseph.

Josephus habebat in Christum jus paternum, puta omnia jura quæ habent parentes respectu filiorum. (*Cornel. c. i. in Matth.*)

"Joseph had a parental authority over Jesus." (*Cornel.*)

Non est in coelestibus agminibus qui Dominum Jesum filium suum audeat nominare. (*S. Cyp. in Bapt. Christi.*)

"There is not one among the blessed spirits who would presume to take the title of 'Father,' with regard to Jesus." (*St. Cyprian.*)

Pater Christi erat jure conjugii atque affinitate. (*St. Jerome.*)

"He was the father of Jesus Christ in virtue of his marriage and the affinity between them." (*St. Jerome.*)

Vocabis nomen ejus Jesum; tu vocabis, utpote pater. (*Theod. c. i. in Matth.*)

"And thou (as being His father) shalt call His name Jesus." (*Matt.* i. 21.)

Pater Domini meruit   " He merited to be
appellari. (*S. Hier. con-*   called the father of our
tra Helvid.)   Lord.

Third Day—March 12.

"He was subject to them."—*St. Luke,* ii. 51.

Titles to consider in St. Joseph.—1. How glorious
to St. Joseph was the dignity of father of Jesus
Christ, which made him the master of the Saviour,
and gave him the power to dispose of Him as a father
disposes of his son. 2. Jesus was the king of heaven,
and yet Joseph's authority over Him was boundless,
because Jesus, in becoming his Son, made a voluntary
resignation of His entire liberty to him. 3. He was
actually served by Jesus Christ for the space of three
and thirty years; he employed Him as any other
artizan would his assistant, and made Him a sharer
in all his labours and hardships.

Virtues to imitate in St. Joseph.—1. His profound
respect for the adorable person of Jesus Christ, and
the reverential awe and humility which he evinced
in the exercise of his authority over Him. 2. The
extreme meekness with which he delivered his orders.
3. The lively faith with which he viewed Jesus
Christ reduced to the condition of a child and a
menial.

Practices of devotion and mortification.—1. Perform
an act of humility towards an inferior. 2. Practise
meekness and gentleness of demeanour in giving your
orders. 3. Recall to your mind with extreme confusion the many occasions on which you spoke in a
haughty and impatient manner to your inferiors; and

on the other hand, when called on to obey, the mur-
muring and interior resistance you have been guilty
of. Say five Paters and Aves, and kiss the ground
five times as a penance for your faults.

Graces to ask of St. Joseph.—O blessed saint!
would that I possessed the wisdom of the cherubim,
and the zeal of the seraphim, that I might worthily
extol and magnify the dignity which elevates you to
the high privilege of commanding Him whom the
angels in heaven adore with respectful awe, and before
whom the pillars of heaven bow down and tremble!
I honour and revere this incomparable dignity; I rejoice on beholding the Son of God listening with great
attention and docility to your last wishes; I rejoice
when I behold an incarnate God sacrifice His entire
liberty, and place it at your disposal; and how can I
any longer hesitate to relinquish mine into your
hands, that you may dispose of it as it may please
you? In consideration of the humble obedience and
the all-divine services which Jesus rendered to you
during so many years, whether as your son in the
house of Nazareth, or as a workman in your shop,
obtain that my will, henceforth docile and submissive,
may never again resist the orders of God, or those of
the constituted authorities who hold in my regard the place of God. Graciously obtain also
that, imitating your example, I may learn how
to command my inferiors with all humility; and
seeing in them the person of Jesus Christ, I may
ever treat them with respect, kindness, and charity.
Amen.

Spiritual Lecture.—Read the third chapter of the
First Book, and some examples of the Second.

Ant. Descendit cum eis, et venit Nazareth, et erat subditus illis.

Ant. " And he went down with them and came to Nazareth, and was subject to them." (*Luke,* ii. 51.)

Prayer as above.

Sentences relating to the virtues and titles of St. Joseph.

Josephus habuit omnia jura veri domini ac patris in Jesum, ut erat homo. (*Tirin. in* i. *Matth.*)

" Joseph was invested with all the authority of a father and of a master over Jesus Christ in His sacred humanity."

Subjectio, sicut inæstimabilem notat humilitatem in Jesu, ita dignitatem incomparabilem signat in Josepho. (*Gerson.*)

" If the dependence of Jesus supposes a humility that knew no bounds, it likewise supposes an incomparable dignity in Joseph." (*Gerson.*)

Ad illum familiæ gubernatio pertirebat.

" The government of the family belonged to Joseph." (*St. Thomas.*)

Labores corporis omnes æquo animo, una cum illis, Jesus obediens tolerabat.

" Jesus, in this state of abjection, cheerfully took part with Joseph and Mary, in all those occupations which were most laborious and fatiguing to the body." (*St. Justin.*)

Sœpè focum, crebroque cibum parat officiosus.

" One of His ordinary employments, was that of making the fire and preparing their food." (*Gerson.*)

FOURTH DAY.—MARCH 13.

" Whereupon Joseph her husband being a just man."—
St. Matt. i. 19.

Titles to consider in St. Joseph.—1. According to
the opinion of a great number of doctors, he was
sanctified even in his mother's womb. He is the
first saint who has been canonized in the Gospel.
The Holy Ghost bestowed upon him the title of
Just, thus giving us to understand that he possessed
the plenitude of all virtues. 2. His sanctity was
commensurate with his high dignity, viz., that of
being Mary's spouse, lieutenant of the Eternal Father,
guardian, foster-father, and father of the Man-God.
3. No other saint approached the source of all sanctity so closely, or for so long a period, as St. Joseph.
He made rapid and continual progress in virtue
under the eyes of Jesus and Mary, his living models.
Virtues to imitate in St. Joseph.—1. The purity
of his heart, which was exempt from the least shadow
of sin. 2. His detachment from all transitory things.
3. His persevering and untiring zeal for his own
advancement in perfection.
Graces to ask of St. Joseph.—You are truly the
just man by excellence, O blessed St. Joseph! The
Holy Ghost Himself, who can neither deceive nor
be deceived, has declared you to be such. Yes,
you are truly just, for you were adorned with grace
and sanctity, even before your entrance into this
exile. You are the just man by excellence, enriched
by the " great Creator " with a degree of sanctity

fully proportioned to the eminence of your dignity, for to Jesus you were the representative of His Eternal Father, and by the alliance which you contracted with the immaculate Virgin, you became, in her regard, the representative of the Holy Ghost. But, then, by your faithful co-operation with such' overflowing graces, with what indefatigable zeal did you not labour to render yourself worthy of so glorious a function, and by the constant exercise of every heroic virtue, to increase your store of merits and sanctity! Having had perpetually before your eyes two models of consummate perfection, with what love and assiduity did you not study them, and endeavour to form yourself according to their counsels and example! I honour and revere that eminent sanctity which distinguishes you from all the other saints; but in order that my homage may contribute no less to my own spiritual advantage than to your glory, obtain, O my dear father and patron! that I may become worthy to receive that inestimable treasure of holiness, without which I can neither hope to please God, nor to prove the solidity of my devotion towards you. Amen.

Practices of devotion and mortification.—1. Examine your conscience more carefully than usual, in order to discover the chief obstacles to your progress in Christian perfection. 2. Make frequent acts of contrition, in order to acquire an increase of purity of heart. 3. Perform some painful act of penance, in order, through the merits of Christ, to atone for your past negligence, and your little zeal for your perfection.

Spiritual Lecture.—Read the fourth chapter of the First Book, and some examples of the Second.

Ant. Joseph cum esset justus et nollet eam traducere, voluit occulto dimittere eam.

Ant. "Whereupon, Joseph her husband, being a just man, and not willing publicly to expose her, was minded to put her away privately." (*Matt.* i. 19.)

Prayer as usual.

Sentences relating to the titles and virtues of St. Joseph.

Joseph sanctificatus est in utero, baptismo flammis, sicut Joannes Baptista.

"Joseph was sanctified in his mother's womb, like St. John the Baptist, by a baptism of desire." (*Gerson.*)

Joseph vocare justum attendite propter omnium virtutum perfectam possessionem.

"Remark that St. Joseph was called 'Just,' because he possessed all virtues in perfection." (*SS. Jerome and Chrysostom.*)

Quos Deus ad aliquid delegit, ita præparat et disponit, ut ad illud inveniantur idonei.

"Those who are destined by Almighty God for any particular function, are always prepared and qualified by Him before hand for its discharge." (*St. Thomas.*)

Non existimo esse temerarium neque improbabile, sed pium potius et verisimile, si quis fortasse opinetur sanctum

"The opinion of those persons is not considered by me either rash or improbable, but rather as pious and most credible,

hunc reliquos omnes in gratiâ ac beatudine.

who hold that this saint surpassed all the other saints in merit and glory; because, as far as I can see, there is nothing either in Scripture or the Holy Fathers which is contrary to such an opinion." (*Suarez on the Mysterious Question*, 29.)

FIFTH DAY.—MARCH 14.

" Joseph her husband, being a just man."—*Matt.* i. 19.

Titles to consider in St. Joseph.—1. He was a model of justice in his duties to God : he obeyed in all things His commandments and inspirations; his only desire was to see the divine will perfectly accomplished. 2. He was a model of justice with regard to his neighbour, in thought, word, and action. Being ignorant of the mystery of the Incarnation, he, nevertheless, judged most favourably of the Blessed Virgin ; and, in like manner, never did the slightest murmur or complaint escape him against Herod, who sought to destroy the Divine Infant. 3. He was a model of that justice which is due to oneself ; he never flattered his senses in the least ; he knew no other interest than that of imitating, as closely as possible, a God incarnate : therefore, St. Joseph may be justly considered as our Divine Lord's first disciple, and the first Christian.

Virtues to imitate in St. Joseph.—1. The exact observance of the law of God, and perfect docility to

His holy inspirations. 2. The love of our neighbour, and a great desire to serve him to the utmost of our ability. 3. A resolute determination to imitate Jesus Christ in this mortified and laborious life.

Graces to ask of St. Joseph.—O my glorious patron! my heart is filled with joy when I contemplate the indefatigable zeal and ardour with which you pursued the path of perfection. You were truly a mirror of justice; you were just towards God, by devoting your whole life, heart, and strength, to the perfect accomplishment of His most amiable will; you were just towards your neighbour, by loving all creatures, without exception, in God, and God in all His creatures; you were just as regarded yourself, desiring no other advantages than those which tended to your advancement in perfection, and which enabled you to imitate more closely the virtues of humility, obedience, poverty, mortification, and charity, as you beheld them reduced to practice by Jesus and Mary. I humbly beseech of you, O thrice just and blessed Joseph! that you will deign yourself to become my master, teaching me thus to fulfil all justice; but I particularly conjure you, by the plenitude of your virtues and your boundless credit with God, that you will obtain for me grace to begin now in earnest to lead the life of a true Christian, that I may become a perfect imitator of a God who lived in poverty, humiliation, and patient suffering. I acknowledge that I have hitherto been the reverse of all this, but now I am firmly resolved to begin a new life, with the assistance of your prayers, and those of your ever-immaculate spouse, the ever-glorious and blessed Virgin Mary, the mother of mercy. Amen.

Practices of devotion and mortification.—1. As a reparation for the injustice you have been guilty of towards God, make a visit to the most holy Sacrament, and humbly ask of Jesus the pardon of your sins, which are so many acts of injustice against His divine will. 2. As a reparation for the faults you have committed against your neighbour, you will endeavour to do him good, in thought, by esteeming him better than yourself; in words, by speaking to and of him with fraternal affection and kindness; and in deed, by assisting him in his spiritual and corporal necessities. 3. In order to expiate the injustice you have been guilty of towards yourself, by gratifying your sensuality in many ways, you will abstain from the indulgence of the senses on some occasions at your choice.

Spiritual Lecture.—The fifth and sixth chapters of the First Book, and some examples of the Second.

Ant. Joseph fili David, noli timere accipere Mariam, conjugem tuam, quod enim in ea natum est de Spiritu Sancto est, pariet autem filium, et vocabis nomen ejus Jesum.

Ant. "Joseph, son of David, fear not to take unto thee Mary thy wife, for that which is conceived in her is of the Holy Ghost. She shall bring forth a son, and thou shalt call His name Jesus."

Prayer as usual.

Sentences relating to the titles and virtues of St. Joseph.

Justus in verbo, justus in facto, justus in

"Joseph was just in his words, just in his actions,

lege, justus in judicio gratiæ. (*Orig. Hom.* i.)

just in the observance of the law, just by a perfect fidelity to grace.

Totum desiderium Joseph fuit obectire voluntati Dei. (*St. Brig. Rev.* l. vi.)

"Joseph's sole ambition was to obey the law of God, which he observed even in its most minute details, to his last breath, though suffering from the infirmities consequent upon his advanced age." (*St. John Damasc.*)

Integram atque inviolatam legem ad senectutem usque servaverat. (*St. Damas. Hom.* i.)

Sic mortuus erat mundo et carni, ut nihil desideraret sed cœlestia.

"So perfectly was he dead to the world and the flesh, that he desired nothing but the things of heaven." (*St. Bridget.*)

In suâ paupertate lætantur vixit.

"He lived content in his poverty." (*St. Bonaventure, Vita J. C.* cvii.)

SIXTH DAY.—MARCH 15.

"Simeon blessed them."—*St. Luke*, ii.

Titles to consider in St. Joseph.—1. He was the crown of all the patriarchs, and of all the ancestors of the promised Messiah. He inherited and enjoyed the fruition of their united benedictions. 2. He was the crown of the saints of the Old Law; all their prerogatives, all their virtues, were concentrated and perfected in his person. 3. He is the crown of the saints of the New Testament: he surpasses them all in dignity, as being head of the Holy Family, of which Jesus Christ, the Son of God made man, was

a member; and as, in the discharge of this function,
he acquitted himself so as to deserve the title of the
prudent and faithful servant by excellence, so should
he also surpass all the other servants of God in glory.
Virtues to imitate in St. Joseph.—1. His faith,
which was most lively and most fruitful in good
works. 2. His equanimity whether in prosperity or
adversity. 3. His zeal for the honour of God, and
the salvation of man.

Graces to ask of St. Joseph.—Most blessed St,
Joseph, who alone were destined to enjoy and to
witness the accomplishment of all the blessings of
the patriarchs, you who were raised to the supreme
dignity of father of the Messiah, in whom all nations
were to be blessed; behold now the patriarchs themselves approaching to place a crown of glory on your
head, and to acknowledge you for their king; they
are followed by all the saints of the Old Law, who
also wish to present you, as their chief, with a crown
composed of as many brilliant stars as you have surpassed them in degrees of perfection; and lastly, the
saints of the New Law—the apostles, martyrs, con-
fessors, and virgins—come with their palms mingled
with lilies and roses, to crown the chief of the family
of God on earth, the first disciple of Jesus Christ, the
first imitator of His divine example, the first confidant of the secrets of Jesus and Mary, and the first
saint whom the law of grace produced, even pro-
claimed such by the sacred writings. We praise and
bless you a thousand and a thousand times, thrice
blessed patriarch of all the saints! Elevated as you
now are in bliss, forget not your poor, miserable
client here on earth, but deign to bestow on me some
small portion of that abundance of good things with

which you will be eternally replenished in the mansion of your heavenly Father. The most ardent of my desires, my glorious patron! is, that you would bestow upon me the salutary fruits with which the tree of life is laden—that tree on which Jesus Christ consummated the redemption of the world. Enriched with these precious fruits of benediction on earth, I shall confidently hope to taste one day the fruits of glory with which the elect shall be¯satiated for all eternity. Amen.

Practices of devotion and mortification.—1. A more rigorous fast than usual. 2. Perform one of the works of mercy, either spiritual or corporal. 3. A visit to our Divine Lord, at which beg to be made a sharer in the blessings enjoyed by St. Joseph; and for that intention recite the " Te Deum."

Spiritual Lecture.—Read the seventh chapter, First Book, and a few examples of the Second.

Ant. Invenerunt Mariam et Joseph, et Infantum positum in præsepio.

Ant. " And they came with haste; and they found Mary and Joseph, and the Infant lying in the manger." (*Luke*, ii. 15.)

Prayer as usual.

Sentences relating to the titles and virtues of St. Joseph.

Magnus magnæ virtutis ac pietatis Jacob. Vèrum quam supra modum magnus patriarcha noster Joseph.

" The patriarch Jacob was considered great on account of his eminent virtues and piety; but how far was he surpassed

Major Noe, et cæteris patriarchis. In viris benedictus unde B. Virgo in mulieribus benedicta. (*Navæus, Serm. 2 in S. Joseph.*)

Duobus privilegiis, id est ut vir Mariæ et pater Christi, auctus est super omnes patriarchas et prophetas. (*Tolet, c. i. in Luc.*)

Primus a tempore missionis, persecutionem propter justitiam passus est, ita ut ferum pertransiret animam ejus.

Eo fuit excellentior quo ad altiorem ordinem pertineat Joseph. (*St. Thom.*)

in this respect by our holy patriarch, St. Joseph!"

"Yes, he was greater than Noah and all the other patriarchs; he is blessed among all men, for the same reason that Mary is blessed among all women."

"He enjoyed two wonderful privileges, of which neither patriarchs nor prophets could boast; for St. Joseph was the spouse of Mary and the father of Jesus Christ."

"He was the first person persecuted for justice sake under the law of grace, for his soul was pierced with a sword of sorrow." (*Rupert, c. ii. in Matth.*)

"Joseph was so much the more excellent that he belonged to a higher order." (*St. Thom.*)

SEVENTH DAY.—MARCH 16.

"Behold an angel of the Lord appeared in sleep to Joseph."— *Matt.* ii. 13.

Titles to consider in St. Joseph.—1. He was singularly favoured, assisted, and honoured by the angels. From them he received comfort in his anguish, light and direction in his difficulties, and help and solace in his labours. St. Joseph was appointed to discharge the function of guardian-angel towards Jesus and Mary. 2. No saint was ever so intimately associated with Jesus as St. Joseph, who so often caressed and fondled Him in his arms. 3. The life which he led in the society of Jesus and Mary, was more a celestial than an earthly life, more divine than human; it was a tissue of simplicity, innocence, and fervour; it was a foretaste of the felicity of the blessed.

Virtues to imitate in St. Joseph.—1. His respect for the ministers of God. 2. The peace and tranquillity of his soul. 3. The truth and sincerity of his words, and the modesty of his demeanour.

Graces to ask of St. Joseph.—To behold you so singularly favoured by the angels, is to me no matter of surprise, O glorious saint! for you are as one of them by your angelic purity. Why marvel to behold them even vieing with each other in rendering service to one whom they consider superior to themselves in dignity? Ah! if envy could find a place in their hearts, it might well have been excited on seeing the happy privilege which you enjoyed of living on terms of such intimate familiarity with our Divine Lord, the Infant God, the wondrous mystery of love, the centre of joy, the source of felicity. Blessed be that mouth, which has so often praised and glorified Him; blessed those arms, which so lovingly embraced Him; blessed that bosom, on which He so often sweetly reposed. By conversing day and night with your Infant Saviour, you learned to become a child like Him, and to imitate the innocence, simpli-

city, purity, and all the other amiable virtues of the
"WORD Incarnate." Ah! you were fully sensible
of His ardent desire to see all Christians become like
little children, that they may thus be enabled to
enter by the low and narrow gate that leads to the
kingdom of heaven. I also burn with an ardent
desire to conform myself perfectly to the Divine
Infant Jesus: obtain, then, for me all the virtues
suited to that happy state of Christian childhood;
may my heart be guileless, my thoughts pure, my
intentions upright, my words innocent, and the whole
tenor of my life and conduct conformable to true
Christian simplicity and humility; obtain for me, in
fine, grace to become once more, by sincere repent-
ance and a truly penitential life, the little child of
Christianity which I was once made by the waters
of regeneration, but whose fair and noble lineaments
have, alas! been so often defaced and abused by the
ravages of sin, the only real evil. Amen.

Practices of devotion and mortification.—1. Excite
yourself to sincere contrition for all your past sins,
kneeling before an image of the Child Jesus, offering
up to Him the innocence, simplicity, and purity of
St. Joseph. 2. Make a visit to the Most Blessed
Sacrament, at least in spirit, for the purpose of conversing with the Lord Jesus, and of making Him an
offering of all the caresses which St. Joseph bestowed
upon Him. 3. Give alms to a poor child, a lively
image of Jesus in His adorable infancy.

Spiritual Lecture.—Read the eighth and ninth
chapters of the First Book, and some examples of the
Second.

Ant. Facta est cum   *Ant.* "And suddenly
angelo multitudo militiæ   there was with the angel

cœlestis laudantium Deum et dicentium : Gloria in excelsis Deo, et in terra pax, hominibus bonæ voluntatis.

a multitude of the heavenly army, praising God, and saying : 'Glory to God in the highest ; and peace on earth to men of good will.'" (*Luke*, ii. 13, 14.)

Sentences relating to the titles of St. Joseph.

Tanto Angelis melior effectus, quanto differentius præ illis nomen hereditavit. (*S. Paul. ad Heb.*)

"Which of the heavenly spirits could address Jesus in the following terms: 'My Son'?" (*St. Cyprian.*)

Jesus paternâ ope et piâ vectatione indigebat. (*Rupert.*)

"St. Joseph was the only being on whom Jesus depended for a father's care and tenderness, the only one to bear His infant form in his arms, until it acquired sufficient strength to walk." (*Rupert.*)

O quantâ dulcedine audiebat Joseph parvulum se patrem vocare. (*S. Bernardin.*)

"Oh! who can conceive St. Joseph's feelings, on hearing himself called 'father' by the child Jesus?" (*St. Bernardin.*)

Cœlum erat domus illa. (*Rupert.*)

"The house of Nazareth was truly a heaven upon earth." (*Rupert.*)

Post mortem reliquos gloria consecrat; tu vi-

"It is not until after death that the other saints

vens, superis par, frueris Deo. (*Hym. S. Joseph.*)

enter into glory, but St. Joseph's glory commenced on earth ; for, like the blessed in heaven, he enjoyed the visible presence of God even in this wretched place of exile." (*Hymn of the Church to St. Joseph.*)

EIGHTH DAY.—MARCH 17.

Titles to consider in St. Joseph.—1. He is considered the master and model of the contemplative life, for he was remarkable for an interior spirit, for his love of silence, retirement, and prayer. His soul was consumed with love ; his sleep was rather an ecstacy than a state of simple repose. 2. He is also a model of the active life, by his assiduous care of the Holy Family, and his content in poverty, with its labour, contempt, and privations. 3. He is a model of the mixed or apostolic life, ever ready to assist his neighbour, to console him in his afflictions, to enlighten him in his doubts, and to instruct him in the law of God, as necessity or occasion may require.

Virtues to imitate in St. Joseph.—1. His recollection and the care with which he shunned all useless conversations. 2. His vigilance and exactness in acquitting himself of all the duties allotted to him by Divine Providence. 3. His zeal in promoting the happiness and advantage of his neighbour, according to the means and opportunities afforded to him by Divine Providence.

Graces to ask of St. Joseph.—All ye holy contemplatives and solitaries, all ye holy anchorets, come, and learn of our glorious patriarch the art of leading a celestial life on earth : a life of contemplation, silence, love and union with God. O glorious patriarch! can we find among all the saints an individual who could boast of faith so strong and lively, charity so ardent, and a knowledge of the mysteries of our redemption so clear and comprehensive, as that which so eminently distinguished you? Saints John and Paul were great contemplatives, the former in sweet and profound ecstasies while reposing on the bosom of his adorable Master; the latter exalted even unto the third heavens, there beholding what eye hath not seen, nor ear heard, nor hath it entered into the heart of man to conceive! But what was all this to the innumerable ecstasies, secrets, and lights with which you were favoured during the many years that Jesus Himself, the true Paradise of pleasure, was all your own? When you enjoyed the transporting vision of Incarnate Beauty itself, when you so often enjoyed the happy privilege of reposing your aged head upon His bosom, His adorable heart, the true sanctuary of the Divinity, and of receiving Him into your arms, which, during His childhood especially, were His ordinary resting-place? Ah! how sweet were His slumbers thus cradled in your arms, and how profound the repose which you enjoyed upon His bosom? Surely, it is only of you that the eagles and the doves—that is, those souls who are possessed of the greatest purity and elevation—ought to learn to direct their flight towards heaven, and to contemplate the "Sun of Justice." And again, who so qualified as you to give useful lessons to those saints who are called to the active and apostolic life ? Can anything be more perfect than the example which you have given them, in the exercise of the painful and laborious duties of your profession, in your anxious solicitude to provide for the comfort and welfare of the Holy Family, on your journeys and pilgrimages, in the instructions, consolations, and multiplied acts of kindness which you so cordially rendered to your neighbour, whether in Egypt, the land of strangers, or at Nazareth, your native home ?   Oh ! thou most perfect of saints, obtain grace for me to imitate thee in the practice of an interior life.   I. earnestly implore the spirit of recollection, which will enable me to pray with greater faith and fervour.   St. Theresa calls you the great master of prayer; permit me, then, though unworthy, to become one of your disciples; initiate and perfect me in the science of the saints, that by learning to converse with God on earth, I may be prepared to glorify Him eternally with you and all the elect in a happy eternity.   Amen.

Practices of devotion and mortification.—1. Endeavour to overcome any inclination to spiritual sloth or sleep with which you may be molested at meditation.   2. Persevere in prayer, notwithstanding dryness and distractions.   3. Form a sincere resolution to devote yourself henceforth to the study and practice of the interior life, and to the use of mental prayer, choosing St. Joseph as your patron, whom spiritualists consider the model of the hidden life.

Spiritual Lecture.—Read the tenth chapter of the First Book, and some examples of the Second.

Ant. Erant pater ejus   *Ant.* "And all that had et mater mirantes super   heard Him were astonish-

his quæ dicebantur de illo.

ed at His wisdom and His answers. And seeing Him they wondered. (*Luke*, ii. 48.)

Sentences relating to the titles and virtues of St. Joseph.

Joseph tota vitæ series fuit oratio. (*Marcel. Pis.*)

" The whole life of St. Joseph was a continual prayer."

Vidimus lumen admirabile multoties circum fulsisse eum. (*Rev. Sta. Brig.* l. vi. ch. 38.)

" We often saw him surrounded with a marvellous light."

Quid aliud Joseph facere posset, quam mente cœlestia meditari. (*St. Atha.*)

"What could Joseph do, save meditate on the things of heaven."

Fuit altissimus in contemplatione. (*S. Bern. S.*)

" He had the gift of contemplation in the highest degree."

In universâ educatione Christi gaudens obsequium præstitit. (*S. Irén.* l. iv. *Contra Hær.*)

" He employed himself joyfully in the education of Jesus Christ."

Joseph apostolorum habet speciem, quibus Christus circumferendus est creditus. (*S. Hil.*)

" Joseph resembled the apostles, because the office of carrying Christ everywhere was confided to him."

Putandum est disseruisse Joseph de verâ religione cum senioribus Taneos. (*Gerson*).

" It is believed that Joseph spoke with the sages of Egypt about the true religion."

NINTH DAY.—MARCH 18.

"Enjoying the happiness of heaven even in this life, you continually behold the blessed vision of God."—*Hymn of the
Church.*

Titles to consider in St. Joseph.—1. The Church
compares the happiness which St. Joseph enjoyed on
earth to that of the saints in heaven, because he
beheld the Man-God face to face during thirty years;
and it is piously believed that our Lord manifested
the glory of His divinity to His good foster-father,
from time to time, as He did to His favourite disciples afterwards on Mount Thabor. 2. St. Joseph
was blessed, because in Jesus Christ he beheld an
exemplification of the eight beatitudes, those infallible marks of eternal beatitude; and he was thus
more easily enabled to reduce them to practice. 3.
He was blessed because he practised all those virtues
in the most- perfect manner to the end of his life,
under the eyes of Him who was one day to reward
them.

Virtues to imitate in St. Joseph.—1. Make choice
of one of the beatitudes to practise in imitation of St.
Joseph. 2. Aim at the practice of all the beatitudes,
as occasion may require. 3. See in which of them
you are most deficient.

Graces to ask of St. Joseph.—"Even in this life
you are equal to the blessed in heaven, being already
in the enjoyment of God Himself!" To you only, O
gracious saint! does the Church address these words
of praise; to other saints it was not given to live
here below with a God incarnate, to fondle the meek
Jesus in their arms like an ordinary child, and to

receive His infantine caresses, and with them such an abundance of heavenly light and consolation !   O ineffable happiness ! and truly do I rejoice, O glorious saint ! in this your anticipated beatitude. Doubtless no one possessed a stronger claim to it than yourself, who for the space of thirty years ceased not to imbibe with holy curiosity the waters of these eight sources of sanctity, which the example of Jesus kept continually open for you. As you know I am also commanded to drink of these salutary streams, though I have as yet neglected doing so, obtain for me now a great love for this heavenly doctrine, and grace to live according to it. I know that I never can be happy until I shall have become poor in spirit, meek, pure, peaceable, and merciful; until I shall be able to rejoice in persecution for justice sake, seeking above all else the kingdom of God and His justice. But alas ! how shall I be able to overcome nature, to devote my whole mind and heart to the contemplation of things altogether spiritual and heavenly; I who am accustomed to flatter my senses, to gratify all my inclinations ? I stand in need of a very strong and lively faith, in order to become detached from all earthly objects ; and I most earnestly implore this faith, O amiable saint ! through your charitable intercession.   It will sanctify and render my good works meritorious through Christ Jesus ; and by the exercise of the beatitudes I shall enjoy in this vale of sorrow a foretaste of the happiness which will constitute their reward exceeding great for an endless eternity. Amen.

Practices of devotion and mortification.—1. A stricter fast than usual, as an immediate preparation for the feast. 2. Some other corporal austerity.

3. Give dinner or other alms to three poor persons, in honour of the Holy Family.

Spiritual Lecture.—Read the eleventh chapter of the First Book, and some examples of the Second.

Ant. Euge, serve bone et fidelis; quia super pauca fuisti fidelis, supra multa te constituam: intra in gaudium Domini tui.

Ant. "Well done, thou good and faithful servant."

Prayer as usual.

Sentences relating to the virtues and titles of St. Joseph.

Infans imprimebat Joseph ineffabiles jucunditates cum filiali aspectu, affectu et amplexu. (*S. Bern. S.*)

"The child Jesus was a source of ineffable sweetness to St. Joseph. Had he not reason to be enraptured when he beheld the sweet and benign Jesus smiling on him; when he received His endearing caresses, and at each moment some new token of His filial tenderness!" (*St. Bernardin of Sienna.*)

Filius meus sic occultabat deitatis suæ potentiam, ut nisi a me, et quandoque a Joseph sciri non posset.

"So thick was the veil in which my Son enveloped His power and divinity, that to all but Joseph and myself He was unknown." (*Rev. S. Bridget.*)

Ipse patientissimus fuit in paupertate, sollicitus in labore ubi necesse fuit, mansuetissimus ad objurgantes, obedientissimus in obsequio meo. (*Rev. S. Bridg.* l. xi.)

"Joseph was patient in poverty, assiduous in work, full of sweetness towards those who insulted him, full of zeal and devotion in serving me."

TRIDUUM IN HONOUR OF ST. JOSEPH.

Among the following considerations, those may be selected which are most in accordance to the particular object of the feast, or most suited to the special wants of the individual :—

First Consideration.—St. Joseph, Spouse of Mary. (See the first day of the preceding Novena, or the Meditation on the Feast of the Espousals of the most holy Virgin.)

Second Consideration.—St. Joseph, Father of Jesus. (See the second or third day of Novena.)

Third Consideration.—Life of St. Joseph. It affords us an example of justice. (See the fifth day of Novena.)

It is the pattern of an active, contemplative, and mixed life. (See eighth day of Novena.)

It is poor, laborious, and meritorious. (See the Meditation of St. Joseph of Chêne.)

It was singularly favoured. (See the seventh day of Novena.)

It was blessed among the lives of men. (See ninth day of Novena.)

Fourth Consideration.—Holiness of St. Joseph. (See the fourth day of Novena.)

Fifth Consideration.—St. Joseph surpasses all the other saints. (See sixth day of Novena.)

Sixth Consideration.—Death of St. Joseph. (See the first exercise for the feast of the 19th of March.)

Seventh Consideration.—St. Joseph in Heaven. His Glory. (See second exercise for the 19th of March, or the first or second Point of Meditation on the Patronage.)

His Protection. (See third exercise for 19th of March, or the third Point of Meditation on the Patronage.)

Practices for the Feasts.—The saints were the friends of God upon earth, whose cause they maintained. His divine bounty showered upon them His choicest gifts: to honour them is to honour God Himself. This is what our holy faith teaches us. But if this may be said with truth of any saint, to whatever degree of perfection they may have attained, with how much greater reason may it be said of St. Joseph, who was peculiarly favoured by God, and whose whole life was one of self-immolation to the glory of God. The Church, in multiplying the feasts in honour of the glorious patriarch, calls upon us to increase our devotion to him; it would not be following her spirit to remain cold and indifferent whilst she gives us an example of an ever-increasing devotion.

In all the feasts of St. Joseph, whatever may be their special object, you will best contribute to the homage paid to him, by meditation, a worthy reception of the sacraments, alms-deeds, and the consecration of yourself to his service.

Meditation.—The subject may be selected from the

preceding Novena, if the ones given below for the
feasts are not found suitable.   Let not the difficulties
which you may experience in this holy exercise dis-
courage you—have recourse to St. Joseph.   St.
Theresa assures us, that, with the assistance of this
faithful guide, prayer, and even contemplation, will
soon become easy to us.

Confession.—Place your confession under the protection of St. Joseph, and bring to it a hearty desire
of amendment.   The saint takes pleasure in seeing
souls devoted to him acquire that purity which tends
to a closer union with God, according to that promise
of the Holy Spirit: "Qui diligit cordis munditiam
habebit amicum regem." (*Prov.* ch. xxiii.)

Ven. Sister Agatha of the Cross, preparing one day
for confession, was visited by the Blessed Virgin,
with her Divine Son in her arms, and accompanied
by her chaste spouse, St. Joseph.   Full of confusion
at this vision, she asked their pardon for having reprimanded some one too severely : it was immediately
granted, with a celestial sweetness and gentleness.
From this moment she retained a peculiar affection
for St. Joseph.

Communion.—During this most precious moment,
invite Mary and Joseph to keep company with Jesus
in your heart.   Tell them affectionately that to-day
is your Feast of the Presentation, that their Divine
Child has been given to you by the Eternal Father,
that they must ransom Him in bringing to you
purity, represented by the dove, and contrition, represented by the plaint of the turtle-dove.

Alms-deeds.—This work of mercy should accompany your Communion.   Invite to your table St.
Joseph, and with him the Divine Child and His holy

mother, following in this the pious practice of the worthy merchant, whose history we have related above. If the smallness of your means or other obstacles should prevent your doing this, try, at least, to give alms to an old man, a woman, and a child, in honour of the Holy Family.

Consecration of yourself to the service of St. Joseph. —This is a worthy manner of crowning the day: the choice of St. Joseph for your special protector, after Mary, will not fail to draw upon you the choicest blessings. If you are the head of a family, or of a community, follow the example of the College of Sienna, which, in 1707, on the feast of the holy patriarch, solemnly placed itself under his protection, presenting to him the names of the students enclosed in a silver heart, which remains to this day suspended in the chapel, as a perpetual memorial of filial affection. Offer to him in the same manner your heart, and in your heart the hearts of all your family. To render your offering more acceptable to him, make it at the foot of his altar, or before one of his images, reciting the prayer at the end of the third meditation for the 19th of March.

And since the feasts of Jesus and Mary are also those of St. Joseph, particularly those of the first mysteries of our redemption, in which he holds so prominent a place, honour him likewise in these. "I do not know," says St. Theresa, "how one can meditate on the care which the Blessed Virgin took of the Divine Child, without thanking St. Joseph for the care he likewise took of both the mother and the Child."

Besides remembering him on these days, keep with great devotion the following feasts :—

FEAST OF ST. JOSEPH.—MARCH 19.

The 19th of March is the principal feast instituted in the honour of St. Joseph. We find traces of this feast as early as the eighth century, in different parts of Christendom. Gregory XV., by a decree of the Congregation of Rites, extended it to the whole Church.

The special subject brought before us in the liturgy of the day, is the greatness of St. Joseph. Can we better prepare ourselves for the commemoration of the august mystery of the Incarnation, which follows a few days after, than by meditating on him who was entrusted with this most sublime of secrets, and with the care and guardianship of the Son and His mother?

You may contribute to the glory of St. Joseph by the five methods proposed above; namely: Meditation, Confession, Communion, Alms-deeds, and the Consecration of yourself to his service.

EXERCISES DURING THE DAY.

The second or ninth of the preceding Novena, or one of the three following, which may likewise be used as a preparatory triduum:—

FIRST EXERCISE—DEATH OF ST. JOSEPH.

" Precious in the sight of the Lord is the death of His saints.".— *Psalm* cxv. 15.

A reflection on St. Joseph's happy death.—1. How ruly precious was it not, when we consider the immense weight of merit which his virtues had acquired for him, the perfection with which he discharged the functions of the ministry entrusted to him, and finally, the well-grounded hope of the great rewards prepared for him in heaven.   2. His death was ennobled by the presence of the angels and of Jesus and Mary, who remained with him to his last sigh. 3. It was a truly sweet and consoling death, on account of the peace which he enjoyed, the depth and tenderness of his love, and the ineffable consolations which the presence and words of Jesus and Mary were so calculated to impart.   It is, indeed, of him that it may be truly said : " He died in the embraces of the Lord."

To honour his death, imitate his virtues.—1. Pray and labour to make new progress daily in the interior or spiritual life.   2. Make your happiness consist in a perfect conformity to the will of God in all things. 3. Endeavour to acquire a strict union of love and confidence with Jesus and Mary, all the days of your life, that you may find them propitious to you at the hour of death.

Graces to ask of St. Joseph.—See the prayer at the end of the twelfth chapter, First Book.

Practices of devotion and mortification.—1. Mortify your extreme curiosity to see all that is passing, and place a guard over your eyes in honour of St. Joseph, who was content to behold Jesus alone, and never cared to look at any other object.   2. Mortify your taste in some little thing, to honour St. Joseph's poverty.   3. Mortify your desire to speak, in order to honour the prudence with which St. Joseph governed his tongue.   The Blessed Virgin revealed to St. Bridget, " that a useless or impatient word never escaped him."

Spiritual Lecture.—Twelfth chapter of the First Book, and some examples out of the Second.

PRAYER.

Sanctissimæ Genitricis tuæ Sponsi, quæsumus, Domine, meritis adjuvemur, ut quod possibilitas nostra non obtinet, ejus nobis intercessione donetur: qui vivis et regnas in sæcula sæculorum. Amen.

Vouchsafe, O Lord, that we may be helped by the merits of thy most holy mother's spouse, and that what of ourselves we cannot obtain, may be given to us through his intercession. Who livest and reignest, world without end. Amen.

Sentences relating to the death of St. Joseph.

Beati qui in Domino moriuntur. (*Apocal.*)

Voluit Deus ipsum mori ante Dominicam Passionem, ne in morte Christi immenso dolore cruciaretur. (*S. Bern. S.*)

Quantas consolationes, promissiones, illuminationes, inflammationes et æternorum bonorum revelationes accepit in transitu suo a sanctissimâ sponsâ suâ et dulcissimo Filio Dei Jesu! (*Id.*)

"Blessed are the dead who die in the Lord."

"God was pleased to take to Himself St. Joseph before our Saviour's Passion, to spare him the overwhelming grief it would have caused him."

"What consolations, promises, supernatural lights, flames of divine love; what a clear view of eternal joys St. Joseph received in his last moments, from his holy spouse and the most amiable Jesus, the Son of God!"

SECOND EXERCISE.—GLORY OF ST. JOSEPH.

" St. Joseph is the glory and ornament of heaven."—*Hymn.*

1. How sublime is his glory, if we consider his great merits and eminent sanctity. 2. How sublime, if we consider his eminent titles : spouse of the Queen of heaven, reputed father of the King of kings. 3. How sublime, if we consider that God has promised a reward to a cup of cold water given in His name ; for Joseph toiled to the last day of his life, in order to minister to the wants of Jesus.

To honour St. Joseph in his glorified state, imitate his virtues.—1. Endeavour to become daily more closely united to God by love. 2. Perform the particular duties of your state with great perfection; they have been allotted you by God Himself. 3. Often think of heaven, and aspire after that glorious life, in which you hope to enjoy the happiness of seeing and loving God, never again to be separated from Him.

Graces to ask of St. Joseph.—Prostrate at your feet, O glorious saint! I am penetrated with feelings of joy and profound veneration, when I behold you receiving from the adorable Trinity the diadem of virginity, and also the first rank among the heavenly choirs, next to the ever-blessed Queen of virgins. The divine title of the " Father " of Jesus Christ, which was your great privilege here below, must impart additional lustre to your glory in heaven. Pharaoh's courtiers were struck with amazement, seeing Joseph of old invested with the purple, wearing the golden crown and ring of royalty, and seated in the monarch's own chariot. But all those

honours were mere shadows to those which the Most
High has been pleased to bestow upon you in the
celestial court. The blessed in heaven, admiring
the great things that are done for you, pour forth
canticles of praise and thanksgiving to God. I seem
to hear them sing in concert these words: "Glory
to the faithful and prudent servant, whom his Lord
has appointed to reign over His family." How munificent the reward bestowed on you by the Eternal
Father, for your faithful guardianship of His beloved
Son. With what sublime gifts have you not been
endowed by the Holy Ghost, for your devotedness
to His chaste spouse; and how great must be the
honours conferred by the Son, on one whom He
called by the name of father here below. "Father,"
said the young Tobias, "can we ever sufficiently
express our gratitude for all the blessings he has
bestowed on us? The half of all we possess would
not repay him." And Tobias spoke here only of the
services which he received from his guide, during a
very short journey. Ah! surely no one can doubt
for a moment, but that Jesus Christ, who infinitely
surpasses young Tobias both in riches and generosity, has admirably rewarded the care and solicitude
of His adopted father, during a period of thirty
years. May we not even suppose, that in your
favour He changed the laws of nature, by raising,
upon the day of His resurrection, that body which
had been worn out in His own service, and making
it a partner with your soul in glory. I rejoice in
your glory, O great saint! in union with all your
devout clients; obtain for me a holy desire of death,
and an efficacious yearning after my heavenly country, where I hope one day to witness your triumph,

and to pour forth my thanksgiving to the Lord Jesus for all that He has done for you. Amen.

Practices of devotion and mortification.—1. Patience under the tribulations of this life, which are the precious purchase-money of the consolations of heaven. 2. Fidelity in the daily practice of some corporal mortification. 3. Implore pardon of God for all earthly or inordinate attachment.

Spiritual Lecture.—Third chapter, Second Book. Prayer as before.

Sentences relating to the prerogatives of St. Joseph.

Beatæ Virgini debetur cultus hyperduliæ, Josepho summæ duliæ. (*Corn. a Lap.* c. 1 *in Matth.*)

"That species of homage called *hyperdulia*, is given to the Blessed Virgin; and St. Joseph receives that called *dulia*."

Dubitandum non est quod Christus familiaritatem, reverentiam et sublimissimam dignitatem, quam exhibuit illi dum ageret in humanis tanquam filius patri suo, in coelis utique non negavit, sed potius complevit ac consummavit. (*S. Bern. S.*)

"It cannot be doubted that Christ, who, during His life on earth, showed St. Joseph the love and respect of a child, would not only not deny him this affection in heaven, but would complete and perfect it."

Profecto cum Christus dicat : Ubi sum ego, illic et minister meus erit, ille proximior videtur collocandus in coelis, qui vicinior atque fidelior

"Since Christ has said : 'Where I am, there shall also my servant be,' the one who, after Mary, was the most intimate with Him on earth, will be

post Mariam inventus est in terris. (*Gerson.*)

Pie credendum est quod piissimus Filius Dei Jesus, sicut Matrem assumpsit in cœlum corpore et anima gloriosam, sic etiam in die resurrectionis suæ sanctissimum Joseph. (*S. Bern. S.*)

also the nearest to Him in heaven."

" It is piously believed, that as our Lord glorified the body of His Blessed Mother after her death, piety may have led Him to confer the same privilege on St. Joseph on the day of His resurrection."

THIRD EXERCISE.—PATRONAGE OF ST. JOSEPH.

1. St. Joseph's intercession is all-powerful with Jesus, in whose regard he held the place of father. It is all-powerful with Mary, his immaculate spouse. St. Joseph was invested with authority over both. 2. His own characteristic goodness inclines him, independently of everything else, to assist and comfort his devout clients; and being the chief instrument in the work of man's salvation, next to the Blessed Virgin, he bears a truly paternal love to all men. 3. His patronage is liberal and universal; it knows no distinction of age or condition, and readily ministers to all kinds of necessities, whether of soul or body.

Virtues to imitate in St. Joseph, thereby to merit his patronage.—1. Choose him as your special patron for life, but particularly at the awful hour of death. 2. Acquire the habit of invoking him at least twice a-day. 3. Endeavour to inspire others with a devotion to him. The Blessed Virgin expressed her gratitude to St. Theresa, for her zealous exertions in extending this devotion throughout the Church.

Graces to ask of the saint upon choosing him as patron.—O great St. Joseph! whose sublime perfection, power, and glory have entitled you to our veneration, love, and confidence above all the other saints, I, *N.*, in the presence of Jesus, who chose you to be His father, and of Mary, who received you as her spouse, make choice of you this day for my spiritual father, the guide and master of my interior, my model, and my advocate. I resolve never to forget you, and to render you every day of my life at least some slight mark of the honour and confidence to which you are so justly entitled. I now most earnestly conjure you to take me under your special protection, and to admit me into the happy number of your devoted servants. Intercede with Jesus and Mary on my behalf; assist me in all the actions of my life, and do not abandon me for a moment at any time; but I especially implore you to assist and comfort me at the hour of my death. Amen.

Practices of devotion and mortification.—1. Prepare to receive worthily the most holy Sacrament on to-morrow, by an exact examen of conscience, and more than ordinary compunction. 2. Practise fasting or some other austerity. 3. Apply to prayer more closely than usual, and give alms to a poor person.

Spiritual Lecture.—Second chapter of the Second Book.

Prayer as above.

Sentences relating to the virtues and prerogatives of St. Joseph.

Dum vir, dum pater   " A favour solicited by
orat uxorem et natum   a wife or a son, may be

velut imperium reputatur. (*Gerson.*)

Sume igitur peculiarem tuum protectorem amicum bonum, intercessorem potentem sanctum Joseph. (*Gerson.*)

Solum in terris magni consitu coadjutorem fidelissimum. (*S. Bernard.*)

Ite ad Joseph et quidquid vobis dixerit facite. (*Genesis.*)

considered in the light of a command."

"Take St. Joseph for your first patron, your most intimate friend, and most powerful advocate."

"He was the chosen one of all men to be the faithful co-operator in the greatest of all the works of God."

"Go to Joseph, and do all that he shall say to you."

FEAST OF THE ESPOUSAL OF ST. JOSEPH.—JANUARY 23.

The espousals of Joseph and Mary, under whose shadow the sublime mystery of the Incarnation was accomplished, has an intimate connexion with the work of our salvation. It is not, then, astonishing that we should have a day set apart for its special commemoration. The pious Gerson was chosen to be the instrument of its establishment, under the following circumstances. A Canon of Chartres, who had become acquainted with Gerson at the Council of Constance, was at the point of death. This worthy ecclesiastic had a particular devotion to St. Joseph, and wished to leave a last proof of his affection. He left, therefore, in his will, a considerable legacy to his church, with this condition, that on the day of his death a special commemoration should be made of St. Joseph, and that the Holy Sacrifice should be offered in his honour. Gerson was consulted about the execution of the will of the deceased; he proposed three methods; but advised that a petition should be presented to the Holy See, to authorize the celebration of the Feast of the Espousals. The Chapter approved of this idea, and the Holy Father gave his sanction.

Later, Paul III. gave permission, likewise, to the Franciscans and Dominicans to celebrate this feast, with a special office, which was soon adopted in several other churches. An indult of Benedict XIII., in 1725, extended it to all Christendom. It was in consequence of a petition of the Dominicans that this feast was finally established on the 23rd of January, by Paul III. (*See Boll.* 19*th March, and Benedict XIV. de Canonisat. Sanct.*).

Spiritual exercises during the day.—The meditation may be made on the glorious prerogatives of St. Joseph (first day of Novena), or on the following considerations, which will be found suitable.

In your spiritual exercises this day, ask grace to know your vocation, or, if you have already chosen it, ask, through the intercession of St. Joseph, for great fidelity in all the duties of your state. You may use the prayer, Chap. V. No. 2, for this intention.

FEAST OF THE PATRONAGE OF ST. JOSEPH.—THIRD SUNDAY AFTER EASTER.

A decree of the Congregation of Rites has fixed this feast on the third Sunday after Easter; its first origin was among the Carmelites, in 1680. In 1621, in a general chapter of the Carmelites, St. Joseph was chosen patron and father of the whole order. Several churches began, soon after this date, to keep this feast. By virtue of a decree of the 10th September, 1847, it was commanded to be solemnised throughout the Church. Among the Redemptorists, Passionists, Jesuits, and the Society of Mary, it is kept as a double of the first class, with an octave and proper office.

We will give here the decree of the Sovereign Pontiff. The clients of St. Joseph will be glad to find in it a beautiful panegyric, from the pen of Cardinal Patrizzi, of their holy patron.

URBI ET ORBI.

Inclytus Patriarcha Joseph, quem omnipotens Pater singularibus gratiis auxit, ac charismatibus cœlestibus abunde cumulavit, ut Unigeniti Filii sui putativus Pater esset, ac verus sponsus Reginæ mundi et Dominæ angelorum tam sublimis electionis partes omnes, muniaque adeo perfecte explevit; ut boni, fidelisque servi encomium meruerit, et præmia. Etenim memor semper præcellentis dignitatis suæ ac sanctitatis nobilium officiorum queis a divina sapientia proficiebatur, ipsius Dei conciliis et vo-

TO THE CITY AND THE WORLD.

The glorious patriarch Joseph was enriched by the Eternal Father with numberless gifts, and replenished with an abundant supply of grace, in order that he might fulfil the double office of reputed father of the only begotten Son of God, and spouse of the Queen of angels and Mistress of the world. He fulfilled the duties and functions of his state of life so perfectly, that he merited to receive the reward of a good and faithful servant. Having the thought constantly before his mind of the eminent

luntatis alacritate pro-
pemodum inenarrabili in
omnibus indesinenter pa-
ruit, placensque Deo
factus est dilectus, do-
nis gloria et honore
coronatus in cœlis, no-
vum susciperet officium,
nimirum ut copiosis me-
ritis, et orationis suffragio miserrimæ subveniret
hominum conditioni, at-
que validissima interces-
sione, quæ possibilitas
humana obtinere nequit,
mundo impetraret. Hinc
passim misericors vene-
ratur ad Deum mediator,
efficaxque patronus, ejus-
que patrocinii festum cum
officio ac missa longe la-
teque instituitur domi-
nica tertia, quæ a pas-
chalibus gaudiis occurrit.
Verum quod unum adhuc
exoptandum supererat,
nimirum ut officium pa-
trocinii sancti Joseph de
præcepto ad universalem
extenderetur Ecclesiam,
id Eminentissimus et Re-
verendissimus Dominus
cardinalis Constantinus
Patrizzi a sanctissimo

dignity and sacred obli-
gations of the trust con-
fided to him by the Di-
vine Wisdom, he obeyed
with promptitude and
inexpressible joy every
indication of the Divine
Will. By striving to
please God, he became
daily more and more
pleasing in His sight,
till crowned with glory
and honour in heaven,
he received a new office,
that of consoling and
succouring the children
of men, by his continual
prayers and abundant
merits, and to obtain for
them fresh supplies of
grace, by which they are
enabled to persevere in
the way of salvation.
This is the reason why
he is honoured every-
where as a merciful
advocate and a powerful
patron, and that the feast
of his patronage is kept
in several churches, with
a Proper Mass and Office,
on the third Sunday after
Easter. There was only
one thing left to be

Domino nostro Pio Papa IX., humillimis precibus proprio, et aliorum sanctæ Romanæ Ecclesiæ cardinalium ac quam plurium etiam exteriorum fidelium nomine porrectis enixe imploravit. Quas quidem preces apprime conformes singulari pietati suæ erga sanctum Josephum apostolica benignitate excipiens sanctissimus idem Dominus, referenti me subscripto sacrorum Rituum Congregationis secretario, benigne in omnibus annuit præcepitque ut deinceps ab utroque clero Urbis et Orbis sub vito duplicis secundæ classis persolvatur officium proprium cum missa patrocinii sancti Joseph dominica tertia post Pascha, qua impedita alio officio potioris ritus vel majoris dignitatis, indulsit ut officium patrocinii sancti Joseph transferatur ad primam diem liberam juxta rubricas, contrariis non obstantibus quibus-

desired, namely, that the office of St. Joseph should be imposed upon the whole Church. The very eminent and Right Rev. Cardinal Constantine Patrizzi presented a most earnest petition to the Holy Father Pius IX. for this purpose, in his own name and in that of the cardinals of the Holy Roman Church, and of a great number of the faithful, Italians as well as foreigners. The Holy Father receiving these supplications, so conformable to his own devotion towards St. Joseph, with apostolical benignity, upon the report of the secretary, signed by the Congregation of Rites, gave his formal consent to the petition, and ordered that from henceforth the Mass of the Patronage of St. Joseph should be celebrated by the clergy of Rome and of the whole Church, as a double of the second class, on the third Sunday after

cumque. Die 10 Sep- Easter; and if on the said
tembris, 1847. day a feast of greater
solemnity should occur,
it should be transferred
to the first free day conformable to the rubrics.
September 10, 1847.

Spiritual exercise during the day.—The second
and third of the Feast of St. Joseph, and the following
reflections, will serve as subjects for meditation.

Exaltation of St. Joseph.—The exaltation of St.
Joseph is worthy of Jesus; glorious for him; advantageous for us.

1st. *Worthy of Jesus.*—Suarez and other theologians are of opinion, that St. Joseph was one
of those saints who are spoken of as appearing
at Jerusalem at the time of the resurrection of
our Lord, and that to honour His triumph he
then entered into heaven in body as well as
soul. (*Suarez de Myst. Quœst. 29. Bern. de S.*
Pie credendum est quod piissimus Filius Dei
Jesus sicut matrem assumpsit in cœlum corpore et
anima gloriosam sic etiam in die resurrectionis
sanctissimum Joseph.) Without doubt, no one had a
greater claim to this favour. " Was it not just,"
says St. Bernardin of Sienna, " that after having
lived familiarly with Jesus and Mary on earth, he
should reign with them eternally in body and soul
in heaven ?" (Sicut illa sancta familia in laboriosa
vita et amorosa gratia simul vixerunt in terris; sic
in amorosa gloria nunc corpore et anima regnant in
cœlis.—*S. Bern. de S.*) Would our Blessed Saviour
have left in the forgetfulness of the tomb those arms

which had carried, those members whose strength
had been spent in providing subsistence for Himself?
The mere notion of such indifference seems impossible, and contrary to our idea of the tenderness of
the heart of Jesus. Hear the words which St.
Francis of Sales, rejecting all doubt upon this subject,
puts into the mouth of St. Joseph, on the occasion of
the descent of Christ into Limbo : "Remember that
when Thou camest from heaven to redeem mankind,
I received' Thee into my house and into my family,
and as soon as Thou wast born, into my arms. Now
that Thou art about to ascend into heaven, take me
thither also. I received Thee into my family;
receive me also into Thine, whither Thou art now
returning. I carried Thee in my arms; carry me
now in Thine; and as I took care of Thee, and
ministered to Thy support during the course of Thy
life on earth, so take care of me, and sustain me in
that life which is eternal" (19th Entertainment).
This is the language of a saint, and, without doubt,
that of truth also. It was most fitting that the
foster-father of the Saviour should receive this
supreme honour which alone could render his exaltation perfect; let us follow him in spirit, and rejoice
in his triumph.

2nd. *Glorious for him.*—Pharaoh said to the first
Joseph : "Tu eris super domum meam et ad tui
oris imperium cunctus populus obediet, uno tantum
regni solio te præcedam....Ecce constitui te super
universam terram Ægypti....Fecitque eum ascen-
dere super currum suum secundum, clamante præcone
ut omnes coram eo genuflecterent et præpositum esse
scirent universæ terræ Ægypti....Clamavit populus
ad regem alimenta petens. Quibus ille respondit.

Ite ad Joseph." (*Gen.* xli.) "Thou shalt be over
my house, and at the commandment of thy mouth
all the people shall obey; only in the kingly throne
will I be above thee.... Behold, I have appointed
thee over the whole land of Egypt.... He made him
go into his second chariot, the crier proclaiming that
all should bow their knee before him, and that they
should know that he was made governor over the
whole land of Egypt.... When the people cried to
Pharaoh for food, he said: Go to Joseph."

Now, according to St. Bernardin of Sienna, and
other celebrated theologians, the triumph of the
minister of Pharaoh is a type of the triumph of
Joseph, the spouse of Mary. What glory and power
must he not have, then, in heaven! The sun so far
transcends the brightness of the other planets, that
they disappear when it appears; but, according to
St. Gregory of Naz., St. Joseph is the sun in which
God has placed the light of the other saints. According to Bernardin of Bustis, our Lord has given one
key of paradise to St. Joseph, and the other to His
blessed mother, wishing that from henceforth no one
should enter there save through their mediation.
We may add, that this is the spirit of the Church,
who presents him to us as a prudent and faithful
servant, presiding on earth over the Holy Family,
and in heaven over the gifts of God. Without
doubt, says St. Bernardin of Sienna, our Lord, who
lived on earth in such great intimacy with St. Joseph,
who treated him with such respect, and raised him
to so high a dignity, has not changed towards this
august patriarch, but has completed and perfected
the work begun in him. So we have just reason to
say, with the Church, of St. Joseph: "Enter thou

into the joy of the Lord." The joy of celestial
beatitude inundates the hearts of all men, when
they are called to the possession of eternal life; but
to show the abundance of that which St. Joseph
enjoys, he was not merely put in possession of
interior joy, but was plunged into an ocean of
delights, by which he was penetrated and surrounded, and, as it were, submerged into an infinite
abyss.*

Let us unite ourselves to so much glory, and let us
rejoice in his happiness; and, after having given
thanks to our Divine Saviour, who is the source of
all, let us supplicate St. Joseph to make use of his
power in our favour, for it is for us as well as for
himself that he has obtained such credit with
God.

3rd. *Advantageous for us.*—The glory of Joseph
was a homage to his merits, a recompense for
his services; the power which he enjoys is a
resource for our numerous wants.   Our interests
are confided to him, his heart sympathises with
our sorrows; for he, like us, has passed through
this valley of tears, he has experienced all the rigours
of exile, he knows the perils of life, the malice of
the enemies who surround us.   How tenderly, then,

---

* Profecte dubitandum non est; quod Christus familiaritatem,
reverentiam atque sublimissimam dignitatem, quam illi exhibuit,
dum ageret in humanis, tanquam filius patrisno in cœlis utique
non negavit, quin potius complevit et consummavit. . . . Unde
non immerito in verbo, proposito a Domino, subinfertur.   Intra
in gaudium Domini tui.   Unde licet gaudium æternæ beatitudinis in cor hominis intret, maluit tamen Dominus ei dicere.
Intra in gaudium ut mystice innuatur, quod gaudium illud non
solum in eo sit intra, sed undique illum circumdans et ipsum
velut abyssus infinita submergens.   (*S. Bern. S.*)

does he receive those who confide in him—with
what zeal does he recommend them to Jesus and
Mary. Father of one, spouse of the other, he fears
not to be refused; for the requests of a father to a
son, a husband to a wife, is a command, and not a
prayer.* St. Francis of Sales says, in the same
entertainment: "How happy should we be, were we
worthy to have a share in his intercessions, for our
Blessed Lady and her glorious Son will refuse him
nothing. If only we have confidence, we shall certainly obtain a great increase in every virtue, especially in those which he possessed in a very high
degree, namely, extreme purity of body and mind,
the lovely virtue of humility, constancy, strength,
and perseverance—virtues which enable us to overcome our enemies in this life, and which will merit
for us the eternal enjoyment of the recompense prepared for those who follow the example of St. Joseph
in these virtues, which will be nothing less than the
perpetual enjoyment of the clear vision of the Father,
of the Son, and of the Holy Ghost." We will conclude with these words of Gerson: "Take St. Joseph
for your first patron, for your most intimate friend.
You, above all, happy inhabitants of Villedieu,
among whom this great saint has chosen a sanctuary,
come often to his shrine to renew the offering of
yourself and of your family. Go to Mary through
Joseph; and assisted by so devoted a patron, so
tender a mother, you will obtain from the heart of
Jesus all your desires, for time and eternity."

* Quanta est fiducia, quanta vis impetrandi, quia dum vir,
dum pater orat uxorem et natum, velut imperium reputatur.
(*Gers. in Orat. Joseph.*)

FEAST OF ST. JOSEPH OF CHENE.—AUGUST 24.

As we have said above, in the last chapter of the
Second Book, the sanctuary of Villedieu was established on the 24th of August. The inhabitants
of the country keep the anniversary with great
solemnity; a large concourse of strangers are attracted
thither by their devotion to St. Joseph, and by
the plenary indulgence granted by his Holiness
Pius IX.

The following considerations may perhaps assist
these fervent crowds to pass the day profitably.

Considerations on the life of St. Joseph.—The life
of St. Joseph was poor, laborious, and meritorious; let
us study it, and try to sanctify our own.

1st. *The life of St. Joseph was poor.*—Although
this holy patriarch was descended from the royal
family, which, for several centuries, had reigned over
Judea, he was born in poverty; his ancestors had
experienced many reverses, which had reduced them
to great indigence; and, to procure a scanty subsistence, St. Joseph was obliged to embrace the trade of
an artizan. His alliance with Mary did not better
his condition, for her ancestors likewise had been
unfortunate. The presence of the Saviour only increased their needs. From rich He had made Himself poor, in order that He might enrich us by His
poverty. He did not, therefore, bring to His family
what He despised for Himself; on the contrary, He
did but increase their poverty: for, as Bossuet says,
in his admirable panegyric of St. Joseph: "Wherever

Jesus enters, He enters with His cross; He brings
with Him His crown of thorns, and shares them
with those who love Him. Joseph and Mary were
poor, but, till His coming, they had never been left
houseless. But as soon as this Child came into the
world, they had to shelter themselves in a stable.
Joseph, by his poverty, was confounded with so
many others, who have no other resource than the
labour of their hands—no other riches than their
health and the strength of their arm; but his great
and generous heart knew how to aspire after solid
happiness, unknown by those whose brilliant career
is envied by the multitude." " Soft and voluptuous
souls," continues Bossuet, " Jesus loves not to be
with you; His poverty is ashamed of your luxury;
His flesh, prepared for so many torments, cannot
abide your extreme delicacy. He seeks for strong
and courageous souls, who will not refuse to carry His
cross, and who will not blush to be the companions
of His poverty and misery. Because those who are
contented with a scanty pittance, earned by the sweat
of their brow, are generally far more grateful towards
God than those who live in riches and abundance, and
who, forgetful of their souls and of eternity, think
only of their own interests and of their sensual gra-
tification."

Console yourselves, then, you to whom God has
refused the riches of this world; He treats you as
His best friends, in calling you to tread thus in the
footsteps of your Saviour. When you are tempted to
complain of the hardships you suffer, look at Joseph:
are you as poor as he was? Enter in spirit into the
house at Nazareth; you see everywhere indications
of poverty and indigence; and ask yourself: Am I

worthy of a richer dwelling than Jesus, Mary, and Joseph?

2nd. *The life of St. Joseph was laborious.*—Holy Scripture tell us that St. Joseph was an artisan; and it is generally believed that he followed the trade of a carpenter, in which Jesus likewise assisted him.

But why so hard a life? This is the question we often ask ourselves when we think of the trials of our state : let us ask it to-day in the presence of these two poor artisans, who are bending under the weight of their constant toil, we shall receive a salutary answer to our complaints and to our murmurs : Jesus and Joseph earn the bread they eat by the sweat of their brow, because they are the children of Adam, and they conform to the sentence passed against him and his posterity. Have we not incurred the same penalty? Are we not liable to the same sentence, since we have added to the sin of our first parents many and far more grievous crimes?

Jesus, by His voluntary toil, expiates these sins of which we have been guilty : ought we, then, to leave Him to tread the way of sorrows alone, and seek only for an idle and useless life? Jesus and Joseph embrace the life of artizans : learn, then, not to blush at your condition, how lowly soever it may be, and not to despise others if you yourself belong to a higher class. The Divine Child is pleased to learn the trade of His foster-father. Does He not, then, condemn those who blush at the humble condition of their parents, and would rather do nothing than render themselves useful in the employments of a low station.

Nevertheless, Jesus and Joseph, descendants of Solomon, remain during the whole of their lives

among the labouring class. Mary, equally illustrious by her birth, serves with pleasure these two
poor artizans, and shares in their humiliations.
What eloquent lessons upon the distinctions of this
world are found at Nazareth! and what cause of con-
demnation to those who, proud of their position, fortune, or birth, do not deign to work, and think themselves justified in leading a useless life, and despising
the labouring classes of society!

It is not the trade of a man which degrades him,
but the corruption of his heart, by which he separates
himself from the Author of all good, to attach himself
to sin. The eyes of the Almighty look with complacency upon the humble and submissive heart. His
anger pursues the guilty who resist His commands
and despise His providence.

Let us examine whether our lives are industrious
and laborious; and yet more, let us try the inward
dispositions of our hearts: Would we not willingly
exchange the labours and trials we meet with here
below, for the pleasures even of a guilty and sensual
life?

3rd. *The life of St. Joseph was meritorious.*—This
great saint, condemned to a life of privation and toil,
submitted with joy and thankfulness to the designs
of Divine Providence. When his thoughts turned to
the ancient splendour and opulence of his ancestors, a
cry of loving resignation escaped immediately from
his lips. "The Lord," said he, with holy Job, "gave,
and the Lord hath taken away: blessed be the name
of the Lord" (i. 21). In this manner, St. Joseph
sanctified his indigence and his prayers, and turned
his trials and contradictions to profit by increasing
his merits.

Happy the poor who take this great saint for their example, and who submit with joy to the privations of their state, painful, it is true, for the moment, but fruitful and sweet for eternity! Happy those who eat not with murmurings the bread gained by the sweat of their brow, and who do not despair under the toil and heat of the day; but who, on the contrary, always humble and submissive, accept the privations and sacrifices imposed upon them as so many favours of Divine Providence! The children of this world are inebriated with the transitory joy of this world, and aspiring only after terrestrial joys, shun all trouble and pain; but this life passes like a dream: at the moment of their waking, they will find nothing but sorrow, bitterness, and deception; they will have nothing to present to God, who is going to take account of their actions, and to render to each according to their merits. How different will it be with the simple laborious man, who has toiled cheerfully during this short life! His days have been full days, because he has taken advantage of the numerous occasions which presented themselves of working, suffering, and mortifying himself; already he contemplates with the eye of faith that eternity where, for a moment of trial, we receive an eternal weight of glory; where, for a small sacrifice, we enjoy an incomparable felicity; where, for our fidelity of a few years, we enter into possession of infinite happiness. These considerations fortify his mind and raise his courage; he embraces with a joyful heart the humble and laborious condition in which he is placed, not only because it is the lot assigned him by God, but, also, because it is more advantageous for him, and more conducive to his eternal interests.

If we find in ourselves these feelings of conformity to Divine Providence, let us offer our thanks to God at the altar of St. Joseph; but if, on the contrary, we find that we have a great aversion for suffering, and a great desire to escape from toil and trouble, let us throw ourselves at the feet of St. Joseph, begging of him to fortify our hearts, and to obtain for us detachment from the transitory joys of this life, and ardent desires for the true and solid joys of heaven.

CHAPTER III.

Confraternities and Associations in Honour of St. Joseph.

THE utility of associations is beyond all question; they unite in favour of the same cause the different members of which they are composed, and the result is generally proportioned to the number and union of the associates. It may be said that every nation is but a vast association with one common interest, under the shadow of which smaller societies and different branches of industry are formed; established it is true for the private interest, but which concur to the public good, and in return for the protection afforded them, maintain the state in opulence and life. These associations exist in the Church, which is the work of God, and therefore the most wisely constituted of all societies. We find them in every age, under the names of confraternities, societies, congregations, &c.; their organization and their means vary according to the different ends proposed by them; but as long as they preserve the spirit of their institution, they bring forth fruit to eternal life, and from time to time lend a powerful aid to the Church, in the warfare in which she is perpetually engaged against the world. Whilst, on the one hand, these closely-united phalanxes of Christian warriors oppose a barrier to the progress of vice, they, on the other hand, lend a friendly support to the weak and feeble, and secure the triumph of justice by the lustre of their examples. By protecting these associations, the Church contributes to her own support. Amongst those highly favoured by her in our own days, several have been placed under the patronage of St. Joseph, and have proposed to themselves, as one of their objects, the extension of the devotion to the holy patriarch. In a work like ours they cannot fail to find a place. By making them known, we shall point out to the clients of our saint an excellent way of honouring him; and we shall thus contribute to the end which we proposed to ourselves in publishing this little work.

The Confraternity of the Bona Mors claims the first place, from its antiquity and importance : we shall therefore give it the same precedence as in former editions. About the others we shall not speak at any length, contenting ourselves with a short notice of them, sufficient to make them known to those who might wish to become members. For further particulars, we refer them to the directors of the several associations.

I.—CONFRATERNITY OF THE BONA MORS.

Its Origin, and the End for which it was established.
If the whole life of a Christian should be a prepara-

tion for death, the best and most infallible means for
promoting that all-important object is the frequent
recollection of Christ's passion, especially of His last
agony upon the cross, of the bitter anguish and deso-
lation of His most blessed mother on receiving His
last sigh, and of the privileged death of St. Joseph,
who was so fortunate as to expire actually in the
arms of Jesus and Mary. These means become still
more efficacious in those associations where so many,
united together in the bonds of charity, continually
implore for one another the most precious of all
graces—that of dying in the peace of the Lord. Such
at all times has been the object of the confraternity
or congregation commonly called the Bona Mors,
established in the "Gesu" at Rome, in 1648, by F.
Vincent Caraffa, seventh General of the Society of
Jesus, and soon after confirmed by Pope Innocent X.
From Rome, the new confraternity, together with the
devotion which was the object of it, was diffused
throughout Italy and other countries, especially since
Benedict XIII., in 1729, permitted the indulgences
which are attached to it to be also enjoyed by the
members of other associations formed on the same
plan. This grant was again confirmed by Pius VII.,
in 1821; and in 1827, Leo XII. granted to the fathers
by whom it was conducted the power of affiliating to
it all the other confraternities of the same nature
already established throughout the Christian world,
and of making them thereby partakers of the same
spiritual favours. Although the Confraternity of the
Bona Mors has been established at Rome under the
invocation of our Saviour agonising on the cross and
of our Lady of Sorrows, nevertheless, St. Joseph has
been chosen for a secondary patron. This is the reason

why we have placed this exercise in a work consecrated to him, and which contains the principal
devotions practised in his honour.

Practices observed by the members.—1. The first
thing to be done in order to establish the congregation canonically, is to obtain the consent of the
bishop of the diocese.   Then, in order to enjoy the
advantage of the indulgences granted by the Sovereign
Pontiffs, it will be necessary to obtain from the
director of the congregation of the Bona Mors, at the
Gesu in Rome, a diploma of affiliation, and to mention to him also the particular Sunday which has
been fixed for it, besides the Friday or any other
convenient day for the general meeting once a
month.

Persons wishing to join the confraternity, will
give in their names to the director to be inscribed in
the catalogue, after which they will receive a ticket
of admission, containing the act of consecration which
is made use of by the associates.   It is as follows :—

" Most sweet Jesus ! adorable Saviour ! confiding in
the merits of Thy bitter Passion and cruel agony on
the cross, I offer to Thee my whole being, as a sacrifice of love and gratitude ; I most humbly supplicate
Thee, by Thine infinite merits, and by the intercession of Mary and Joseph, to grant me, as well as all
the members of this congregation, the inestimable
grace of a happy death ; by which we may attain to
the possession of eternal bliss, that we love Thee for
all eternity.   Amen."

One Sunday of each month, and all Fridays
throughout the year, are the usual meeting days of
the associates.   The Sunday meeting, when held in
the parochial church, is the most solemn.   On these

occasions, after reciting the *Veni, sancte Spiritus,* the celebrant gives a short instruction or exhortation on death; then the following prayers are said for all the associates, whether living or deceased:

"Adorable Lord Jesus! we conjure Thee, by Thy sacred wounds, by Thy precious agony and death, and by the intercession of Thy holy mother and St. Joseph, to grant us, and all the members of this congregation, an invincible courage and fortitude in repelling the attacks of our spiritual enemies, perfect contrition for our sins, persevering self-denial, and fidelity to grace; and vouchsafe to crown all Thy other favours by bestowing on us the precious blessing of a holy and happy death, that thus all Thy sufferings may not prove fruitless, and that Thy most precious blood, the great price of our ransom, may not have been shed in vain.   Amen.

"O my crucified Saviour! hope and refuge of those who are in their last agony, by the inconceivable torments which Thou wert pleased to undergo upon the cross, vouchsafe to assist all our associates in their last moments with such abundant and efficacious graces, that the enemy of Thy glory and their salvation may not prevail against them, but that they may be worthy to obtain admission into the eternal tabernacles, where with all the elect they may have the happiness to love and enjoy Thee for an endless eternity.   Amen.

"Omnipotent God! who willest the salvation of all men, we beseech Thy infinite goodness, by the merits of our Blessed Redeemer's Passion, and the intercession of the Blessed Virgin and St. Joseph, to grant to all the deceased members of this congregation the bliss of being speedily admitted into the

mansions of eternal glory, where Thou livest and
reignest world without end. Amen."

Then follows exposition of the most holy Sacrament, during which the following hymn is sung, to
obtain the blessing of a worthy communion at the
hour of death :

> "Ave verum corpus natum,
>   De Maria Virgine ;
> Vere passum immolatum
>   In grace pro homine :
> Cujus latus perforatum
>   Fluxit unda et sanguine :
> Esto nobis prægustatum
>   Mortis in examine.

" ℣. Panem de cœlo præstitisti eis. Alleluia.
" ℞. Omna delectamentum in se habentum.
Alleluia.
" ℣. Thou hast given them bread from heaven.
" ℞. Abounding with ineffable sweetness."

THE PRAYER.

Deus qui nobis sub
sacramentum mirabili
passionis tuæ memoriam
reliquisti ; tribue quæsumus, ita nos corporis et
sanguine tui sacra myste-
ria venerari, ut redemp-
tionis tuæ unctum nobis
jugiter sentiamus. Qui
vivis, &c.

O God, who in this
wonderful sacrament hast
left us a memorial of Thy
passion ; grant us so to
reverence the sacred mys-
teries of Thy sacred body
and blood, that our souls
may be always sensible
of the fruit of Thy redemption Who livest,
&c.

Interveniat pro nobis quæsumus, Domine Jesu Christe, nun cet in hora mortis nostræ, apud tuum clementiam beata Virgo Maria mater tua, cujus sacratissimam animam in hora passionis tuæ, doloris gladius pertransivit.

Sanctissimæ Genitricis tuæ sponsi, quæsumus Domine meritis adjuvemur, ut quod possibilitas nostra non obtinet, ejus nobis intercessione donetur : qui vivis et regnas in cum Deo Patre, in unitate Spiritus Sancti Deus, per omnia sæcula sæculorum. Amen.

℣. Benedicamus Domino.
℟. Deo gratias.
℣. Fidelium animæ per misericordiam Dei requiescant in pace.

℟. Amen.

We beseech thee, O Lord Jesus Christ, that the Blessed Virgin Mary may effectually intercede for us with Thy clemency, both now and at the hour of our death, who at the hour of Thy passion had her most holy soul pierced with the sword of sorrow.

We beseech Thee, O Lord, that we may be assisted by the merits of the spouse of Thy most holy mother, and that what we cannot obtain may be granted to us by His intercession, who livest and reignest with God the Father, in the unity of the Holy Ghost, world without end. Amen.

℣. Let us bless the Lord.
℟. Thanks be to God.
℣. May the souls of the faithful departed, through the mercy of God, rest in peace.
℟. Amen.

The following is sung before or during Benediction:—

Bone Pastor, panis vere,
Jesu, nostrî miserere :
Tu nos pasce, nos tuere;
Tu nos bona fac videre
In terrâ viventium.

Jesu! Shepherd of the sheep,
Thou Thy flock in safety keep ;
Living bread! Thy life supply,
Strengthen us, or else we die :
Fill us with celestial grace.

Tu qui cuncta scis et vales
Qui nos pascis.hîc mortales
Tuos ibi commensales,
Cohæredes et sodales
Fac sanctorum civium.

Thou who feedest us below !
Source of all we have or know !
Grant that with Thy saints above,
Sitting at the feast of love,
We may see Thee face to face.

Or,

O salutaris Hostia,
Quæ cœli pandis ostium,
Bella premunt hostilia;
Da robur, fer auxilium.

Or,

O saving.victim ! opening wide
The gate of heav'n to man below,
Our foes press on from every side,
Thine aid supply, thy strength bestow.

Uni trinoque Domino
Sit sempiterna gloria,
Qui vitam sine termino
Nobis donet in patriâ.
Amen.

To Thy great name be
endless praise,
Immortal Godhead, one
in three!
Oh! grant us endless
length of days
In our true native land
with Thee.

℣. Benedicamus Domino.

℟. Deo gratias.

℣. Fidelium animæ
per misericordiam Dei
requiescant in pace.

℟. Amen.

℣. Thanks be to God.

℟. Let us bless our
Lord.

℣. May the souls of
of the faithful departed,
through the mercy of
God, rest in peace.

℟. Amen.

N.B.—For less solemn occasions, the devotional
exercises marked for Sunday may be retrenched at
pleasure.

On the Sundays which are appointed for the
solemn meeting as above described, it would be
desirable for the associates to make some particular
preparation for death, according to each one's devotion. We here give a method which may be used
with advantage. It consists in putting yourself in
the dispositions in which you would wish to be found
at the hour of death, and in making use of those
devotions which you would wish to make use of then.

1. On awaking in the morning, imagine that your
guardian angel addresses you in the words of the
Prophet Isaias to King Ezechias: "Take order with

thy house, for thou shalt die and not live" (*Isaias,*
xxxviii. 1). Ponder these words whilst dressing,
and return thanks to God for having given you time
to prepare for death. Perform all your morning
devotions with as much fervour as if you were certain
you should not survive the day. At your morning
prayer, offer your heart to God, together with all
your thoughts, words, actions, and sufferings, whether of mind or body, in union with the bitter agony
of Christ Jesus expiring on the cross; and beseech of
Him, through the merits of His well-beloved Son,
and the intercession of the Blessed Virgin and St.
Joseph, to give you every necessary grace in order to
make a salutary preparation for death.

2. Prostrate before a crucifix, or, if possible, in the
presence of the most holy Sacrament, reflect calmly
and seriously upon the following points : The blessing of life is still granted to me, but how soon shall
all trace of my existence have passed away for
ever ! .... I shall die, as well as such and such a
friend.... How shall I then esteem all that is most
prized by the world and the flesh—riches, honour,
and pleasures ?.... What shall be then my estimation
of virtue?....Am I ready to appear before God ?....
What is the state of my conscience?....Is there
nothing in me which is opposed to the love of
God, or that would prevent me from dying in His
love ?....Do I at this moment cherish any dangerous affection or any lurking aversion in my
heart ?....Have I paid all my debts, or withheld
from my neighbour that which justly belongs to
him ?....Have I endeavoured to make reparation
for the injury I may have done him in his person or
character?....Have I arranged all my temporal

affairs, and were I this moment summoned to appear before the judgment-seat of God, am I free to attend solely to the all-important affair of my eternity?.... Answer all these questions, or any others your conscience may suggest; and having discovered whatever may prove a source of uneasiness to you, were you to die before the end of the day, resolve firmly to apply an immediate remedy to it.

3. Penetrated with these sentiments, make your confession as if it were to be your last; and should you feel any particular uneasiness about any one of your past sins, set your conscience at rest by confessing it now again with greater exactness and contrition than ever.

4. Receive the holy Communion as viaticum. Resolve to be scrupulously exact in obeying the good inspirations you may receive from our blessed Lord for the good of your soul. Beg of Jesus Christ crucified to establish and fortify you in the holy dispositions which are requisite in order to die happily, and conjure Him to form your death on the model of His own. Address yourself then to Mary, as to your good mother and advocate, and ask her to assist you in your last moments. Recur, also, to the intercession of St. Joseph, as protector of the agonizing and patron of a happy death; and conclude these preparatory acts by the following spiritual testament, composed chiefly by St. Charles Borromeo:—

✠

"In the name of the Father, and of the Son, and of the Holy Ghost. Amen.

"I, *N. N.*, a miserable sinner, redeemed by the most precious blood of Jesus Christ, being uncertain as to the hour of my death, now resolve, for the love of God and my own eternal salvation, to make the following acts with all the fervour of my soul, as a preparation for appearing before the tribunal of the sovereign Judge.

1. "In the presence of my omnipotent Creator, and the whole court of heaven, I protest that it is my ardent desire and firm determination, with the aid of divine grace, to live and die a member of the holy Roman Catholic Church, and to preserve to my last sigh the same faith of which I now make a solemn profession.

2. "I fully and most cheerfully pardon all my enemies, for the love of Jesus Christ; firmly hoping, through His infinite mercy, to obtain forgiveness of all my sins, which I detest from the bottom of my heart, because they have offended His adorable sanctity and infinite goodness.

3. "To the five precious wounds of my amiable Saviour I commend my soul; to Him it belongs by every title. I beg of Him now to receive it as the work of His hands, and the purchase of His blood, that, at its departure out of this world, it may find an asylum in His sacred heart. My body I consign again to the earth, whence it sprung, until that period when God, in His infinite goodness, shall be pleased to resuscitate and reunite it to my soul, and mercifully introduce it into the mansions of everlasting peace. I also desire to be made a partaker in all the prayers and good works which shall be performed after my death in the Confraternity of the 'Bona Mors,' in those of the Sacred Hearts of

Jesus and Mary, and in all other pious associations, to the end of time.

4. "I most ardently desire to receive the holy viaticum immediately previous to my death; and I most humbly entreat of my Divine Redeemer not to refuse me this happiness, that my soul, being nourished and fortified by this heavenly bread, may terminate its journey to eternity in security and peace.

5. "Having bequeathed my soul to God and my body to earth, a few short moments of time now only remain to me : I consecrate them entirely to you, O my Jesus ! I desire no longer to live but in you, and by you. Ah ! do not refuse me grace to love and serve you to the end, and to expire with your sweet and saving name upon my lips.

6. "I choose the ever-blessed mother of my Saviour-God as my powerful protectress. She is the refuge of sinners ; I commend myself, with filial confidence, to her maternal tenderness, both now and at the hour of my death. I also specially recommend myself to the glorious St. Joseph, the patron of the agonizing. May I not cease to invoke the august names of Jesus, Mary, and Joseph, during my last agony !

7. "I sincerely thank my holy angel-guardian for his charitable attention to my interests during my whole life, and I earnestly ask his powerful aid in struggling against the enemy of my soul at the hour of death. Finally, I humbly beg, O my Divine Redeemer ! that you would be graciously pleased to accept of this my last will and testament. I now once more ratify and confirm it in your sacred presence, and implore the graces necessary to persevere in the same dispositions to my last sigh ; and

that during my last conflict, neither life, nor death, nor hell, nor any other creature, temptation, or accident, shall be able to separate me from the love of God in Christ Jesus our Lord. In these dispositions I desire and hope to die on the day and at the hour by you decreed, that I may live eternally with you in heaven. Amen."

4. On the evening of the same day you will make a short reflection on the sacrament of extreme unction, and receive it spiritually. For this purpose, you will apply your crucifix to all the parts which are usually anointed, saying at each : "May our Lord, by His tender mercy, pardon me all the sins I have committed by my sight, hearing," &c., &c. ... In conclusion, you will place the sacred image on your heart, saying : "Divine Jesus! pardon all the thoughts, affections, and desires of this poor weak heart, which have not been for Thee alone ; pardon all its ingratitude, and deign to apply to it all the satisfaction and merits of Thine own adorable heart.

5. The last exercise for this day, before retiring to rest, shall be the recital of the prayers of the agonizing, at least a part of them. When lying down, reflect that many persons who now, like you, are retiring to rest in good health, and not thinking of death, will actually die this very night ; and that, perhaps, even you yourself will be among the number of those who will never see to-morrow ! Enter your bed as you would your tomb, saying : "Into thy hands, O God, I commend my spirit ;" and, after having made such acts as you would wish to do were you actually about to expire, repeat the saving names of Jesus, Mary, and Joseph, with as great fervour as you hope to do when breathing your last. Should

you awaken in the course of the night, I would recommend you a very pious practice, and which, doubtless, if observed not only on the day of preparation for death, but every day of your life, will bring you much peace and holy confidence at the hour of death. This practice consists in rising from bed, should you awake in the night, and, prostrate, adoring our Divine Redeemer, really present in the most adorable Sacrament of His love. For that purpose you can transport yourself in spirit to some church where the most holy Sacrament reposes during the night, and recite the following prayer :

"Ave verum, corpus natum," &c. ; or, "I adore thee, O true body of Jesus ! which was born of the Virgin Mary; which has truly suffered and been immolated on the cross for the salvation of men; whose side was pierced with a lance, whence issued forth water and blood. Grant us grace to receive Thee worthily at the hour of death. O sweet Jesus! O merciful Jesus! O Jesus, Son of the Virgin Mary, have mercy on us. Amen."

This earnest and persevering petition during so many years, can neither be rejected nor forgotten; it will surely obtain for you the most precious of all graces next to final perseverance—that of a holy and fervert Communion at the approach of your last hour; and as an immediate preparation for a saintly death, what means can be better calculated to insure a favourable issue at that most awful and most decisive of all moments ?

Indulgences.—1. A plenary on being admitted as a member, provided the sacraments are approached, and the usual prayers recited for the intentions of the Church. 2. At the hour of death. 3. Any one Friday

of each month. 4. Christmas Day, Epiphany, Easter
Sunday, Ascension, Pentecost, Trinity Sunday, Corpus
Christi, the Immaculate Conception, Nativity, Annunciation, Purification, Assumption, St. John the Baptist, St. Joseph, Feasts of Apostles, and of All Saints.
All these indulgences are plenary. 5. Each time a
member assists at the public devotions of this confraternity, seven years and seven quarantines. 6. Each
time a member performs any of the following good
works, one year's indulgence : attending a funeral ;
visitation of the sick poor; reciting a Pater and Ave,
kneeling if possible, for the sick or departed ; visiting
those in prison ; hearing Mass on a week day ; nightly
examen of conscience. 7. Every day in Lent, and on
other days when the stations are performed at Rome,
as found at the beginning of the Mass of the day in
the Roman Missal, by visiting a church of the confraternity, and there saying the usual prayers, the
same indulgences are gained as would be by visiting
the churches at Rome where the stations are performed : the indulgence for each day of the stations
is ten years and ten quarantines. All the above-
named indulgences are applicable to the souls in
purgatory ; they were granted by Benedict XIII. to
perpetuity. Those persons not residing near the
church of the Confraternity of Bona Mors, may gain
the same indulgences by visiting their parochial
church, and performing there, as nearly as possible,
the same exercises as those made use of at the church
of the confraternity.

Abstract of the Rules.—1. All persons anxious to
honour in a special manner the death of our Divine
Lord upon the cross, and the dolours of His sorrow-
stricken mother assisting at His last agony, having

got their names inscribed in the catalogue, will offer up all their good works in union with the associates, in order to obtain for each the grace of a happy death: this will be done kneeling before a crucifix. 2. They will recite daily five Paters and Aves for the same intention, before an image of Jesus Christ crucified, and His afflicted mother. 3. They will endeavour to receive holy Communion at least one Friday in each month, for the same intention, and every Friday if possible. 4. Every Friday they will perform some act of mortification in memory of the agony of Jesus, and the dolours of His blessed mother, offering up all the actions of that day for the same intention. 5. All will make an effort to attend the public meetings as regularly as possible : those who cannot conveniently do so, should perform some similar devotion in private. 6. On hearing of the death of one of the members, each should offer up a Communion, or some prayer or good work, for the repose of the soul of the deceased.

These rules do not bind under pain of sin; but those who neglect them are of course deprived of their share in the communication of all good works accomplished by the associates.

II.—CONFRATERNITY OF ST. JOSEPH,

Established at the Church of St. Nizier, at Lyons.

The aim of this confraternity is—1. To honour in a special manner the glorious patriarch St. Joseph, as the head of the Holy Family, and to put this parish under his protection. 2. To preserve and strengthen faith among men. 3. To induce married people mutually to honour each other, and to live holily.   4. To give to those who aim at true piety a perfect example in the virtues of the holy patriarch.

His Holiness Pope Gregory XVI. has granted to this confraternity the following indulgences, applicable to the dead :—

Plenary Indulgences.—The day of reception, the hour of death, January 1st, March 19th. Indulgence of sixty days for every pious work performed with devotion.

His Holiness has likewise granted the favour of a privileged altar to all the Masses said at any of the altars of St. Nizier for deceased members. To become a member of this confraternity, it is only requisite to have one's name inserted in the registers of the confraternity.

III.—Association of Perpetual Devotion to St. Joseph.

The aim of this association, which Pius IX., by a rescript of the 20th of January, 1856, has authorised and enriched with indulgences, is to honour St. Joseph every day of the year; and since the year is composed of 365 days, an equal number of associated members choose a day on which to offer a special homage to our saint.   Those who wish to enter this congregation have their names inscribed in a register kept for this purpose, with the day they have chosen, and receive a ticket of the confraternity, on which their names and the day chosen are written.   If the number of the associated should exceed 365, two members may have the same day; if, on the contrary, there should be fewer members than days of the year, each person may take two or more days of the year. Thirty-one persons would suffice to form an association, if each took one day in the month.

The Association of the Perpetual Devotion is a new fountain of grace opened to the faithful; to endeavour to extend it, is to procure the protection of the great saint in whose honour it is founded.

Exercises of the Association.—The associated of the Perpetual Devotion should, at their convenience, perform the following exercises on the day assigned to them :—1. Confess and communicate; if prevented, they should supply by a hearty act of contrition and a spiritual Communion. 2. Hear with devotion the holy Mass, in memory of the presentation of the Child Jesus in the temple. 3. Meditate for at least a quarter of an hour on the sufferings and sorrows of St. Joseph. 4. Endeavour to keep recollected during the day, and to think from time to time of St. Joseph. 5. Perform in his honour some act of mortification, or some work of spiritual or corporal charity; say the exercise of his Seven Dolours and Seven Joys, in the Third Book, chap. 1, No. viii. 6. Finish the day by a visit to the blessed Sacrament, and by the offering of your heart to St. Joseph.

Indulgences granted by his Holiness to the members of the association :—

Plenary Indulgences.—1. The day of admission. 2. The day chosen for the exercises of the Perpetual Devotion. 3. At the hour of death. 4. The 19th of March, Feast of St. Joseph; the third Sunday after Easter, Feast of his Patronage; 23rd of January, Feast of the Espousals of the Blessed Virgin and St. Joseph. 5. The feasts of the Purification, Annunciation, Assumption, Nativity, and of the Immaculate Conception of the Blessed Virgin.

N.B.—To gain these indulgences it is necessary to confess, communicate, and pray for the usual intentions.

Indulgences of seven days and seven quarantines once a day, for the performance of any of the practices mentioned above.

Ticket of the Congregation.

N—— has chosen for the exercises of the Perpetual Devotion to St. Joseph, the day or the days following:—

January.........	July.............
February	August..........
March....	September...,...
April............	October.........
May.............	November......
June...	December......

Inscribed the —— the day of ——, 186 , in the register of the Association.

           Director——————.

CHAPTER IV.

Manner of Sanctifying the Month of March, and of Extending the Devotion to St. Joseph.

WE have already said, that the two principal means of honouring St. Joseph, are to consecrate the month of March to his honour, and to labour for the extension of this devotion. We will give some details about these two practices, which will form a suitable conclusion to a work undertaken for the glory of this great saint.

Month of St. Joseph.

This is the name given by several devout Christians to the month of March, which they now consecrate to his honour.   This devotion commenced a few years ago, and is already wide-spread, and brings forth abundant fruits.

The aim is self-evident; it is simply to honour St. Joseph.   The means are easy : at the beginning of the month prescribe to yourself certain prayers and practices, and, if possible, erect a little altar of St. Joseph.   If a parish or community practise these devotions, they may join to the former, hymns and a consideration under the form of lecture or meditation. By these means, St. Joseph will receive the same honours as the Blessed Virgin during the month of May.   The following is a table of the exercises best suited for every day of the month :—

March 1.

Consideration.—First motive of honouring St. Joseph—the Example of our Blessed Lord (First Part, chap. i.).

Hymn.—Te Joseph celebrent (Hymn iii.).

Prayer.—Blessed St. Joseph (Pr. 7).

[One or two prayers only are named in this list; others may be used according to time and devotion.]

March 2.

Consideration.—Second motive—Example of the Blessed Virgin (chap. ii. part 1).

Hymn.—O custos matris Domini (Hymn ii.).

Prayer.—O holy St. Joseph! father and guardian (Pr. 2).

March 3.

Consideration.—Third motive—Example of the Angels (chap. iii. part 1).
Hymn—Cœlitum Joseph (Hymn iv.).
Prayers.—Litanies of St. Joseph.

March 4.

Consideration.—Fourth motive—Example of the Church.
Hymn.—Iste quem læti colimus fideles (Hymn v.).
Prayer.—O Joseph! who, by your fidelity (Pr. 4).

March 5.

Consideration.—Fifth motive—Devotion to St. Joseph is a source of benediction to the whole universe.
Hymn.—Salve, pater Jesu mei (Hymn vi.).
Prayer.—What consolation do I feel (Pr. 5).

March 6.

Consideration.—Sixth motive—Power and benevolence of St. Joseph.
Hymn.—Quicumque (Hymn i.).
Prayer.—Domine Jesu (Pr. 8).

March 7.

Consideration.—Seventh motive—Our own interest.
Hymn.—O custos (Hymn ii.).
Prayer.—What consolation (Pr. 5).

MARCH 8.

Consideration.—Eighth motive—Example of religious orders.

Hymn.—Te Joseph celebrent (Hymn iii.).

Prayers.—Jesus, Joseph, Mary (Pr. 1). Domine Jesu Christi (Pr. 8).

MARCH 9.

Consideration.—Ninth motive—Example of princes, kingdoms, &c.

Hymn.—Iste quem læti (Hymn v.).

Prayer.—3.

MARCH 10.

Consideration.—Tenth motive—Example of a great number of pious writers.

Hymn.—Salve Pater.

Prayers.—O holy names (Pr. 6). Ave Joseph, imago Dei Patris (Pr. 14).

MARCH 11.

[On this day the exercises of the Novena preparatory to the Feast of St. Joseph are commenced.]

Consideration.—St. Joseph, spouse of Mary.

Hymn.—O custos matris (Hymn ii.).

Prayers.—Those of the Novena and Prayer 2.

MARCH 12.

Consideration.—St. Joseph, father of our Lord.

Hymn.—Te Joseph celebrent (Hymn iii.).

Prayers.—Those of the Novena and Prayer 2.

MARCH 13.

Consideration.—Obedience of our Lord.
Hymn.—Salve, pater Jesu (Hymn vi.).
Prayers.—Those of the Novena and the Litanies.

MARCH 14.

Consideration.—Holiness of St. Joseph.
Hymn.—Cœlitum Joseph decus (Hymn iv.).
Prayers.—Those of the Novena and Prayer 12.

MARCH 15.

Consideration.—St. Joseph, model of justice.
Hymn.—Iste quem læti (Hymn v.).
Prayers.—Those of the Novena and the Litanies.

MARCH 16.

Consideration.—St. Joseph surpasses all the other saints.
Hymn.—Cœlitum Joseph (Hymn iv.).
Prayers.—Those of the Novena and Prayer 14.

MARCH 17.

Consideration.—Favours granted to St. Joseph.
Hymn.—Salve, pater Jesu (Hymn vi.).
Prayers.—Those of the Novena and Prayer 6.

MARCH 18.

Consideration.—The life of St. Joseph is one example.
Hymn.—Iste quem læti (Hymn v.).
Prayers.—Those of the Novena and Prayer 4.

MARCH 19.
FEAST OF ST. JOSEPH.

Consideration.—Happiness of St. Joseph in this life.

Hymn.—Te Joseph celebrent (Hymn iii.).

Prayers.—Those of the Feast, and Prayers 5, 6, 8.

MARCH 20.

Consideration.—The life of St. Joseph was poor, laborious, and meritorious.

Hymn.—O custos matris (Hymn ii.).

Prayer.—4.

MARCH 21.

Consideration.—Death of St. Joseph.

Hymn.—Iste quem læti (Hymn v.).

Prayers.—Litanies.

MARCH 22.

Consideration.—Glory of St. Joseph.

Hymn.—Cœlitum Joseph decus (Hymn iv.).

Prayer.—14.

MARCH 23.

Consideration.—Protection of St. Joseph.

Hymn.—Quicumque sanus (Hymn i.).

Prayer.—7.

MARCH 24.

Consideration.—The exaltation of St. Joseph is worthy of Jesus—glorious for the holy patriarch—advantageous for men.

Hymn.—Te Joseph celebrent (Hymn iii.).

Prayer.—9.

MARCH 25.

Consideration.—For religious : St. Joseph, protector of the Order of Mount Carmel.   For other persons : St. Joseph, protector of those who aspire to interior perfection.
Hymn.—O custos Matris Domini (Hymn ii.).
Prayer.—Domine Jesu Christi (Pr. 8).

MARCH 26.

Consideration.—St. Joseph, protector of the salvation of his clients.
Hymn.—Salve, pater Jesu (Hymn vi.).
Prayers.—Litanies and Prayer 2.

MARCH 27.

Consideration.—St. Joseph, protector of the welfare and health of his clients.
Hymn.—Quicumque (Hymn ii.).
Prayer.—5.

MARCH 28.

Consideration.—St. Joseph, protector of his clients on their journeys.
Hymn.—O custos Matris (Hymn ii.).
Prayer.—11.

MARCH 29.

Consideration.—Protection of St. Joseph at the hour of death.
Hymn.—Iste quem læti (Hymn v.).
Prayer.—6.

MARCH 30.

Consideration.—St. Joseph, protector in every necessity.
Hymn.—Salve, pater Jesu (Hymn vi.).
Prayers.—5 and 12.

MARCH 31.

Consideration.—Increase of the devotion to St. Joseph.
Hymn.—Te Joseph celebrent (Hymn iii.).
Prayer.—14.

At the meetings of the association for honouring St. Joseph, and for extending this devotion, the first hymn is to St. Joseph, the second to the Sacred Heart, the third to the Immaculate Conception. We confine ourselves, however, here to marking the hymns to St. Joseph; the two others may be chosen by the director.

EXTENSION OF THE DEVOTION TO ST. JOSEPH.

Were there no other motive for this than the wish to please our Lord and His holy mother, it would surely be sufficient for every Christian heart. But we have a further motive, namely, that by making known this great saint, we give to men an example in several conditions of life, a powerful patron, and a generous friend. No further motives can be required to urge us to use our utmost endeavours to spread this devotion. (What are the best means to adopt for this

end?) A zealous soul takes advantage of every
opportunity which present itself, and often creates
opportunities; and with that energy which charac-
terises her, employs her utmost endeavours to complete and perfect her work. To endeavour to spread
the devotion to St. Joseph, is to do the work of God,
and, consequently, to expose oneself to contradictions
and difficulties. Constancy, however, will triumph
in the end, and will, moreover, draw down the blessing of heaven on our work. To make known St.
Joseph is the necessary preliminary to the increase
of this devotion. The best way of doing this, is to
distribute books about this great saint. This work,
of which we venture to present a translation, will
be found suitable to the wants of most persons: its
solidity will please the well educated; its historical
nature, those who are less cultivated; whilst the
moderation of its price will render it accessible to all.

To distribute images and medals of St. Joseph.—
These are acceptable to all classes of people, and are
like the book of the ignorant. A print with verses
or texts is another excellent means of increasing this
devotion; they are attractive in themselves, and
speak to simple hearts.

If the distribution of these medals, pictures, &c.,
be accompanied with anecdotes of the protection of
this saint, and words spoken in favour of this devotion, it will redouble their power, and will open
the hearts of those to whom we speak to dedicate
altars and statues to him. Neglect no opportunity
of establishing public devotions to him, and patronise
those already commenced in your neighbourhood.

Heads of families and superiors of communities,
in erecting in their houses an humble sanctuary to

St. Joseph, being satisfied even to place his statue in an honourable position, have gained as many hearts as there were persons in their house. This is a great good acquired at a very small cost. Good priests, in giving to St. Joseph an altar, a statue in their church, or a chapel in their parish, have caused piety to revive. And often this first germ of devotion has, in developing itself, produced a confraternity, and, in a few years, entire parishes have been converted.

Confraternities.—All confraternities established under the patronage of St. Joseph, produce the most happy results. We find, in studying this illustrious patriarch, an inexhaustible source of virtue and incomparable qualities, which speak to the mind and heart. It may be said, that labourers have generally a great devotion to this great saint. The best results may be obtained by uniting them under his banner.

In reading the preceding chapter, we may take notice of the different confraternities which have been established in honour of St. Joseph.

Month of St. Joseph.—If, by our position, we have it in our power to establish, during the month of March, a series of devotions in honour of St. Joseph, let us eagerly embrace this opportunity of causing him to be honoured. The study of this beautiful model offers considerations capable of implanting solid virtue in the members of a house or parish. A few moments taken from our ordinary occupations, will be amply repaid by the spiritual advantages we shall derive therefrom.

Consecration of the Wednesday to St. Joseph.— Clients of St. Joseph have the pious custom of consecrating Wednesday to St. Joseph, and of performing some practice on this day in his honour. We have heard, with great edification, of what takes place in the parish of Our Lady at Rennes. The venerable priest of that parish offers his Mass every Wednesday in honour of St. Joseph, for all those who assist at it. An ever-increasing concourse of the faithful from the surrounding parishes attend at it.

At Vitré, there is a society of ladies who meet on the same day; a Mass is said for the same intention. One of the most eminent ecclesiastics of the town has accepted the presidency of this society.

Before separating these fervent Christians, uniting themselves in spirit to the pilgrims of St. Joseph of Chêne, recite a prayer for the extension of the devotion to the holy patriarch.

The priest of Villedieu has adopted the same exercises, which are also established at Angers, in the chapel of St. Joseph of Mercy, and in several other churches of Poitou. Several communities and schools have asked to have a share in the pious works of this association, which promises the happiest results. We hear, also, with pleasure, that several cottages in France and Belgium honour St. Joseph in a particular manner on Wednesday.

Persons who may be residing at places where this devotion is not established, can assist at Mass on Wednesdays for this intention, till they can inspire a sufficient number of persons to enable them to have the Holy Sacrifice offered for their intention, which they might begin with having on the first Wednesday in the month, and afterwards increase to every week, as circumstances might permit.

The following prayer is recited at the meetings after Mass. The Bishops of Angers, Tours, Beauvais,

Rennes, Poitiers, and Nantes have attached to it an indulgence of forty days :—

"Holy St. Joseph! you, who by your fidelity to the inspirations of heaven, in the midst of toil, contempt, and the many trials of this life, have merited to receive from the Holy Spirit the title of just, and to be entrusted by the Eternal Father with the care of Mary, the Queen of virgins, and with Jesus, His only begotten Son; we implore you, now that you have entered into the bliss of eternal life, to remember us who are still languishing in this valley of tears, exposed to the snares of most cruel enemies. Obtain for us a holy contempt for the false pleasures of this world, victory over our passions, constant devotion in the service of God, and a burning love for Jesus, thy Son, and Mary, thy spouse. Holy St. Joseph! be our guide, our protector, our defender at the hour of our death : this we ask for the love you bear to Jesus and Mary. We entreat you also to obtain the same graces for all those who are associated with us in this pious work. Hearken to their prayers, second their efforts, and reward their zeal, by obtaining for them a place near your throne in heaven, at the feet of Jesus and Mary. Amen.

"Sacred Heart of Jesus, have mercy on us.

"Immaculate Heart of Mary, pray for us.

"St. Joseph, pray for us."

A Pater and Ave is afterwards said for the special intentions of the associates.

At the end of the Mass, a meeting may be held to concert means for the propagation of the devotion to St. Joseph, of which the ones mentioned above will be found very efficacious. This union in prayer and good works is all-powerful with God, and produces great results among men. Often those who would otherwise have been carried away by the world, have, through the prayers and examples of their companions, become true saints.

CHAPTER V.

Prayers and Hymns to St. Joseph.

THESE prayers and hymns are so many means which we may make use of to honour St. Joseph, either in private or in associations, as also in pilgrimages to the sanctuaries of this holy patriarch. Our attraction and our necessities regulate us in the prayers which we make in private. As to those in pilgrimages, they vary with the inspirations which lead us to make them. They depend besides upon the objects of veneration which are to be met with in the place that we visit.

After having given a certain number of prayers to St. Joseph, we will add some others to the Sacred Heart, and in honour of the Immaculate Conception; because the sanctuary of Villedieu, which we have especially in view in our work, proposed to our veneration these three objects, which a true Christian ought always to unite in his heart and in his devotions.

§ I.—PRAYERS.

I.—Prayers to St. Joseph.

1. *Ejaculatory Prayers.*

Jesus, Joseph, and Mary, I give you my heart and my life. Jesus, Joseph, and Mary, assist me in my last agony. Jesus, Joseph, and Mary, grant that I may die in your holy company.

(Three hundred days' indulgence, applicable to the souls in purgatory.—Pius VII., 1807.)

2. *A Prayer for Purity.*

O holy St. Joseph! father and guardian of virgins, to whose fidelity was confided Jesus, innocence itself, and Mary, the Virgin of virgins; I supplicate and conjure you, through Jesus and Mary, this sacred deposit which is so dear to your heart, to grant that, preserved from all sin, and perfectly pure in mind, heart, and body, I may have the happiness of always serving Jesus and Mary very faithfully. Amen.

(Indulgence of one year for priests, applicable to the souls in purgatory.—Pius VII., 1807.)

3. *Prayer for a Person who has a Laborious Occupation.*

Blessed Joseph! who have passed your life in the painful labours of an humble profession, I take you as my model and my protector. Obtain for me that I may bear patiently the pains and fatigues of my state, that, like you, sanctifying my labours, I may merit a crown in heaven. Amen.

(Forty days' indulgence in the dioceses of Angers, Tours, Beauvais, and Rennes).

4. *Prryer for a Family or any other Reunion.*

O Joseph! you who, by your fidelity to the inspirations of heaven, have merited, in the midst of the hardest labours, the contempt of the world, and the trials of this life, that the Holy Spirit should give you the title of just, that God the Father should confide to you, together with Mary, the Queen of virgins, Jesus, her dear Divine Son; we implore you now that you are all-powerful before God, to remember us who still languish in this valley of tears, exposed to the snares of the most cruel enemies. Obtain for us the contempt for the false goods of this world, the victory over our passions, an unbounded devotion to the service of God, a tender confidence in Jesus, your Son, and in Mary, your spouse. O Joseph! be our guide, our patron, and our model, during the course of this life; be our defender in death: this we implore of you by the love which you bear to Jesus and Mary. Amen.

(Forty days' indulgence in the dioceses of Angers, Tours, Beauvais, and Rennes.)

5. *Prayer to implore the Protection of St. Joseph.*

What consolation do I feel, O my admirable and powerful protector! in hearing your servant, St. Theresa, assure us that no one ever invoked you in vain, and that all those who have a true devotion to you, and who seek your help with confidence, are always heard! Animated with a like confidence, I have recourse to you, O worthy spouse of the Virgin of virgins; I take refuge at your feet; and a sinner though I am, I dare to present myself tremblingly before you. Do not reject my humble prayers, O you that have borne the glorious name of Father of Jesus! listen favorably to them, and deign ,to intercede for me with Him who has been willing to be called your Son, and who has always honoured you as His father. Amen.

6. *Invocation of the Holy Names of Jesus, Mary, and Joseph.*

O holy names of Jesus, of Mary, and of Joseph! be always on my lips and in my heart; let the most constant and most tender love ever engrave you upon it. Let these sweet names, unceasingly repeated, be the delight of my soul in all my aspirations; may I pronounce them with respect, love, and confidence, till my last sigh, in order that I may sing them eternally in heaven. Amen.

7. *Act of Consecration to St. Joseph.*

O blessed St. Joseph! I consecrate myself to your honour, and give myself entirely to you. Be always my father, my protector, and my guide, in the way of salvation. Obtain for me a great purity of heart, and a practical love of the interior life. After your example, may I do all my actions for the greater glory of God, in union with the divine hearts of Jesus and Mary. And, in fine, deign, blessed Joseph! to make me participate in the delights of your holy death.

8. *Oratio Cardinalis P. d'Ailly.*

Domine-Jesu Christe, æternaliter Deus de Deo et ineffabili humilitate temporaliter homo factus de Virgine, qui sanctum Joseph beatæ Mariæ matri tuæ, virginem virgini desponsari et humilem humili sociare voluisti, et eum de parvo magnum, de humili excelsum, multis virtutibus et magnis honoribus augmentatum, mirabiliter sublimasti : da nobis, quæsumus, ejus exemplis, meritis et precibus, cum cordis et corporis munditiâ, veram humilitatis virtutem, nobisque in humilitate fundatis, da fidei, spei et caritatis omniumque virtutum augmentum ; uti per virtuosa merita, gloriosa secum præmia consequi valeamus, qui cum Patre vivis et regnas in unitate Spiritûs Sancti, per omnia sæcula sæculorum. Amen. (*Ex Bollandistis.*)

9. *Sanctus Joseph in patronum advocatur.*

O sancte Joseph, qui tanquam pater et manuductor Christum Jesum in pueritia et juventute per omnes peregrinationes humanæ vitæ fidelissime deduxisti, et mihi, obsecro, in vitæ meæ peregrinatione tanquam comes et ductor assiste ; nec unquam permitte me a viâ mandatorum Dei declinare. Sis in adversis præsidium, in ærumnis solatium, donec tandem ad terram viventium perveniam, ubi tecum et sanctissima sponsa tua Maria, omnibusque sanctis et Deo Jesu meo æternum exsulter. Amen. (*Vade-Mecum sacerdotum.*)

10. *Ad S. Joseph ante missam.*

O felicem virum, beatum Joseph, cui datum est

Deum, quem multi reges voluerunt videre et non viderunt, audire et non audierunt, non solum videre et audire, sed portare, deosculari, vestire et custodire.

℣. Ora pro nobis, beate Joseph.

℞. Ut digni efficiamur promissionibus Christi.

Oremus.—Deus, qui dedisti nobis regale sacerdotium, præsta, quæsumus, ut, sicut beatus Joseph Unigentium Filium tuum, natum ex Mariâ Virgine, suis manibus reverenter tractare meruit et portare : ita nos facias cum cordis munditiâ et operis innocentiâ tuis sanctis altaribus deservire, ut sacrosanctum Filii tui corpus et sanguinem hodie digne sumamus et in futuro sæculo præmium habere mereamur æternum, per Christum Dominum nostrum. (*Analecta et P. Morel*).

(*Indulg.*—1 anni cuilibet sacerdoti hanc precem ante missam dicenti. Animabus purgatorii potest applicari.—Pius VII., 1802.)

11. *Consecratio sui ad S. Joseph.*

Sancte Joseph, Domini mei Jesu nutritie ac beatæ Mariæ Virginis sponse, ego, *N...*, te in singularem patronum ac tutorem eligo et quoniam constituit te Deus præpositum sanctæ familiæ suæ, oro te atque obtestor, ut in vocatione meâ mihi adsis benignus et intercessione tuâ faveas. Doce me, quæso, Mariam venerari ut advocatam, colere ut Dominam, amare ut matrem. Te duce, juxta legem christianam in viâ pietatis ac virtutis ambulem et ita merear patrocinio tuo, verus Jesu et Mariæ filius, perpetuo vivere et mori. Amen.

12. *Ad felicem mortem obtinendam.*

O sancte Joseph, qui in suavissimo Jesu clientis
tui et dulcissimæ sponsæ tuæ Mariæ complexu ex
hâc vitâ emigrasti : succurre mihi, ô sancte Pater,
cum Jesu et Mariâ, tunc potissimum quando mors
vitæ meæ finem imponet, illudque mihi solatium
mihi impetra, ut in iisdem sanctissimis Jesu et Mariæ
brachiis expirem.   In manus vestras vivens et mo-
riens, commendo spiritum meum, Jesu, Maria, Joseph.
(*Cœleste Palmetum.*)

13. *Pia invocatio.*

Protector noster, aspice nos ; beate Joseph, in ad-
jutorium nostrum semper intende, ut, imitatione tuî,
Jesum et Mariam debito cultu et amore constanter
prosequentes in terris, æternum contemplari et bene-
dicere tecum mereamur in cœlis.

14. *D^{ni.} Olier invocationes.*

Ave Joseph, imago Dei Patris.
Ave Joseph, pater Dei Filii.
Ave Joseph, sacrarium Spiritûs Sancti.
Ave Joseph, dilecte sanctæ Trinitatis.
Ave Joseph, magni consilii coadjutor fidelissime.
Ave Joseph, Virginis Matris sponse dignissime.
Ave Joseph, pater omnium fidelium.
Ave Joseph, custos sanctarum virginum.
Ave Joseph, paupertatis amantissime.
Ave Joseph, exemplum mansuetudinis et patientiæ.
Ave Joseph, speculum humilitatis et obedientiæ.
Et benedicti oculi tui, qui viderunt quæ tu vidisti.

Benedictus es tu inter omnes homines.

Et benedictæ aures tuæ quæ audierunt quæ tu audisti.

Et benedictæ manus tuæ quæ contrectaverunt Verbum incarnatum.

Et benedicta brachia tua, quæ portaverunt omnia portantem.

Et benedictum pectus tuum, in quo Filius Dei dulcissime requievit.

Et benedictum cor tuum ardentissimo amore succensum.

Et benedictus Pater æternus qui te elegit.

Et benedictus Filius qui te amavit.

Et benedictus Spiritus Sanctus qui te sanctificavit.

Et benedicta Maria, sponsa tua, quæ te ut sponsum et fratrem dilexit.

Et benedictus Angelus qui te custodivit.

Et benedicti in æternum omnes qui benedicunt tibi et qui diligunt te.

15. *Litaniæ sancti Joseph.*

Kyrie, eleison.

Christe, eleison.

Kyrie, elieson.

Christe, audi nos.

Christi, exaudi nos.

Pater de cœlis, Deus miserere nobis.

Fili Redemptor mundi Deus, miserere nobis.

Spiritus Sancte, Deus, miserere nobis.

Sancta Trinitas, unus Deus, miserere nobis.

Sancta Maria, sponsa sancti Joseph, ora pro nobis.

Sancte Joseph, vir Mariæ de quâ natus est Jesus, ora pro nobis.

Sancte Joseph, vir virgo virginis matris,
Sancte Joseph, custos virginitatis Mariæ,
Sancte Joseph, pater Filii Dei,
Sancte Joseph, nutritie pueri Jesu,
Sancte Joseph, organum Verbi silentis,
Sancte Joseph, redemptor Redemptoris nostri,
Sancte Joseph, salvator Salvatoris nostri,
Sancte Joseph, dux Christi fugientis,
Sancte Joseph, hospes Dei peregrinantis,
Sancte Joseph, gubernator incarnatæ Sapientiæ,
Sancte Joseph, minister magni consilii,
Sancte Joseph, quæstor thesauri cœlestis,
Sancte Joseph, vir consummatæ justitiæ,
Sancte Joseph, exemplar perfectæ obedientiæ,
Sancte Joseph, lilium intemeratæ castitatis,
Sancte Joseph, zelator animarum nostrarum,
Sancte Joseph, protector domorum religiosarum,
Sancte Joseph, defensor agonizantium,
Sancte Joseph, patrone in Domino morientium,

Ora pro nobis.

Agnus Dei, qui tollis peccata mundi, parce nobis,
Domine.
Agnus Dei, qui tollis peccata mundi, exaudi nos,
Domini.
Agnus Dei, qui tollis peccata mundi, miserere nobis.
Christe, audi nos.
Christe, exaudi nos.
    ℣. Ora pro nobis, sancte Joseph.
    ℞. Ut digni efficiamur promissionibus Christi.

OREMUS.

Sanctissimæ Genetricis tuæ Sponsi, quæsumus,
Domine, meritis adjuvemur, ut quam possibilitas
nostra non obtinet, pretiosa mors Sanctorum nobis

ejus intercessione donetur: qui vivis et regnas, Deus, in sæcula sæculorum. Amen.

Memento nostrî, beate Joseph, et tuæ protectionis suffragio apud tuum putativum filium intercede; sed et beatissimam Virginem sponsam tuam nobis propitiam redde, quæ Mater est ejus qui cum Patre et Spiritu Sancte vivit et regnat per infinita sæcula sæculorum. Amen. (*S. Bernardin de Sienne.*)

15. *Litany of St. Joseph.*

Lord, have mercy on us.
Christ, have mercy on us.
Lord, have mercy on us.
Christ, hear us.
Christ, graciously hear us.
God, the Father of heaven, have mercy on us.
God the Son, Redeemer of the world, have mercy on us.
God the Holy Ghost, have mercy on us.
Holy Trinity, one God, have mercy on us.
Holy Mary, spouse of St. Joseph,
St. Joseph, spouse of Mary, the mother of Jesus,
St. Joseph, virgin spouse of a virgin mother,
St. Joseph, guardian of the virginity of Mary,
St. Joseph, father of the Son of God,
St. Joseph, nurse of the Child Jesus,
St. Joseph, organ of the Word reduced to silence,
St. Joseph, redeemer of our Redeemer,
St. Joseph, saviour of our Saviour,
St. Joseph, guide of Jesus in His flight,

Pray for us.

St. Joseph, teacher of incarnate Wisdom,
St. Joseph, minister of the great council,
St. Joseph, depository of the celestial treasure,
St. Joseph, man of consummate justice,
St. Joseph, model of perfect obedience,
St. Joseph, lily of spotless purity,
St. Joseph, zealous lover of our souls,
St. Joseph, protector of religious houses,
St. Joseph, defender of the agonizing,
St. Joseph, patron of those who die in the
    Lord,

Pray for us.

Lamb of God, who takest away the sins of the world,
    spare us, O Lord.
Lamb of God, who takest away the sins of the world,
    hear us, O Lord.
Lamb of God, who takest away the sins of the world,
    have mercy on us.

℣. Pray for us, O holy St. Joseph.

℞. That we may be made worthy of the promises of Christ.

LET US PRAY.

We beseech Thee, O Lord, to assist us, through the merits of the holy spouse of Thy most holy mother, and to grant us, by his intercession, the precious death of the saints, which of ourselves we are not able to obtain. Grant us this grace, O God: who livest and reignest for ever and ever. Amen.

LET US PRAY.

Be mindful of us, O blessed Joseph! and grant us the assistance of your protection with Him who has called you father; and also render favourable to us the most Blessed Virgin, your spouse, and the mother of Him who, with the Father and the Holy Ghost, liveth and reigneth for ever and ever. Amen. (*St. Bernardine of Sienna.*)

II.—PRAYERS TO THE SACRED HEART.

After having honoured St. Joseph, patron of the chapel of St. Joseph-du-Chêne, let us turn our devotion to the Sacred Heart of Jesus, which is admirably represented in one of the stained windows.

The Venerable Margaret Mary, of whom our Lord was pleased to make use in order to make known the excellence of the devotion to His Divine Heart, speaks thus, in one part of her writings : "I can say with certainty, that if it were known how pleasing this devotion is to Jesus Christ, there is not a Christian, however little love he might bear to this loving Redeemer, who would not practise it. Our Lord has discovered to me, that He reserves treasures of love and grace for those persons who shall consecrate themselves to procure for His Heart all the honour, love, and glory which shall be in their power. He reserves incomprehensible treasures for all those who shall occupy themselves in establishing this devotion."

1. *Consecration to the Sacred Heart.*

O my Divine Saviour! Thou presentest Thyself to me under the emblem of the Good Shepherd, bearing on Thy shoulders the stranger sheep, and showing me Thy Heart. I understand this language, inspired by the love with which Thou burnest for me. "See, O my child!" Thou wouldst say to me— "see how much I have loved thee. I have sought thee when thou didst flee from me; I received thee when thou wert covered with wounds; I brought thee back to my sheepfold, the sheepfold of the children of God, which thou hadst quitted by sin. Dost thou understand at last the mercy, the tender solicitude of My Heart? Wilt thou flee from me again?" No, Oh my Saviour! No, I will never again separate myself from Thee. To whom should I go, Thou hast the words of eternal life? My heart is Thine; I give it to Thee, but purify it, strengthen it. May the love of creatures, and of the false goods of the earth no more penetrate into this sanctuary, which is consecrated to Thee! Do Thou command there as a sovereign, and banish from it that which displeases Thee. Henceforward, let it follow Thy inspirations alone; let thy desires be its desires also. Grant that sweetness, patience, humility, obedience, a contempt for the frivolities of the earth, and all the virtues which are pleasing to Thee, may also be the delight of my heart. Be my guide through the dangers of this world, my consoler in my pains, my asylum in persecutions, my defender against the powers of hell. I conjure Thee, by this precious blood which Thou hast shed for my salvation, inflame me with the fire which Thou didst come to bring upon the earth. And, if I cannot recover again those years which I have lost by sin, in order to consecrate them to Thee, at least let me give Thee every instant which shall be granted to me in future. I wish to live only to love Thee; happy if it is granted to me to make some heart enter into Thy love, and to live till my last sigh a victim to Thy glory and Thy good pleasure.

To obtain this grace, I offer Thee, O Heart of Jesus! the pure and burning hearts of Mary and Joseph : accept their love in reparation for my tepidity and infidelities. Sacred Heart of Jesus! mayest Thou be honoured, loved, and adored, by all creatures, now and in all ages. Amen.

2. *Offering to our Lord.*

My loving Jesus, as a proof of my gratitude, and in reparation for my infidelities, I give Thee my heart; I consecrate myself entirely to Thee, and I purpose, with Thy holy grace, never more to offend Thee.

This offering should be made before a picture of the Sacred Heart.

Indulgence of 100 days is granted once a day to recite this prayer.

Plenary indulgence once a month, if they say it every day for a month, go to confession and holy Communion, and pray for the intention of the Sovereign Pontiff, applicable to the souls in purgatory.— Pius VII., 1817. (*P. Maurel.*)

3. *Offering to God the Father of the Merits of our Saviour.*

Eternal Father, in union with all the heavenly court, the most holy Hearts of Jesus, Mary, and Joseph, I would wish to have offered Thee during all past ages; and I would wish to offer Thee during all future ages, the most precious blood of Jesus

Christ, His infinite merits, and those of the whole
Church, in payment for my sins, and the sins of the
world; for the deliverance of all the souls in purgatory; in thanksgiving for all the gifts, favours, and
mercies which Thou hast vouchsafed as well to us as
to all men, having regard rather to Thy great glory,
and our sanctification in the midst of the trials of
this life, than to the punishments which we have
deserved by our sins; in thanksgiving to Thee for
having made of the entire world one only fold, under
one and the same Shepherd : in order that, all
living on this earth in the faith, hope, and
charity of our Saviour Jesus Christ, we may be
admitted to celebrate Thy divine mercies in heaven.
Amen.

4. *Prayer to the Sacred Heart of Jesus, to obtain His love.*

Heart of Jesus, which burnest with love for men,
consume our hearts with the love of Thee.

O Sacred Heart ! which didst pour forth on Calvary from Thy open wound the torrents of Thy
charity ! O generous Heart ! which, from the altar
where Thou immolatest Thyself each day, and from
the tabernacle where Thy love reposes, dost not
cease to shed Thy blessings on the earth ! O
tender Heart ! which has so much loved men, which
lovest them still, who will always love them, unworthy though they be of Thy goodness ! inflame
with Thy warmth our dry, hard, icy hearts, or rather
take from us these " hearts of stone," and give us
hearts which know how to love Thee, which love
Thee alone, or which love nothing but in Thee and

for Thee; hearts like to Thy heart: in order that,
consumed in Thy unity, and united in Thy
charity, we may one day be crowned in Thy glory.
Amen.

5. Prayer to the Sacred Heart of Jesus, for the agonising.

O clementissime Jesu,
amator animarum, obse-
cro te per agoniam Cordis
tui sanctissimi et per
doloris Matris tuæ imma-
culatæ, lava in sanguine
tuo peccatores totius
mundi, nunc positus in
agoniâ et hodie moritu-
ros. Amen.

O most merciful Jesus,
lover of souls, I beseech
Thee, by the agony of Thy
most holy Heart, and by
the sorrows of Thy im-
maculate Mother, wash
in Thy blood the sinners
in the whole world who
are in their agony, and
who will die this day.
Amen.

6. Litaniæ Sacri Cordis Jesu.

Kyrie, eleison.
Christe, eleison.
Kyrie, eleison.
Christe, audi nos.
Christe, exaudi nos.
Pater de cœlis, Deus,
Fili, Redemptor mundi, Deus,
Spiritus Sancte, Deus,
Sancta Trinitas, unus Deus,
Cor Jesu,
Cor Jesu, in sinu Matris Virginis formatum,
Cor Jesu, Verbo Dei substantialiter unitum,

Miserere nobis.

Cor Jesu, Divinitatis sanctuarium,
Cor Jesu, sanctissimæ Trinitatis tabernaculum,
Cor Jesu, sanctitatis templum,
Cor Jesu, fons omnium gratiarum,
Cor Jesu, mitissimum et humillimum,
Cor Jesu, fornax amoris,
Cor Jesu, origo contritionis,
Cor Jesu, sapientiæ thesaurus,
Cor Jesu, bonitatis oceanus,
Cor Jesu, misericordiæ thronus,
Cor Jesu, virtutum omnium exemplar,
Cor Jesu, domus Dei et porta cœli,
Cor Jesu, thesaurus nunquam deficiens,
Cor Jesu, de cujus plenitudine nos omnes acce-
    pimus,
Cor Jesu, dives in omnes qui invocant te,
Cor Jesu, pax et reconciliatio nostra,
Cor Jesu, host.ɪ vivens, sancta, Deo placens,
Cor Jesu, propitiatio pro peccatis nostris,
Cor Jesu, fons aquæ salientis in vitam æternam,
Cor Jesu, puteus aquarum viventium,
Cor Jesu, in horto anxiatum,
Cor Jesu, sudore sanguineo debilitatum,
Cor Jesu, saturatum opprobriis,
Cor Jesu, attritum propter scelera nostra,
Cor Jesu, usque ad mortem crucis obediens
    factum,
Cor Jesu, lancea perforatum,
Cor Jesu, in cruce sanguine exhaustum,
Cor Jesu, refugium peccatorum,
Cor Jesu, fortitudo justorum,
Cor Jesu, consolatio afflictorum,
Cor Jesu, robur tentatorum,
Cor Jesu, terror dæmonum,

Miserere nobis.

Cor Jesu, perseverentia bonorum, miserere nobis.

Cor Jesu, spes morientium, miserere nobis.

Cor Jesu, gaudium beatorum, miserere nobis.

Cor Jesu, rex et centrum omnium cordium, miserere nobis.

Ab omni peccato, libera nos, Jesu.

A duritia cordis, libera nos, Jesu.

A morte perpetua, libera nos, Jesu.

Agnus Dei, qui tollis peccata mundi, parce nobis, Jesu.

Agnus Dei, qui tollis peccata mundi, exaudi nos, Jesu.

Agnus Dei, qui tollis peccata mundi, miserere nobis, Jesu.

Jesu, audi nos.

Jesu, exaudi nos.

6. *Litany of the Sacred Heart of Jesus.*

Lord, have mercy on us.

Christ, have mercy on us.

Lord, have mercy on us.

Christ, hear us.

Christ, graciously hear us.

God the Father of heaven,

God the Son, Redeemer of the world,

God the Holy Ghost,

Holy Trinity, one God,

Heart of Jesus,

Heart of Jesus, formed in the womb of a virgin mother,

Heart of Jesus, hypostatically united to the Word of God,

Heart of Jesus, sanctuary of the Divinity,

Have mercy on us.

Heart of Jesus, temple of the Holy Trinity,
Heart of Jesus, temple of holiness,
Heart of Jesus, fountain of all graces,
Heart of Jesus, full of sweetness and humility,
Heart of Jesus, furnace of love,
Heart of Jesus, source of contrition,
Heart of Jesus, treasure of wisdom,
Heart of Jesus, ocean of goodness,
Heart of Jesus, throne of mercy,
Heart of Jesus, model of all virtues,
Heart of Jesus, house of God and gate of heaven,
Heart of Jesus, inexhaustible treasure,
Heart of Jesus, of whose fullness we have all received,
Heart of Jesus, liberal to those who invoke Thee,
Heart of Jesus, our peace and our atonement,
Heart of Jesus, living sacrifice, holy and agreeable to God,
Heart of Jesus, propitiation for our sins,
Heart of Jesus, fountain of water, springing up into everlasting life,
Heart of Jesus, spring of living water,
Heart of Jesus, sorrowful in the garden, even unto death,
Heart of Jesus, weakened by a sweat of blood,
Heart of Jesus, saturated with revilings,
Heart of Jesus, filled with sorrow for our sins,
Heart of Jesus, made obedient, even to the death of the cross,
Heart of Jesus, pierced by a lance,
Heart of Jesus, exhausted of Thy blood on the cross,

Have mercy on us.

Heart of Jesus, refuge of sinners,
Heart of Jesus, strength of the just,
Heart of Jesus, consolation of the afflicted,
Heart of Jesus, support of those who are tempted,
Heart of Jesus, terror of the evil spirits,
Heart of Jesus, perseverance of the just,
Heart of Jesus, hope of the dying,
Heart of Jesus, joy of the saints,
Heart of Jesus, king and centre of all hearts,

Have mercy on us.

From all sin, Lord Jesus, deliver us.
From hardness of heart, Lord Jesus, deliver us.
From everlasting death, Lord Jesus, deliver us.
Lamb of God, who takest away the sins of the world:
 spare us, O Jesus.
Lamb of God, who takest away the sins of the world:
 graciously hear us, O Jesus.
Lamb of God, who takest away the sins of the world:
 have mercy on us, O Jesus.
Jesus, hear us.
Jesus, graciously hear us.

7. *Act of Reparation to the Sacred Heart of Jesus.*

Heart of Jesus! adorable sanctuary of the love of
God for men! how can we sufficiently lament the
excess of our ingratitude towards Thee? O God,
Thou hast loved us from all eternity; Thou hast
created us in Thine own image; Thou hast given us
our being, only that Thou mayest crown us with
those blessings of which Thou Thyself art the source,
and that Thou mayest fully satisfy, in giving us
eternal happiness, Thy burning love for our salvation. When man had, by sin, despised Thy love,
more liberal and more merciful than ever, Thou didst

humble Thyself to take upon Thee our nature, in order to redeem us; Thou didst appear upon earth as the most amiable among the children of men; Thou didst take a heart like unto ours, in order to constrain us to love Thee.   Divine Heart of my Jesus! Heart consumed with the ardent fire of charity! Thou hast taken upon Thyself our griefs and our sorrows.   Heart infinitely holy! most pure fountain of justice and innocence! Thou hast carried the iniquities of the whole world.   Thou hast tasted the bitterness thereof; Thou hast been wounded for our crimes; and by the shedding of Thy most precious blood, Thou hast spread over the earth those blessings which console it, those graces which purify it. Nothing has extinguished Thy love: neither the sufferings and labours of Thy whole life, nor the grief and ignominy of Thy cross, nor the monstrous ingratitude with which we have repaid Thy benefits; Thou hast crowned all Thy other blessings by giving Thyself to be the food of the children of men.

And we, O Lord, have but repaid Thy love by ingratitude; we have despised Thee, we have forgotten Thee, and have not ceased, by new outrages, to fill up the measure of our iniquities.   Alas! men wish no longer to know Thee, they will not love Thee; every day Thy commandments are transgressed, and the remembrance of Thy holy name is well-nigh blotted out.   Thy temples are deserted, Thy sacraments abandoned, Thy religion despised. Christians, inebriated by the love of false pleasures and perishable goods of this world, only remember Thy love to grieve it by their indifference, or to outrage it by their crimes.   O my God! dost Thou still find faithful hearts upon earth? Are there any yet to be found who return love for love?

For us, whom Thou hast deigned to remember in Thy mercy, if we do not love Thee as much as Thou deservest, at least Thou knowest that we desire to do so. From the height of Thine eternal throne, deign to cast Thine eyes upon the small number of faithful souls brought to Thy feet through gratitude and love. Alas! why cannot we, by the entire sacrifice of ourselves, render to Thee all the glory which the world and hell strive to deprive Thee of. Yes, we would efface by our tears those crimes which pierce Thy Divine Heart with grief; happy, indeed, should we count ourselves, were we permitted to wash them out by our blood. But who, O my God! can repair Thy outraged glory? There is none, save Thyself. It is, then, to Thy adorable Heart that we have recourse in this our necessity.

O most merciful Heart! pardon the blind and the ungrateful; or, if Thou willest to take revenge upon them, revenge Thyself in a manner conformable to Thy glory, by casting upon them, not the scourges of Thine anger, but the burning darts of Thy love, in order that, conquered by this infinite love, we may all become its apostles and disciples, and, after having practised the virtues Thou commandest, we may partake one day of the happiness Thou promisest. Amen.

8. *Consecration to the Sacred Heart, by the Rev. F. Colombière.*

[It may be made use of by Religious at the renewal of their vows.]

O my adorable Redeemer! I give and consecrate myself to Thy Sacred Heart, in the most complete and perfect manner possible.

I am, as it were, nailed to the cross by the vows of my profession; I renew them in Thy Divine Heart, in the presence of heaven and earth.

I give Thee thanks for having inspired me to make them. I confess that the yoke of Thy holy service is neither rough nor heavy; that I do not find its sacred obligations burthensome. On the contrary, I would wish to multiply them, and to bind myself yet closer to Thy service.

I embrace, then, the amiable cross of my vocation, till my death; it shall be my joy, my glory, and my delight. "Absi mihi gloriari nisi in cruce Domini nostri Jesu Christi; per quem mihi mundus crucifixus est et ego mundo." God forbid that I should ever glory or rejoice in anything, save in the cross of Jesus Christ.

God forbid that I should have any other treasure than poverty; any other joy than suffering; any other love than thee, O my God!

No, no, my dearest Saviour, never, never will I depart from Thee. I will attach myself to Thee alone. The narrowest paths of the perfect life to which am called, frighten me no longer, because Thou art my light and my strength.

I trust in Thee, O Lord, that Thou wilt make me unshaken in temptation, victorious over the wiles of

mine enemies; and that, since Thou hast showered
so many blessings upon me, Thou wilt show Thyself
more and more liberal to me. This I ask, O adorable Jesus! through Thy blood, through Thy wounds,
and through Thy Sacred Heart. Grant that by this
consecration of my whole self to Thee, I may become
one day a new work of Thy charity. Amen.

III.—Prayers to Mary.

Before leaving this blessed sanctuary, let us throw
ourselves at the feet of Mary, whom we find represented on the window at the left-hand side. Let us lay
open to her our fears and our desires: who has ever
prayed to her in vain? We shall obtain at her altars
strength to combat our most powerful enemies, grace
to preserve inviolate the flower of innocence, whose
sweet perfume rejoices the heavens.

St. Bonaventure assures us, that no one can pronounce the holy name of Mary without fruit. St.
Stanislaus used to ask Mary's blessing every morning
and evening. St. Bernard advises every one to have
recourse to her in all temptations, trials, and difficulties. St. Theresa made her the mistress of all she
had, and asked her assistance in all her undertakings.
Have a great devotion to her Rosary and Scapular.
Salute Mary every day under one of these titles:
Mother of God, Queen of Angels and of Men, Our
Mother, Our Model, Our Advocate, Our Deliverer,
Mother of Sorrows, Our Refuge, during life and at
the hour of death.

1. *Prayer to the Sacred Heart of Mary.*

Heart of Mary, Mother of God and men, most tender heart, object of complaisance to the Adorable Trinity; heart worthy of the love and respect of heaven and earth; heart which most resembles the Heart of Jesus, of which it is the most perfect image; loving heart, which compassionates our miseries, deign to melt our icy hearts, and to conform them entirely to that of our Divine Saviour. Communicate to them the love of your virtues and the fire of charity, which has always burnt in your breast. Watch over the Church, protect it, be its refuge and defence against the attacks of its enemies. Be the way which conducts us to Jesus, the channel through which He communicates His blessings to us. Be our solace in our necessities, our support in temptation, our refuge in persecution, our succour in all dangers, specially at the hour of death, when hell, let loose, strives to devour our souls. Let us experience, O most compassionate Virgin! at this awful moment, on which our eternity depends, the tenderness of your heart; show your power with Jesus, in opening to us His Sacred Heart, source of all mercy, where, in company with all the blessed, we may dwell with Him for all eternity.

May the Divine Heart of Jesus and the immaculate heart of Mary be known, praised, blessed, loved, served, and glorified in all the universe, for ever and ever. Amen.

(An indulgence of sixty days for every recital. Plenary indulgence on the feasts of Nativity, Assumption, and of the Sacred Heart of Mary, for those who have said this prayer every day for a whole month, and who after confession and Communion pray for the intentions of the Sovereign Pontiff. A plenary indulgence at the hour of death for those who had said it every day. These indulgences are applicable to the dead.)

2. Prayer in honour of the Immaculate Conception of the Blessed Virgin Mary.

Blessed be the holy and Immaculate Conception of the Blessed Virgin Mary.

(A hundred days' indulgence each time, applicable to the dead.—Pius VI., 1793.)

3. Act of Consecration to Mary.

O Domina mea sancta Maria, me in tuam benedictam fidem ac singularem custodiam et in sinum misericordiæ tuæ, hodie, et quotidie et in horâ exitûs mei, animam meam et corpus meum tibi commendo; omnem spem et consolationem meam, omnes angustias et miserias meas, vitam et finem vitæ meæ tibi committo; ut per tuam sanctissimam intercessionem et per tua merita, omnia mea dirigantur et

O holy Mary, my Queen, I put myself with confidence under your special protection; I throw myself into the bosom of your mercy today, and every day, and at the hour of my death. At this last hour I commend into your hands my soul and my body. I commit to you my sorrows and pains, my life and death, that through your merits and most holy intercession, my actions and all my thoughts may

| disponantur opera, secundum tuam tuique Filii voluntatem. | be directed and regulated according to your will and that of your Son. |
| Amen. | Amen. |

4. *Consecratio sui.*

Ave Maria, etc. O Domina mea, ô Mater mea ! Tibi me totum offero, atque, ut me tibi probem devotum, consecro tibi hodie oculos meos, aures meas, os meum, plane me totum.   Quoniam itaque tuus sum, ô bona Mater, serva me, defende me ut rem et possessionem tuam.

Aspiratio in tentatione.

O Domina mea, ô Mater mea, memento me esse tuum, serva me, defende me ut rem et possessionem tuam.

Indulgentia 100 dierum recitantibus mane et vespere has preces.

Indulgentia plenaria semel in mense his qui, quotidie his recitatis, confessi et communione refecti, ad intentionem Summi Pontificis orant.

Indulgentia 40 dierum secundam precem in tentatione dicenti.   Animabus purgatorii applicari possunt.—Pius IX., 1848. (*Analecta, P. Maurel,* &c.)

5. *Sancti Bernardi oratio.*

Memorare, ô piissima Virgo Maria, non esse auditum a sæculo, quemquam ad tua currentem præsidia, tua petentem suffragia esse derelictum. Ego tali animatus confidentiâ, ad te Virgo virginum, Mater, curro ; ad te

venio, coram te gemens peccator assisto. Noli, Mater
Verbi, verba mea despicere, sed audi propitia et exaudi.
Indulgentia 300 dierum semel recitanti.
Indulgentia plenaria his qui, eâ quotidie recitatâ
per mensem, confessi, sacrâ communione refecti, ad
intentionem S. Pontificis orant. Animabus purgatorii applicari potest.—Pius IX., 1846. (*P. Maurel.*)

6. *Ad veniam peccatorum impetrandam.*

Sancta Maria, Regina coelorum, Mater Domini nostri
Jesu Christi et mundi Domina, quæ nullum derelin-
quis et nullum despicis; respice me, Domina, cle-
menter oculo pietatis, et impetra mihi apud tuum
dilectum Filium, cunctorum veniam peccatorum : ut,
qui nunc tuam sanctam Conceptionem devoto affectu
rocolo, æternæ in futurum beatitudinis bravium ca-
piam, ipso, quem Virgo peperisti, donante Domino
nostro Jesu Christo, qui cum Patre et Spiritu Sancto
vivit et regnat in Trinitate perfectâ, Deus in sæcula
sæculorum. (*Cœleste Palmetum.*)

7. *Trina sanctæ Mecthildis salutatio ut bonam
mortem per Mariam obtineret.*

Ave, Maria, &c.
O Domina mea, sancta Maria, sicut *Deus Pater*
per omnipotentiam suam, te potentissimam effecit,
ita mihi, quæso, ad sis, in horâ mortis, omnemque
mihi contrariam potestatem a me potenter averte.
Ave, Maria, &c.
O Domina mea, sancta Maria, sicut *Filius Dei*
divinâ suâ scientiâ et sapientiâ te replevit, ita,
quæso, animam meam lumine fidei in horâ mortis

illustra et corrobora, ut nullo errore aut ignorantiâ
pervertatur et in perditionem inducatur.

Ave, Maria, &c.

O Domina mea, sancta Maria, sicut *Spiritus Sanctus* suum amorem plenè tibi infudit, ita tu, in morte,
divini amoris dulcedinem mihi instilla, per quem
omnis angor et amaritudo tollatur et cor meum
cœlesti consolatione recreetur. (*Cœleste Palmetum.*)

8. Bona Mors quæritur.

O Maria sine labe originali concepta, ora pro nobis
qui confugimus ad te! ô refugium peccatorum, mater
agonizantium, noli nos derelinquere in horâ exitûs
nostri, sed impetra nobis dolorem perfectum, since-
ram contritionem, remissionem peccatorum nostro-
rum, sanctissimi Viatici dignissimam receptionem,
Extremæ-Unctionis sacramenti corroborationem, qua-
tenus securi præsentari valeamus ante thronum justi
sed et misericordis judicis Dei et Redemptoris nostri.
Amen.

Indulgentia 100 dierum cuilibet recitanti.—Pius
IX., 1856. (*Analecta.*)

9. Salutationes P. M. Centurionis.

Ave, Filia Dei Patris!
Ave, Mater Dei Filii!
Ave, Sponsa Spiritus Sancti!
Ave, Templum totius Trinitatis!
Ave, mundi spes, Maria!
Ave mitis!
Ave, pia!
Ave, plena gratiâ!

SPIRITUAL EXERCISES DURING MASS.

In union with the Sacred Heart of Jesus.

The Mass is the sacrifice of love, in which the Sacred Heart of Jesus offers itself for us to the Eternal Father. It is also principally by assisting at this adorable mystery, that we come to the knowledge and love of this Sacred Heart, by considering its most holy dispositions, desires, &c. Penetrated with the deepest sentiments of gratitude, make your offering in the following manner:—

Eternal Father, permit me to offer Thee the Sacred Heart of Jesus as he offers Himself to Thee in sacrifice for us. I supplicate Thee to accept for me all the affections and operations of this Divine Heart. They are mine, since it is for me that He offers them, since I desire to have no other save them. Receive them as a satisfaction for my sins, and as a thanksgiving for all Thy benefits. Receive them, O my God! and, through their exceeding merit, grant me all the graces I have need of. Receive them as so many acts of love, adoration, and praise, which I offer to thy Divine Majesty, since it is by Him alone that Thou art worthily loved, praised, and glorified.

During the Psalm, Judica.

Judge me, O my God, according to Thy great mercy, and cast me not away like the impious. Destroy in me the kingdom of the devil and of self-love, that, enlightened by Thy truth, and inflamed by Thy love, I may approach with confidence to the feet of Thine altar.

When the priest goes up to the Altar.

I have learnt from Thy apostles, O my God, that Jesus Christ is our peace; that He has re-united us to Thee by the effusion of His spirit and His Sacred Heart, with which he has sealed us as a pledge of reconciliation, of which the kiss given by the priest to the altar is the sign.

During the Introit.

Thy Church, O Lord, prepares itself for the sacrifice in praising Thee and in imploring Thy mercy. Unite me to Thy Sacred Heart, in order that I may worthily join with her in praising Thee, and that I may obtain the mercy which she implores.

At the Kyrie.

I know, O my Saviour, that by reason of the depth of my misery I have an extreme need of Thy mercy, which will not suffer Thee to cast me away; but if my countless ingratitudes should constrain Thee to this, I would still cry with the Canaanitish woman—"Lord, have mercy upon me!"

Gloria.

At the Collects.

The whole Church prays to Thee, my God, by the mouth of Thy priest. I unite myself to her, supplicating Thee, through the merits of the Sacred Heart of Jesus, to grant me all that she asks, and that all the desires and designs of Jesus Christ upon our souls may be eternally accomplished. Amen.

At the Epistle.

Grant, O my God, that I may listen attentively when Thou speakest to me, and that I may receive the truths Thou teachest me, submitting my mind and opening my heart; in order that, regulating my life according to Thy Holy Word, I may be able to say from my heart, as the Jews said to Moses, when he preached Thy law to them—"We will do all that the Lord commands us, and we will obey Him."

At the Gradual.

Thou art about, O my Jesus, to speak to us Thyself in Thy gospel; grant that I may listen with a profound respect, a humble docility, and an ardent desire to accomplish all that Thou commandest.

At the Gospel.

That I may never, O Lord, blush at Thy gospel or at Thy cross, I imprint its sacred sign upon my forehead; that I may profess openly with my mouth the truths which I believe in my heart, I sign my lips and my heart therewith; that I may show myself prompt in the execution of Thy holy law, I listen to it standing. May I love it, as the kiss of the priest, after having read it, testifies he does, because, in order to enjoy Thee hereafter, we must desire Thy promises and love Thine ordinances.

Credo.

At the Offertory.

Look, O Lord, we beseech Thee, upon the Sacred Heart of Thy well-beloved Son, which we offer to

Thee with the priest as a victim equal to Thy Majesty; as a gift equal to Thy benefits; as a satisfaction which surpasses our crimes; as a petition which will not admit of a refusal, and which Thou canst not accept without giving us Thyself in exchange.

When the priest inclines himself before the Altar.

Cast Thine eyes upon Thy Christ, O adorable Trinity! remember His sufferings, His death, and His burning love for us. Remember His resurrection, by which He consummated the work of our redemption and glorified Thee; His ascension, which raised Him to the throne of Thy glory; all the miracles He worked for us; all the merits of His holy Mother, and all Thy saints, in order that Thou mayest favourably accept our sacrifice, to the glory of Thy name, the good of our souls, and the welfare of the whole Church.

At the Preface.

During the union which takes place of the Church in heaven and earth, in offering to Thee this sacrifice, I enter into the Sacred Heart of Jesus, to be consumed by its divine flames, and to adore Thy holiness by the holiness of the Victim. I unite myself to the celestial host, saying, with them, Holy, holy, holy, Lord God of Sabaoth! heaven and earth are full of the majesty of Thy glory. Have mercy on us and save us, O Thou that dwellest in the highest heavens.

At the Canon.

We adore Thee, O Eternal Father, and we entreat Thee, by the Heart of Thy Son, to receive the oblation which the priest offers Thee for the universal Church, for our pastors, for our parents, for our friends, and for our enemies, supplicating Thee to give them a lively faith, and so to order their lives that they may attain to a perfect union with Thee in everlasting life. Refuse not, O Lord, Thy mercy to the poor souls who are finishing the work of their purification in the flames of purgatory; they are conquests of the Heart of Jesus. Have compassion above all on those who were most devout to this adorable Heart, and to the glorious Virgin Mary; deliver them from their prisons, and lend a favourable ear to our prayers. We hope for this grace by the offering we now make to Thee of this true, living, and eternal Host.

When the priest spreads his hands over the Oblation.

O Lord, since by the hands of the priest spread over the Oblation is signified Thy acceptance of the Victim immolated for us, and substituted in the place of us sinners, just victims of Thine anger and justice, we ought no longer to consider ourselves, save as victims, destined to die. Give us, then, the grace to die to ourselves, by consecrating to Thee our thoughts, words, and affections, that for love of Him who died and rose for us, we may live in the spirit of continued self-sacrifice, to the glory of Thy name.

At the Consecration.

Transform us into Thee, O Lord, and make us become one with Thee, as Thou changest this bread into Thy body; change, O Lord, our evil hearts, and make them conformable to Thine, that they may have no other will or desire save Thine, O Lord.

At the Elevation of the Host.

O saving Victim, opening to us the gate of heaven! Sacred Heart of my Jesus, inundating the world with inexhaustible treasures of grace! my heart is subject to countless weaknesses, oppressed with numberless sorrows, torn by conflicting passions: give it strength to resist, animate it by Thy virtue, inflame it by Thy love, that it may lose itself, and become one with Thee.

At the Elevation of the Chalice.

O most precious blood, shed in order to kindle in the world the fire of divine love, extinguish in my heart all earthly and profane love. Adorable Heart, who, to wash me from all mine iniquities, hast willingly shed the last drop of Thy precious blood, never permit me for the future to commit any evil.

At the genuflection of the priest before the Pater.

O my God! I acknowledge that we can do nothing without Thy Son, whom Thou hast given to us, and who Himself teaches us to pray; it is by Him, through Him, and in Him that we dare to supplicate Thee to transport this Victim placed by the priest on *our* altars to *Thine altar*, that is to say, to that sublime altar which is Thyself, that it may be carried by Thy Holy Angel, which is Jesus Christ, to the presence of Thy Divine Majesty, in order that all those who assist at this adorable Sacrifice, and the holy souls in purgatory, may feel its virtue in receiving the abundance of Thy grace.

After the Pater.

Deliver me, O Lord, through Jesus Christ, Thy Son, from all evils, past, present, and to come; and grant me the grace to serve Thee in peace, and with unshaken confidence.

When the priest puts a particle of the Host into the Chalice.

This union, O Divine Jesus, of the species of bread and wine changed into Thy adorable body and blood, puts before the eyes of my faith the ineffable union of God and man by Thine incarnation, of man with Thee by the holy communion, and of all the saints transformed into Thee in the kingdom of Thy glory. I bless Thee, and give Thee thanks, through the merits of Thy Sacred Heart, for all the benefits Thou hast conferred upon us; through the first I ask the grace of the second, and I hope to attain, by Thy great mercy, to the happiness of the third.

At the Agnus Dei.

Divine Lamb! I confess with the priest that to Thee alone it appertains to take away the sins of the world. Blot out all my sins, which I detest with my whole heart. Have mercy on me, and give me ever-lasting peace, in order that I may eternally praise and bless Thee.

At the Domine non sum dignus.

It is true, O Lord, that I am infinitely unworthy that Thou shouldst enter into my soul; but this same unworthiness, this same misery, makes me desire this celestial bread, and hunger obliges me to have recourse

to Thy Sacred Heart, to draw from its fulness where-
with to fill the emptiness of mine, and to supply its
wants. Take possession of my soul, which belongs
to Thee by so many titles, and in coming, render it
worthy to receive Thee, and to become a partaker of
Thy grace.

[One of the Acts before Communion may be used as a
Spiritual Communion.]

At the Blessing.

Bless us, O Lord, with Thy most abundant benedictions in Thy Son, and by Thy Divine Son, our
Saviour, in order that Thy Holy Spirit may direct,
animate, and sanctify all our actions, and the whole
course of our life; so that, imitating on earth the
actions of the sacred humanity of Jesus Christ, we
may merit to contemplate in heaven the splendour of
Thy Divinity. Amen.

ACTS BEFORE COMMUNION, WHICH MAY SERVE FOR SPIRITUAL COMMUNION.

Act of Faith.

Adorable Jesus! I believe with a lively faith upon
Thy Word, that Thou art under these sacramental
species, where the ineffable goodness of Thy Heart
has concealed Thee, to give to our souls a living
bread, from which to derive a supernatural life;
that Thou art as a consuming fire, capable of in-
flaming us with love; as a hidden treasure, in which
all the riches of the divine liberality are enclosed;
and in short, as a remedy for all our evils.

Act of Desire.

My soul, O Lord, burns with desire to eat this bread, in order to live in this life; to receive this blood, to be inflamed with Thy love; to find this treasure, and to give up all to purchase it, so as to become enriched by the divine liberality, and to have recourse to this sovereign remedy to be cured of all evils : but to obtain this grace it is necessary to be free from all sin.

O Lord, I detest from the bottom of my heart all the sins I have committed during my whole life, because they have offended Thine infinite goodness. O Divine Jesus, if there be nothing on my conscience which renders the desire I have to receive Thee displeasing, I abandon my whole soul to this desire, and I sigh after Thee with the same ardour as the weary stag pants after the fountains of clear water. Come then, O Lord, give Thyself to me as truly by Thy graces as Thou dost by the real presence of Thy body and blood, which Thou bestowest in this mystery so liberally upon the children of Thy Church. Bury in this precious seed all the sins of the world, particularly my own ; grant me grace no more to commit them, to nourish myself by the imitation of Thy virtues, and to receive and preserve the fruits of the divine Sacrifice, at which I have the happiness of assisting.

Act of Humility.

Who am I, O God of glory! who am I, that thou shouldst deign to cast Thine eyes upon me? Whence comes this excess of happiness, that my God should come to me? I, a sinner, worse than

nothing, approach a God of all sanctity! receive
the bread of angels! Ah! Lord, I do not deserve it; I shall never be worthy! King of
heaven, Creator and Preserver of the world, I
bow down before Thee, and wish to humble myself
as profoundly for Thy glory as Thou dost in this
sacrament for the love of me. I acknowledge with
humility Thy greatness, and my own extreme
unworthiness; the sight of the one and the other
causes me a confusion which I cannot express. O
my God, I can only say, with humble sincerity,
that I am quite unworthy of the grace Thou deignest
to bestow upon me to-day.

Act of Hope.

Thou comest to me, my Divine Saviour! What
may I not expect from one who gives Himself
entirely to me? I present myself, then, before
Thee, O my God! with all the confidence which
Thine infinite goodness inspires me. Thou knowest
my wants, and canst relieve them; Thou wilt do
so, for Thou invitest me to come to Thee, and dost
promise to assist me. Behold me, then, O my God,
I rely upon Thy word, and come to Thee with all
my weakness, blindness, and miseries, hoping that
Thou wilt strengthen, enlighten, comfort, and change
me. Come, then, adorable Jesus, and however
unworthy I may be to receive Thee, say but a word
and my soul will be purified. My heart is ready;
but if it were not, Thou couldst, with a single glance,
prepare and inflame it. Come, Lord Jesus, come.

Acts after Communion.

Act of Adoration.

Adorable Majesty of my God, before whom all
that is great in heaven and on earth is unworthy to
appear! what can I do but be silent and honour Thee
in the inmost recesses of my heart. I adore Thee,
O my God, and pay homage to that supreme greatness before which every knee bends, and compared
to which all power is weakness, and the brightest
light but profound darkness.

Act of Love.

I have at last the happiness of possessing Thee,
O God of love! What a happiness! What return
can I make to Thee! Why am I not all heart to
love Thee as much as Thou deservest! Inflame my
heart, O my God, and make it burn with Thy holy
love. My beloved is mine. Jesus, the amiable Jesus,
gives Himself to me. Angels of heaven, mother of
my God, saints of heaven and earth, lend me your
hearts—give me your love to love my amiable Jesus.
I love Thee, O God of my heart, I love Thee with
my whole soul; I love Thee for Thine own sake,
and with a firm resolution to love none but Thee. I
promise and protest it; but do Thou, O my God,
strengthen these holy resolutions in my heart.

Act of Thanksgiving.

What thanksgiving, O my God, can equal the
favour Thou grantest to me? O God of goodness,
not content with having loved me so as to give Thy

life for me, Thou deignest to honour me with a visit,
and to give Thyself to me! O my soul, glorify
the Lord thy God! Acknowledge His goodness,
extol His magnificence, publish incessantly His
mercy. I will for ever remember that Thou hast
given Thyself to me this day, O my God! and to
prove my gratitude, will, for the remainder of my
life, give myself entirely to Thee.

Act of Petition.

I possess Thee, O inexhaustible source of all
good! Thou art full of tenderness for me, and Thy
hands are filled with graces which Thou art ready
to pour into my heart; give them to me in abundance. O good and liberal God, behold my wants;
take from my heart everything which displeases
Thee, and put there whatever is agreeable to Thee.
Purify my body; sanctify my soul; apply to me the
merits of Thy life and death; live in me, so that I
may live in Thee, and for ever for Thee. Do to me,
O divine Saviour! that for which Thou art come;
give me the graces Thou knowest to be necessary for
me. Grant the same graces to those for whom I am
obliged to pray. Canst Thou refuse me anything
after the favour Thou hast bestowed upon me in
giving me Thyself.

Act of Offering.

Thou overloadest me with Thy gifts, O God of
mercy! in giving Thyself to me. Thou wishest that
I should live but for Thee: this, O my God! is my
most earnest desire. I wish that for the future all
my thoughts and all my actions may be in perfect

submission to Thee; I wish that everything belonging to me—health, strength, talents, goods, reputation—be employed but for the interests of Thy glory. Take possession, then, O King of my heart, of all the powers of my soul; I submit myself to Thy will. After the favour with which Thou hast honoured me, I desire there should be nothing in me which does not belong entirely to Thee.

Act of Amendment.

O best of friends, what can henceforth separate me from Thee? I renounce with all my heart whatever, until now, has kept me at a distance from Thee; and I promise, with the help of Thy grace, no more to fall into the same faults. Therefore, no more thoughts, desires, words, or actions contrary to modesty or charity; no more neglect of my duties, or tepidity in Thy service; no more attachment to my inclinations, or desire for the esteem of the world. May I rather die, O my God, than ever displease Thee. Divine Jesus! it is in Thy presence that I make these resolutions; may the adorable Sacrament which I have received be as a seal which I may never be permitted to break. Confirm the desire which I have to belong entirely to Thee, and to live only for Thy glory. Amen.

HYMNS TO ST. JOSEPH.

No. I.

1 Quicumque sanus vivere
Cursumque vitæ claudere
In fine lætus expetit,
Opem Josephi postulet.

2 Hic sponsus almæ virginis
Paterque Jesu creditus,
Justus, fidelis, integer,
Quod poscit orans impetrat.
Quicumque, &c.

3 Fœno jacentem parvulum
Adorat, et post exsulem
Solatur; inde perditum
Quærit dolens, et invenit.
Quicumque, &c.

4 Mundi supremus artifex
Ejus labore pascitur,
Summi Parentis Filius
Obedit illi subditus.
Quicumque, &c.

5 Adesse, morti proximus
Cum Matre Jesum conspicit,
Et inter ipsos jubilans
Dulci sopore solvitur.
Quicumque, &c.

Gloria Patri et Filio et Spiritui sancto; sicut erat, &c.
Quicumque, &c.

Ant. Ecce fidelis servus et prudens quem constituit Dominus super familiam suam.

℣. Ora pro nobis, beate Joseph.

℞. Ut digni efficiamur promissionibus Christi.

Oremus. Deus qui ineffabili providentiâ beatum Joseph sanctissimæ Genitricis tuæ sponsum eligere dignatus es, præsta, quæsumus, ut quem protectorem veneramur in terris, intercessorem habere mereamur in cœlis, qui vivis et regnas in sæcula sæculorum. Amen.

(Indulgence of one year, applicable to the souls in Purgatory, &c.—Pius VII. 1804.)

No. II.

1 O custos Matris Domini,
   Devotos tuo nomini,
   Joseph alme, per aspera
   Salva semper et prospera.

2 Adesse tuis famulis
   Dignare, dux amabilis;
   Sentiant nostra pectora
   Tua semper juvamina.

3 Tu salus et protectio,
   Nostraque jubilatio
   Sit tibi laus et gloria
   Per cuncta semper sæcula.—Amen.

No. III.

1 Te, Joseph, celebrent agmina cœlitum,
  Te cuncti resonent christiadum chori.
  Qui clarus meritis junctis es inclytæ
      Casto fœdere virgini.

2 Almo cum tumidam germine conjugem
  Admirans, dubio tangeris anxius,
  Afflatu superi Flaminis angelus
      Conceptum puerum docet.

3 Tu natum Dominum stringis; ad exteras
  Ægypti profugum tu sequeris plagas;
  Amissum Solymis quæris, et invenis
      Miscens gaudia fletibus.

4 Post mortem reliquos gloria consecrat,
  Palmamque emeritos gloria suscipit,
  Tu vivens, superis par, frueris Deo,
      Mira sorte beatior.

5 Nobis, summa Trias, parce precantibus
  Da Joseph meritis sidera scandere:
  Ut tandem liceat, nos tibi perpetim,
      Gratum promere canticum.—Amen.

No. IV.

1 Cœlitum Joseph decus, atque nostræ
  Certa spes vitæ, columenque mundi,
  Quas tibi læti canimus, benignus
      Suscipe laudes.

2 Te sator rerum statuit pudicæ
  Virginis sponsum, voluitque Verbi
  Te patrem dici, dedit et ministrum
    Esse salutis.

3 Tu Redemptorem stabulo jacentem,
  Quem chorus vatum cecinit futurum,
  Aspicis gaudens, humilisque natum
    Numen adoras.

4 Rex Deus regum, Dominator orbis,
  Cujus ad nutum tremit inferorum
  Turba, cui pronus famulatur æther
    Se tibi subdit.

5 Laus sit excelsæ Triadi perennis,
  Quæ tibi præbens superos honores,
  Det tuis nobis meritis beatæ
    Gaudia vitæ.—Amen.

No. V.

1 Iste, quem læti colimus fideles,
  Cujus excelsos canimus triumphos,
  Hac die Joseph meruit perennis
    Gaudia vitæ.

2 O nimis felix, nimis o beatus,
  Cujus extremam vigiles ad horam
  Christus et Virgo simul astiterunt
    Ore sereno.

3 Hinc stygis victor, laqueo solutus
   Carnis, ad sedes placido sopore
   Migrat æternas, rutilisque cingit
       Tempora sertis.

4 Ergo regnantem flagitemus omnes,
   Adsit ut nobis, veniamque nostris
   Obtinens culpis, tribuat supernæ
       Munera pacis.

5 Sint tibi plausus, tibi sint honores,
   Trine, qui regnas, Deus, et coronas
   Aureas servo tribuis fideli,
       Omne per ævum.—Amen.

No. VI.

Salve, pater Jesu mei,
Sponse genitricis Dei,
    Quem decorat puritas.

Quænam possit te condigne
Humana vox exaltare
    Quem selegit Trinitas?

Tu patriarcharum decus,
Inter electos electus,
    Virorum justissimus.

Tu consors integræ matris,
Consolator in ærumnis,
    Adjutor fidissimus.

Primùm dubius hæsisti,
Dein particeps fuisti
Secreti perpetuus.

Verbi tu nutritor carnis,
Pueri custos fidelis,
Protector assiduus.

Primus virorum vidisti
Adoransque credidisti
Jacentem fœno Deum.

Pastores lætificâsti,
Ipsosque Magos ditâsti,
Porrigendo filium.

Infantem circumcidisti,
Et in mortem præsignâsti,
Agni fuso sanguine.

Jesu nomen indidisti
Illi datum quod audîsti
Ab æterno numine.

Pius in templum portâsti,
Summo Patri præsentâsti
Natam mundo victimam.

A te Simeon accepit,
Per te Maria recepit
Israëlis gloriam.

Redemptorem redemisti,
Ipsumque nostrum fecisti,
Solvens Deo pretium.

Salvas nobis Salvatorem,
Et dirum vitas Herodem
   Pergens in exilium.

Tuus quàm paternus amor!
Sed quàm studiosus labor
   Quo succurris puero!

Quis non miretur Josephum,
Natum gestantem divinum
   Ac foventem gremio?

Genis genas admovebat,
Juxtà cor suum premebat
   Patris unigenitum.

Modo Deum appellabat,
Modo regem vocitabat,
   Modo dulcem filium.

Quam vivificus tum calor,
Quam mirus, ô Joseph, ardor
   Subibat pectus tuum.

Cùm stringens ulnis infantem,
Sentires in te pulsantem
   Cordis Jesu palpitum!

Sed nulla lingua narrare,
Nec mens valet penetrare
   Tàm sancta mysteria.

Audito cœli mandato,
Jesum reducis Ægypto
   Tecta petens patria.